Pedagogy of Computer

Pedagogy of Computer

Making Effective Learning Designs

Noushad Husain

SHIPRA

I would like to show my gratitude towards all those authors and publishers whose works have been consulted, quoted and abstracted to make the book up-to-date and useful.

With great pleasure, I express my grateful thanks to my beloved father Mr. Zakir Husain, mother, Mrs. Aishya Begum, wife Razda Khan, son Arsh Husain, brother Shahab Husain and other family members for their encouragement and support.

In the end I am grateful to Mr. D. Kumar, Shipra Publications for publishing this book within the shortest time with accuracy and style.

Lastly, I offer this book to all those teachers and teacher educators who want to use computers in teaching-learning process with pedagogical beliefs.

Dr. Noushad Husain

Contents

Introduction

The world is constantly changing and ways in which we function at home, work and school are also changing. The speed at which technology has developed plays a major role in these changes. Computers are definitely influential in our lives and can enhance the learning process in schools in various ways. With the increasing popularity of computer technology, it is essential for administrators to support and encourage computer technology in our education systems.

Computers are important in education because they facilitate us to reconsider how people learn, how they are empowered and what the nature of learning and useful information is. We cannot avoid the presence of computers in our schools because they are forcing educators to re-evaluate the very nature of what and how we teach.

It is time to fully integrate computer technology more into the educational settings since skillful use of technology supports the development of process skills such as, higher order skills, adaptability and collaboration that are essential to success in our rapidly changing information age. I believe in Dewey's words that if we teach today as we taught yesterday, we rob our children of tomorrow (Dewey, 1916).

Computer technology allows us to better serve the diverse learning styles of our students and educate them for a wider range of intelligence. Everybody has different learning styles for meaningful learning but teachers cannot represent all the styles in a traditional classroom environment. However, with the flexibility and help of the computer technologies, we can design learning environments in which students can manage and construct their own representations of knowledge in their minds.

Teachers need to use a variety of teaching activities in their classrooms and that variety should include technology whenever appropriate. Computer technology can be used not only as an information management tool but also as a means of teaching students of diverse backgrounds. Use of computer technology can help teachers to relate today's students, who are very media aware, new approaches to curriculum and encourage developments in teaching skills. It can also assist teachers in helping students to make connections with a worldwide community.

The widespread proliferation of computers in schools is based on the assumption that computers have a significant role to play in education and that their use can and will result in the advancement of education. The nature, the expectations and the importance of the role that the computer has come to play in the classroom has been justified through the embrace of different sets of reasons, principles and beliefs, i.e. different rationales.

Research indicates that the benefits of computer technology integration do not happen in some miraculous way simply because the technology has been provided and computer technology cannot be effective in the classroom without teachers who are knowledgeable about both—the computer technology itself and how to use it to meet educational goals. Therefore, in order to accomplish the profound changes associated with the integration of technology in the overall learning environment, there is a real need for training of teachers.

It is a serious problem of our education system that traditionally teachers play a transmission of knowledge with students taking a fairly passive role, which easily leads to shallow approaches to learning. There is little on how to transfer knowledge or skills to new situations. Many teachers use lectures to deliver knowledge and the final examination is the only main assessment at the end of the course, making students focus more on the examination for getting credits.

From the pedagogical point of view, the learner's learning activities should be directed at activating his/her own prior conceptions and relating it to new knowledge. Accordingly, the learning environment should provide the learner with opportunities to test and try out his/her new conceptual understanding in various applied circumstances like problem solving or project work. The most important task of a teacher lies in the stimulation and coaching of a learner. In this way, the student develops an independent and active attitude of great importance for his or her functioning in a modern, dynamic society

Computer technologies have changed teaching and learning in a number of ways from graphing calculators to online lesson plans to virtual field trips and simulated dissections. Computer technologies can help students to access content in new and often exciting ways. In fact, one would be hard pressed to find there is a significant gap between the presence of computer technology and its usage in the classroom. While some type of technology is present in nearly every classroom in our country, it is rarely used to its fullest potential. Some of this discrepancy is due to a lack of comfort with using computer technology for teaching and learning. Even teachers who are using new technology and report a high degree of comfort with technology tend to use it in fairly rigid ways, such as searching for activities to use with students, communicating with other teachers and word processing. And while students frequently do use computers in the classroom, use is often limited to information gathering and word processing rather than using multimedia tools or digital content to design and create products. Often, learning with technology is teacher-centered rather than student-centered.

While many teachers still feel uncomfortable using computers technology in their teaching practice, it is also likely that teachers feel new technologies are unproven in the classroom. Schools may find themselves stuck in a series of initial implementation efforts, trying one thing after another and not achieving full implementation of a programme. Even high-quality training, if used in isolation, is not sufficient to lead to full-scale implementation of computer technology; for true technology integration, teachers need to do more than simply learn about a new technology tool. If we want teachers to use computer technology to enhance student learning, then it is important to address these issues.

An understanding and incorporation of learning theory is needed for teachers when designing instruction because it adds focus and direction to the process. Instructional designers should address their goals and intentions of designing instruction in order to best incorporate learning 'theory within their programmes. This requires considering the learner's needs and characteristics, content and context, the strengths and weaknesses of the learning theory considering thc scope of the instruction as well as the designer's own intentions, preferences, and expectations.

Learning theories provide a pedagogical basis for understanding how our students learn. Each theoretical perspective offers benefits to designers but the perspectives must be taken into context depending upon the situation, performance goal(s) and learners. And since the context in which the learning takes place can be dynamic and multi-dimensional, some combination of the four learning theories and perhaps others should be considered and incorporated into the instructional design process to provide optimal learning.

Four learning theories, specifically behaviourism, cognitivism, constructivism and connectivism are addressed within the scope of instructional design. This book contains an interpretation of the learning process of each theory along with the implications each has on the instructional design process.

Designing effective instruction goes beyond systematically executing various steps within an instructional design model. Among a host of considerations, effective instructional design should take into consideration the theoretical bases in which it is grounded. This is not to say that learning theory offers instructional designers answers to design problems but instead, offers clarity, direction and focus throughout the instructional design process.

Learning theories do not give us solutions, but they do direct our attention to those variables that are crucial in finding solutions. Thus, understanding theoretical frameworks and properly incorporating them within the scope of instructional design is important for designers to effectively prepare and present instruction as well as for organizational entities to more precisely and efficiently address training-appropriate issues.

Learning is an active process, in which we can speak of learning-activities. We have to focus our attention, decode information and understand the information. Learning takes place in a learning environment. This means that learning occurs under certain conditions that are specially designed to improve learning. This book focuses on four different views on learning environments—behaviourism, cognitivism, constructivism and connectivism.

This book presents the relationship between learning theories and educational technology pedagogy. Theories of learning explain how individuals learn while pedagogy describes the roles of teachers and learners, the relationship between them and kinds of teaching and learning activities they engage in. The central object of study of learning theories thus differs from that of pedagogy.

Integrating technology not only involves the attainment of computer skills but also consists of a process in which learners try, fail, access, evaluate, analyze and apply meaningful tasks including but not limited to researching, analyzing data, applying and representing knowledge, communication and collaborating. Thus, the integration of technology into education means using it as a tool to teach subject matter and to promote problem-solving and higher-order thinking skills. It is neither computer literacy nor computer awareness. It means using the computer where it is the best medium to support the learning goal. It requires changes in a school. The entire school community of students, parents, teachers and administrators has to accept that computers are a part of everyday school life.

1
History of Computers in Education

After studying this chapter, the reader will be able to: Know the important factors that have been changed the world; Categorize the human history into four ages; Know the development of the computer; Discuss the origin of the computers in education; Know the history of automated instruction; List out the major projects related to computerization in education; Discuss the effectiveness of computer-based education; Aware the role of artificial intelligence in education; Distinguish between generative and intelligent CAI

The history of computers in education has been variously characterized as an "accidental revolution" or "unthinking man and his thinking machines." Others have said that the computer revolution has changed the adage that "necessity is the mother of invention" to "in a computer world; invention is the mother of necessity." However characterized, it is clear that innovators in this field have created some of the most provocative and stimulating ideas in the history of education.

A Confluence of Changes

Broadly speaking, the two major functions of education are to transmit the culture, values and lessons of the past to the current generation; and to prepare our children for the world in which they will live. Preparing children for the world in which they will live is becoming more difficult than ever. In retrospect, there has been a confluence of changes that has significantly impacted the direction of modern education.

The Global Economy

Modern, high-speed computers and telecommunications have facilitated the rapid movement of financial resources, goods and services and have created interdependence among the world's economies. To benefit from these markets, nations must be competitive and to be competitive they must have a well-educated work force.

Now, science-based information industries are emerging in which knowledge and human capital are as important as industrial plants. Daniel Bell (1979) says a major characteristic of these industries is that they derive from work in theoretical science and are dependent on the codification of theoretical knowledge. The significance of this development is that if we choose to maintain our current standard of living, our knowledge workers must compete in an international market and must have a good understanding of science.

The Scientific Information Explosion

We are experiencing a scientific information explosion of unprecedented proportions. Today, scientists and engineers use computers to access thousands of rapidly growing data bases that store numbers, words, maps, chemical and physical structures. Today, the base of scientific knowledge is huge.

The Emergence of Cognitive Science

There has been a major paradigm shift in education from theories of "learning" to theories of "cognition." Cognitive science approaches teaching and learning in a different way. It addresses how the human, as an information processor, functions and uses information. Rather than focusing on teaching facts through expository lectures or demonstrations, the emphasis is, instead, on developing higher-order thinking and problem-solving skills.

The cognitive approach is important because it recognizes human information processing strengths and weaknesses and the limits of human perception and memory in coping with the information explosion. It focuses, instead, on organizing information to fit human capacity and has changed the emphasis in education from learning to thinking.

Four Ages of Human History

Human history is sometimes broken into four major time periods or ages:

- *Hunter-gatherer Age*: All of human history, up to about 10,000 years ago.
- *Agricultural Age:* Helped to ensure larger and more stable food supplies.
- *Industrial Age:* Began about 200 years ago; based on engines and their fuels.
- *Information Age:* Began about 40 years ago; based on computers and connectivity.

Until about 10,000 years ago, all people on earth could be classified as hunter-gatherers. Education during the hunter-gatherer age was informal-learn by imitating adults, and learns by doing. Schools and the formal education system that we now take for granted did not exist.

About 10,000 years ago, people began to raise crops and to domesticate farm animals. The ability to store and accumulate food produced major societal changes. After about 5,000 years, cities began to emerge, and reading, writing, and arithmetic were invented. Learning the "three R's" required quite a long period of formal instruction and practice. Thus, formal educational systems were developed. In many ways, the classrooms of 5,000 years ago looked quite a bit like the classrooms of today (Logan, 1995).

Of course, for many thousands of years reading materials were scarce and only a few people received the instruction and practice needed to become proficient at reading and writing. Even then, however, reading and writing contributed greatly to an accumulation of human knowledge. This accumulation was slow because transportation was slow and the electronic communication systems that we now take for granted did not exist.

The Agricultural Age was still continuing when Johannes Gutenberg invented a printing press that made use of moveable type about 550 years ago. This invention made possible the mass production of books. It led to more widespread formal education and the societal changes that accompany having a better-educated population.

The Industrial Age began in the late 1700s, not much more than 200 years ago. The invention of the steam engine made possible the augmentation of human power for manufacturing and transportation.

Mind Tools

Humans have developed a marvelous range of tools-aids to their physical bodies and to their minds. It is people plus their tools that make possible reading, writing, arithmetic, communications satellites and artificially intelligent computer systems. It is people plus their tools that fuel the steady march of science and technology.

The transition from the Hunter-gatherer Age to the Agricultural Age made use of considerable insight into nature, along with some simple tools. This was a long and slow process. Even after the development of reading and writing, the worldwide pace of change remained very slow.

The Industrial Age came about through steadily increasing insight into science and technology, along with the development of more sophisticated tools to aid the human body.

The Information Age is based on a rapid pace of progress in science and technology, supported by steady improvements in computer-related technology. We can think of such technology as aids to the human mind or mind tools. It is these mind tools that are now changing our world.

Development of the Computer

The early history of computers is one of researchers and inventors working to develop faster and more automatic aids to doing arithmetic computations. Mechanical calculators have existed for hundreds of years. When driven by an electric motor, such a calculator required several seconds to complete a multi-digit multiplication or division. Of course, that is far faster than can be done using paper and pencil. However, it is slow relative to the computational demands of modern science and engineering.

Work on the Electronic Numerical Integrator and Computer (ENIAC), began in 1943 and the machine first became operational in early 1946. It is considered to be the world's first fully operational general-purpose electronic digital computer. It could do about 350 multiplications or 40 divisions in one second. Moreover, it could store both the numbers being worked on and the results, so that it could do a sequence of computations without anyone having to re-key in numbers. Roughly speaking, this computer was a thousand times as fast as a person using an electric calculator.

Now-a-days, a medium-priced microcomputer is more than 100,000 times as fast as the ENIAC. This means that it can do arithmetic about as fast as 100 million people working with electric calculators. How can one explain millions of people owning such machines, even carrying portable machines in their briefcases? Who needs to personally own a machine that can do the work of 100 million people working with electric calculators?

The answer lies in how such computers are used. We have moved beyond the first-order effect levels of computer use. Most computers are not used to do calculator-like arithmetic computations. Rather, they are used in more demanding tasks such as the storage and retrieval of databases of information, in creating and manipulating graphics, in developing spreadsheet models of business problems, as switching circuitry in telecommunications systems, and in processing digital information from scientific instruments.

We are continually developing tasks that challenge the capabilities of the most powerful computer systems. For example, the combination of continued progress in the underlying science of speech recognition and in building faster microcomputers is just now making possible reasonably priced voice input systems. You can well imagine how voice input will affect the teaching of reading and writing.

Progress is occurring on the computer translation of spoken natural languages. This is an extremely difficult problem. Some futurists feel that the problem will be solved within 15-20 years. How will it affect education and the societies of the world if such automatic translation systems become readily available?

A virtual reality can be considered as a type of simulation. Continuing progress in the hardware and software used for virtual realities is producing simulations of ever increasing quality. Learn about Mars by taking a walk on the surface of Mars, with scientific instruments in hand. Learn about the

Antarctic or the deepest parts of our oceans by taking simulated trips into these environments. High quality virtual reality systems demand computing power beyond the fastest of today's microcomputers.

Computers in Education

Influence of the Early Greeks on Instruction and Approaches to Teaching

The primary objective of CAI is to provide individualized instruction i.e., one learner and one teacher. Of course this is not a new method of teaching, the system of having one teacher and one pupil can be traced back to early Greek time. In those days, for example, the youth of Athens were taught by the most learned men of the day. Socrates was probably the most famous exponent of this type of instruction and many of the techniques he employed are to be found in modern day CAI. Socrates believed that all ideas are given to a person at birth and that his task was to help the student become aware of these innate ideas. Because he saw himself in the role of a midwife, giving birth to ideas, his method of teaching is sometimes called the 'Maieutic' method: 'Maieutikos' in Greek means 'midwifery'.

The Socratic Approach to Teaching

In the Socratic approach to teaching a small unit of information is presented, followed by a question. Now it is obvious that by asking a question the teacher can determine whether or not the student has comprehended the material he has just received. But the question serves another important purpose, it encourages a dialogue between the student and the teacher and thus maintaining the student in a non-passive role during the lesson. Similarly, the CAI author tries to structure his lessons so that they are conversational and does this by using the basic formula of Socrates: a statement, a question, then a reply to provide feedback to the student. In this way the student benefits by remaining active in the learning situation and progressing at a rate that is directly related to his own performance and comprehension.

The Aristotelian Approach to Teaching

One of Socrates students was Plato, who in turn taught Aristotle. Although little is known about the techniques used by Aristotle in teaching, it is widely believed that he relied mainly on the lecture method. His students would take notes of what he had said, in the same way that students take notes from their lectures today. This method of Aristotle was incomplete contrast to that of Socrates or Plato and there were other things in which he differed from his predecessors. In particular, he did not accept Socrates' belief that all ideas are innate.

Importance of Association in Learning

Aristotle assumed that all knowledge was gained through experience and based on this assumption; he put forward an idea that is of practical interest to CAI authors today. The idea was that learning and memory are based on experience and association. We use association, for example, to teach new terminology-a new word is presented along with its definition. Later, if association has taken place, we can trigger recall of the word definition by presenting just the word by itself. As well as new terminology and vocabulary, CAI authors also use association to introduce students to new ideas and concepts. The CAI author should always be careful, when using association, that new words or ideas are always defined in terms that are already known to the student. If not, Students may well end up by being able to 'parrot' back strings of words without any real understanding of their meaning.

First Steps towards Automated Instruction

We have now seen that methods and ideas introduced over two thousand years ago have an immediate and practical relevance to today's CAI author and teacher. Obviously though, the early Greek teachers could not have envisaged the prospect of instruction being automated. The first step towards automated instruction was taken in the 1920s. Working at Ohio State University in America, an educational psychologist, called Sidney L. Pressey, invented a device that could be used for self-administered, self-scoring tests.

Since testing itself is a form of teaching, Pressey reasoned that a machine could be built to take over some routine teacher functions. As an outcome of this idea, Pressey wrote a paper, published in 1927 called, A Machine for the Automatic teaching of Drill Material. The paper described a machine that could display a menu of answers and which had a mechanism for a student to indicate his selection. The machine could provide feedback on whether the student's answer was correct or not.

Pressey's contribution to CAI development is notable because, as well as describing his machines in terms of labour-saving devices, he also discussed how the machines could be used to implement the principles of learning and instruction. In the same way the CAI author has a similar task of trying to implement known principles when developing instructional material.

Introduction of Programmed Instruction

Although Pressey continued work in this field, little progress was made in the automation of instruction until the 1950s. It was Professor B.F. Skinner, working at Harvard University, who gave a new impetus to the development of CAI technology by pioneering a system of teaching called, programmed instruction. Using the basic idea of Pressey, Skinner invented a mechanical teaching machine, and developed a method of automated teaching, which obliged the student to 'construct' his own response to a question (rather than choosing from a menu of replies as with the Pressey method).

Skinner's approach to teaching placed considerable emphasis on the need for posative reinforcement and his lesson material was organized to minimize the possibility of the student giving an incorrect response and so maximized the amount of positive reinforcement received by the student. This strategy maintained a high level of motivation. However, Skinner's programmed lessons were 'linear' or 'non-branching', each student received the same sequence of instructional units as every other student. There were other researchers who felt that the possibility of the student error should not be excluded from the learning process and that an automated system of instruction should take into account the differences between ability and proclivity.

Non-Linear Programming

At about the same time as Skinner was developing programmed instruction, another researcher, called Norman A. Crowder, was working on a technique of Intrinsic Programming. Intrinsic Programming is also called 'non-linear' to differentiate it from Skinner's 'linear' programming. Using the intrinsic programming technique, the student's response determines the next step in one of several paths through the instructional material.

This differs fundamentally from Skinner's method, where there is no deviation from the 'prime path' of correct answers. The foregoing comparison of Skinner and Crowder reflects a difference of opinion over method but the CAI author should not regard the techniques of 'linear' and 'non-linear' as conflicting alternatives. Both techniques can be used successfully in computer-assisted instruction and the CAI author should apply whichever one he feels is best suited to the subject matter at hand.

The concept of using automation for educational purposes is not much younger than computers themselves. In the 1950's the teaching machine was touted as an incredible new educational breakthrough. The history of the modern computer age is brief one. It has been about 50 years since the first operational computer was put into use: the MARK 1 in 1944 at Harvard University and ENIAC in 1946 at the University of Pennsylvania. Early use of computers in education was primarily found in mathematics, science and engineering as a mathematical problem-solving tool.

Beginning of the Computers in Education: The 1950's

CAL's history began in the late 1950's, when the second-generation computers were built and introduced. These systems were cheaper and more reliable than the earlier models. So digital computers became typical facilities in universities and research centers. Consequently researchers started to find new fields of applications for the computers and CAL was one of these. Certainly at the beginning, like other technical productions, CAL systems, which are a combination of computer hardware, added special purpose peripherals and CAL software, had only scientific and academic applications and were experimental. At that time, before other specialists, psychologists used the computer as an ideal tool for conveying programmed instruction. This branch of CAL was called computer-assisted instruction (CAI) (Hooper, 1975). About that time, large universities began using computers for administrative purposes such as accounting, payroll and student record keeping. At the same time people began using computers for instructional research. In the late 1950's educators at Stanford, Florida State and Dartmouth started using computers to deliver instructional courseware to students (Abell, 1983).

Prophets and Pioneers: The 1960's

The process of computer introduction in instruction has been developed in three directions: computer literacy, computer as technical devices of educational technology and industrialization of computer instruction system. In this period outstanding results were achived by John Kemeny, Patrick Suppes and the group that developed the PLATO system.

John Kemeny with Thomas Kurtz created BASIC (Beginner All Purpose Symbolic Instruction Code). In spite of their original intention to make BASIC a preparatory language for computer literacy it provide to be the most widely used language of computer laymen, contained in the ROM memory of most home computers and the language in which many educational programmes are written.

In 1960s Patrick Suppes, from the Institute for Mathematical Studies in the Social Sciences (IMSS) at Stanford University put his prophetic work on a completely different basis. His efforts were directed towards using the computer as a tool to teach subject matter. His goal to use the computer to individualize instruction for each individual student was not realized in those early years and may be it will not be in the near future. However, his vision is as valid today as it was 30 years ago. It still drives many educators to further research.

By mid 60s interactive courseware with graphics and sound were available. The IBM 1500 system used a minicomputer to drive CRT terminals with an attached random access audiotape and random access 16 mm film projector. Input to the system was by keyboard and light pen. One example implementation of this system is that of a cardiology programme at the University of Alberta in 1969. The student would go through a case scenario such as a walk in-patient with shortness of breath. The student could, for instance, orders an ECG and the projector would display the corresponding ECG. Using the light pen to point to the patient's heart would play back the corresponding heartbeat.

In 1967 Suppes founded Computer Curriculum Corporation (CCC) to deliver computerized instruction to users interested in using telephone connection to computer terminals. The programmes were prepared for groups with special needs, for both handicapped and gifted students. All the programmes were based on exhaustive analysis of the teaching material and equally precise selection of strategies for learning the content. Students receive immediate feedback to their responses before they move ahead to the next step in a sequence. The diagram shows the instructional process.

PLATO Project

In the early 1960's, approximately a dozen years after the first commercial computer became available; a team at the University of Illinois began work on—(1) a flat plasma panel for computer terminals and (2) software for a CAI system which was to become known as PLATO. Funded by numerous federal agencies, including the National Science Foundation and United States Office of Education, this effort eventually produced a training system, which represents some of the most advanced thinking in the interactive process of communicating learning. Many of the PLATO software tools developed to support learning still serve as models for present day efforts and are described in a subsequent section. The primary function of PLATO was to provide a rich environment in which educators and trainers could create and deliver high quality interactive courseware to students in classrooms, homes, and offices with or without the presence of an instructor

The PLATO (Programmed Logic for Automatic Teaching Operations) system was developed by the group at the University of Illinois concurrently with the work at Stanford University. Donald Bitzer guided this project. This was the first large-scale project for the use of computers in education. A mainframe computer located in the university campus using a time-sharing operating system and a network of terminals controls the instruction.

In this system, the mainframe computer was running courseware for a given subject, which was accessed by students through terminals. PLATO is considered a CAI programme, but through later refinements it acquired some characteristics of today's multimedia applications such as interactivity.

In the period of 25 years of its existence, the PLATO system, which was later included in Control Data Corporation (CDC), has prepared over 16000 hours of instruction for 150 subjects and it has nationwide network delivery systems for school and college students with 1100 terminals at 185 locations [Sugarman, 15(8), 1978].

PLATO has a network oriented and interactively organized instructional and programme language TUTOR. The originator of the PLATO system Donald Bitzer had difficulties in generating instruction software. From approximately 16000 hours of instruction software only about 4000 hours are used regularly. But, those 16000 hours resulted from 500000 to 800000 hours of writing. These are used primarily at PLATO original site at the University

Illinois. In that time the only one PLATO system was in active use at the University of Delaware. In spite of difficulties mentioned above Bitzer forced to form a national network with more than million CAI terminals. In Bitzer's estimation the amount on courseware (interactive educational computer programmes) increases exponentially with the number of terminals. Kinzer *et al.* (1986) stated, "the goal of PLATO was to deliver cost-effective, computer-assisted instruction (p. 26).

How was all this accepted in educational institutions?

Each innovation, computers included, has to undergo the process of introduction and antagonism. The attraction of CAI was felt by those who had an interest in "hidden problems" in the area of application educational tools and devices and who belived advanced technology would give them another chance. In the late 1960's it was expected that the computer was going to revolutionize the learning process; the best teachers were supposed to write courseware that would be nationally distributed. Students would learn more rapidly and efficiently. However, reality turned out to be quite different from the dream. Several factors influenced this:

- Few people had time to study the medium's potential and produce courseware.
- The development of CAI remained in the hands of a relatively small numbers of experts who have yet to develop efficient courseware.
- Negative relation of invested time in the preparatory period of writing courseware to the time of courseware lasting.
- Subjective feeling of the teacher to be threatened by technology.

Except for drill and practice the programme for elementary schools, educational institutes did not welcome CAI and it was necessary to do something for its better acceptance in future. Although schools were reluctant in accepting it, nine centers were founded in the USA in this period.

New Insights and Wider Application in the 1970's

From the mid 1960's through the first half of the 1970's third generation computers became available in increasing numbers and at lower cost. More school systems and colleges began using computers for administrative functions. But the instructional use of computers was still largely the domain of universities, with only a few private corporations and the military taking an interest.

TICCIT (Time-Shared Interactive Computer Controlled Information Television)

TICCIT (Time-Shared Interactive Computer Controlled Information

Television) is another major CAI system developed at the University of Texas and Brigham Young University and funded by a grant from the National Science Foundation in 1977 (Kinzer, Sherwood, and Bransford, 1986). This system was designed to teach higher-order concepts using an instructional design system called RULEG. RULEG provides a general statement, or rule, and examples of how the rule is applied. Niemiec and Walberg (1989) stated that this system was innovative because the "instructional tactics were unique to the system and not particular to the authors of programmes" (p. 272-273). The audience using the TICCIT system was intended to be adult learners, but another version was later released for elementary schools.

Intended for adult instruction, TICCIT embodied an instructional philosophy called "Learner Controlled Instruction (LCI)". Lessons on TICCIT always included a variety of information presentations, examples, practice problems, tests and a "map" of the structure of the curriculum. The keyboard had, in addition to the ordinary alphanumeric keys, special keys labeled RULE, EXAMPLE, PRACTICE, EASY, HARD and ADVICE. By presenting these keys the student could change instructional activities, ask for easier or harder activities, or ask for advice as to what to do. Learner-Controlled Instruction had two intended advantages. First, students could adapt the sequence of instruction to their own pace and learning styles. Second, instructional developers did not have to make complex decisions about content sequence, because the students made their own sequencing decisions via the keyboard. The TICCIT system continues to be used in a variety of adult educational environments, chiefly in the military.

TICCIT or Time-Shared Interactive Computer Controlled Information Television System attempted to test the effectiveness of computer-aided instruction (CAI) against the traditional classroom format. (Saettler, 1990). TICCIT, together with PLATO (Programmed Logic for Automatic Teaching Operation) received $60 million in funding from the National Science Foundation, and the Educational Testing Service (ETS) (Chambers, 1983) formally evaluated both.

TICCIT was designed to be the primary, rather than supplemental medium of instruction for 5,000 college students "using minicomputers, colour TV, graphics, and the expertise of content specialists and psychologists well-versed in instructional design (Chambers, 1983, p. 11)." According to Saettler (1990), the MITRE Corporation and the University of Texas (now Brigham Young University) initially intended to implement TICCIT into elementary schools in 1969. Other authors state that TICCIT mathematics and English freshman-level courses were eventually launched at two community colleges, Phoenix College in Arizona and Northern Virginia in Alexandria in 1971-72 (Chambers, 1983; Alessi & Trollip, 1991). ETS's evaluation was mixed: Both the TICCIT mathematics and English course students reported "significant achievement" over the traditional classroom formats; however, more students favoured lecture classes over TICCIT math courses, and fewer students completed the TICCIT math courses as compared to the standard (Chambers, 1983).

Both the design and the implementation of the TICCIT project had influences upon Instructional Technology. "For the first time, a large scale project emphasized innovative approaches to hardware as well as in-depth consideration of learning theory and instructional strategies in the design of the course materials (Chambers, 11)". The CAI research highlighted factors beyond the instruction materials, which influence effectiveness. For example, Chambers concluded that many "students simply did not complete the mathematics CAI course, apparently because the faculty paid little or no attention to their needs." The faculty's minimal interaction may be attributed to fear of technology or inadequate training. Most instructional development plans today analyze the needs of all users, both students and instructors, and try to build in adequate support. Also, TICCIT strongly emphasized the concept of learner control as well as component design theory (Allessi &Trollip, 1991). However, the TICCIT math students did not receive sufficient feedback about their progress, and consequently made poor control decisions about what and when to study, practice, and test. Instructional developers who design a tutorial programme such as this must embed some feedback mechanism either into the programme itself or through instructor training, and they must also evaluate how much learner control is appropriate given the skill base of the targeted learners.

During the early 1970's, the PLATO project introduced PLATO IV, a large time-shared instructional system. Students study on individual terminals, hundreds of which are connected to a large computer on which all lessons and student data are stored. All programme execution occurs on the main computer, which communicates with the terminals by telephone line. PLATO IV allows up to 600 students to use the computer materials at the same time that students are studying lessons.

Other computer-based instruction projects were begun and developed in the early 1970's. Seymour Papert at the Massachusetts Institute of Technology began research on teaching children by having them programme computers (Papert, 1971). Papert, following the educational theory of Jean Piaget (Bybee, 1982; Flavell, 1963), maintained that students can learn many problem-solving skills on their own, given the correct educational environment, which he claimed to be an easily programmed computer. Two major developments of Papert's projects are "LOGO", a powerful but easily learned programmeming language and the "TURTLE", a small robot that children can control using Logo.

Major instructional programmes also began in the U.S. Navy (the Navy Computer Managed Instruction System) (Hansen, Ross, Bowman & Thurmond, 1975) and the U.S. Air Force (the Air Force Advanced Instructional System) (Rockway & Yasutake, 1974). The Ohio State University, the

University of Texas, Florida State University, the State University of New York at Stony Brook and a few other universities also started large computer-based instruction projects during this period.

Minnesota Educational Computer Consortium (MECC) took a different approach to these university and government projects. From its inception in 1972, MECC was oriented toward putting computers and related facilities in the public schools. But MECC, like all the projects, used large and relatively expensive computers because that was all that was available at the time.

Many of these computer projects grew rapidly. The PLATO system at the University of Illinois expended from a classroom of about 20 student workstations to over a thousand terminals throughout the country. Both the PLATO system and TICCIT became commercially available during this period.

In the mid 1970s a few small computer companies began experimenting with microcomputers. Unlike large and medium-sized computers, they could be used by only one person at a time and were thus referred to as dedicated computers.

None of these early microcomputers were very successful. However, in 1977 three microcomputers were introduced that proved to be successful. Two large corporations, Radio Shack and Commodore Business Machines, introduced the TRS-80 and the PET computer, respectively. And a completely unknown company Apple Computer introduced its own computer of the same name.

The introduction of these microcomputers ushered in the microcomputer revolution. Unlike previous microcomputers, these were complete computer systems with all necessary input, output, memory, and processing and permanent storage. They were more reliable and much easier to use than previous microcomputers. Furthermore, all three were well marketed, the unknown Apple Computer best of all.

The 1970's were marked by the appearance and commercial production of the microprocessor and its implementation in microcomputer systems. With the appearance of the microcomputer "computer power" and its application become available to users. In these period different groups of scientists made remarkable advances in CAI. Several research projects at that time are as follows:

SOLO Project at the University of Pittsburgh

Leadership of the Solo Project lay in the hands of Thomas Dwyer. The project was designed for secondary school students and was directed towards giving them control over their own education. The central focus was in mathematics. He called his approach "solo mode" (individual mode). The goal was the emancipation of students from conventional instruction by giving them means of making decisions and solving problems in their own way. One of the approaches used resembles the structure of many computer programmes. In short it was organized in top-down design. The problems are broken down into their components together with an initial basic component that provides overview control of the entire task.

Physics Computer Development Project at the University of California at Irvine

Alfred Bork began this project in 1970 and it coincides with the appearance of microcomputers. The project established measures for the application of stand-alone computers at all academic levels. Although the programmes provide instruction in natural science, the concept underlying them is adaptable to other academic areas. The emphasis is laid on dialogue between student and computer as "teacher" and communication is supported by integrating graphical environment. In Bork's opinion graphics will play an increasing role in "computerized instruction". In keeping with Suppes, Bork belives that all education will eventually include major computer components that are individualized and interactive. Students will be individually engaged in dialogues with computers at least for some part of their education. Bork paid special attention to learning by means of computer simulation and thinks that it should be integrated with other educational tools. Bork thinks that next 25 years "should be an exciting time". (Bork, 1979).

Arthur Luehrmann

Arthur Luehrmann also came into prominence during this decade. He is best identified as an individual with a mission rather than as the imitator of any particular project. (White and Hubbard, 1988). Luehrmann who in 1972 became associated director at the University of California at Barkley supported use of CAI in physics, although his primary interest lay in teaching programming. He believed that computer programming is as much as basic skill in a computer society as the three R's (Reading, Writing, Arithmetic) have been for "Gutenberg's" society. Luehrmann distinguishes learning how to programme from using the computer as means of instructing students in various school subjects. "His junior high school textbook, Computer Literacy: A Hands-On Approach, is the latest in a series of efforts to promote the teaching of programming". (White and Hubbard, 1988).

MIT LOGO Group

Seymour Papert and his colleagues from the laboratory for artificial intelligence at the MIT created a new language LOGO in the late 1950's. His concept of "guided free play" is based on the works the Jean Piaget with whom Papert worked. In contrast to Luerhmann, Papert thinks that main value of CAI lies in encouragement of the intellectual development of students. His goal is to help students to understanding their thought processes better.

What did the Period of Miniaturization Bring?

The 1970's will be remembered as the decade of the hardware triumph. We have become accustomed to orders-of-magnitude thinking. Our expectations are more than mere boosterism; they are reasonable extensions of a history of technical success. We have to reason to doubt that the system of the 80's will indeed do all those wonderful things predicted for them. And if they do not, the failures will be due not to shortcomings in hardware but to deficiencies in the knowledge of those who would use that hardware.

When Time magazine made the personal computer its "Man of the Year" for 1983, the full impact of electronic computing on Americans seemed somehow more authentic. In less than a decade, the powers once exclusive to users of expensive, highly technical mainframe computers had become available to the average customer. During 1982 ownership of personal computers increased 50 percent. Personal computers had found their way into homes for budgeting, into small business for book-keeping and into school for every application, from nuclear reactor simulations to computer games.

In 1980's Computer becomes an Integral Part of Instructional Process

CAI systems became widely used at all levels of education. Besides in the USA remarkable results were achieved in Western Europe. J. B. Rogers (1984) offers data referring to pre-college education in the USA and points out that, computers are much more used than before. The number of secondary schools, which in the period from June 1980 to January 1983 used two to four microcomputers, has risen ten times. In elementary school the use has risen about eight times.

An expert group has been studied the attitude of teachers to CAI. Computers were introduced in 64 per cent of elementary schools and 85 per cent of secondary schools. Besides, programming instruction was studied in 47 per cent of elementary schools and 76 per cent of secondary schools. Computer drill and practice is more used in elementary school–59 per cent and 31 per cent in secondary schools.

On the Clarkson University the number of microcomputers has risen from 50 to over 1700 in less than a year. It was estimated that in 1986 each student would have a computer. Besides this, computers will be included in a campus net and will be connected with mainframe.

The Athena project explores the possibilities of using new computer technology at MIT. Among varied possibilities of its use in instruction the most controversial is its use as an integral part of the instructional process. The global goal of the Athena project is to improve instruction at MIT by organizing and installing the net of working stations with a number of communication services, use of data base management systems, tools for the applications development and graphical environment.

The Effectiveness of Computer-based Education

James Kulik at the University of Michigan performed a meta-analysis on several hundred well-controlled studies in a wide variety of fields at the elementary, secondary, higher and adult education level. He found that computer-based education could increase scores from 10 to 20 percentile points and reduce time necessary to achieve goals by one-third. He found that computers improved class performance by about one-half a standard deviation, less than the one-sigma difference that could be accomplished by peer tutoring. However, this analysis did not include newer studies utilizing advanced technologies and newer educational paradigms. But, this study did answer the question: do computer –based technologies work? They most certainly do.

Artificial Intelligence and Education

Although the idea of intelligent machines is over hundred years old, research on artificial intelligence (Turning test) started in the 1950's with very ambitious goals. However in the 1970's it was found that desirable aims were not realized but the research was continued with more realistic goals mainly restricted to the research and implementation of new programme methods and tools. Besides, a new relationship of industrial and business institutions towards artificial intelligence resulted from the Japanese 5th generation project and achievements in the applications of the artificial intelligence in the expert systems areas. In this environment CAI has undergone transformation. The goal of researchers and designers of CAI systems was to design a curriculum, which may be included in well-prepared teaching materials and adapted to each individual student. Such CAI systems received the prefix intelligent, i.e. Intelligent Computer Assisted/Aided Instruction (ICAI) or Intelligent Tutoring systems (ITS). An intelligent CAI system should be able to present a rich domain knowledge (subject material), which the student should be able to use in a way, which is not defined in advance by the teacher. Besides, the instruction should pay attention to the student's abilities, weakness and preferred styles of learning.

Ad-hoc Frame Oriented CAI

First curricula had different forms and modality of use but all of them followed the same pedagogical paradigm. The student usually has to read the text followed by a question, which requires a short answer. After that, the computer tells him whether his answer is right or wrong. Sometimes his answers ask for repetition of some parts of the material, which the student must repeat and sometimes he is offered further text with new information. The process of learning is branched. The PLATO system distinguishes two kinds of branching.

In author initiated branching the author establishes error criteria while the students can always be directed back or asked for further explanation. The authors of courseware try to predict every wrong answer of the student and adapt further explanation and help to the student's specific purposes.

This branching is the first step towards individualization of instruction. Carbonell (1970) calls this CAI "ad-hoc frame oriented" CAI (AFO CAI) and points out its dependence on information modules which were prepared by the author. AFO CAI design is based on a stimulus-response (S-R) system.

Criticism of CAI

Carbonell (1970) and Rickel (1989) agree that the greatest difficulty in application of CAI lies in the representation of domain knowledge, in building student models and in student diagnosis. This knowledge consists of a canned presentation of the information to the student, canned problems with which to test his knowledge, canned answers and pre specified branches in the presentation based on a pre-remunerate set of possible responses. These systems were criticized for their lack of adaptation to the student. Their pre specified branches present them from adapting the presentation to the needs of the student. They also prevent them from handling unanticipated answers. And their pre specified answers leave them with no criteria for judging student responses other than as right or wrong.

Generative and Intelligent CAI

In most CAI systems of the AFO type the computer does little more than what a programmed textbook can do and one may wonder why the machine is used at all (Carbonell, 1970, p. 194). In contrast to the AFO approach in design and implementation of SCHOLAR tutorial systems Carbonell defines structure oriented information base as a network of facts, conceptions and procedures. Elements of this net are units, which define words and events in the form of a multilevel hierarchical information tree. Carbonell has made a remarkable advancement in designing a structure of CAI when he applied the ISO system to build mixed-initiative dialogue (student-tutor) in SCHOLAR. Mixed-initiative dialogue offers more sensitive and efficient systems and gives better conditions for individualized learning. Carbonell's work in this field is treated by Barr and Feigenbaum (1986) as a pioneer step and in their opinion it defined other types of CAI—intelligent CAI or knowledge based CAI. Besides the above mentioned, early use of the artificial intelligence techniques in CAI systems pointed out the possibilities of generating problems supported by a database with domain knowledge. These systems were called generative CAI. In these systems the problem is generated on the basis of the established rules or other suitable structures.

Syntax and semantics of the problems are determined by the system, which gives more interesting possibilities of one ways of "mixing" problems. The system can direct and control the process of problem generation by establishing the difficulty and the field of interest and by trying to realize the individual abilities of the students. In the 1970's the second phase in the development of ICAI or ITS systems started with the following characteristics: building of the student model and student diagnosis and establishing and developing of the tutorial strategies. The intelligent tutoring systems should pass three tests of intelligence:

1. The subject matter or domain knowledge must be 'known' to the computer system well enough to enable it to draw inferences or solve problems.
2. The system must be able to deduce a learner's approximation of that knowledge.
3. The tutorial strategy must be intelligent as "instructor in the box" can, implement strategies to reduce the difference between expert and student (Burns and Capps, 1998).

Intelligent Tutors

In the 1970's, researchers were looking for new educational paradigms to take advantage of breakthroughs in computer technology. It appeared that the combination of artificial intelligence, cognitive science and advanced technologies could dramatically improve learning and problem solving. Intelligent CAI (ICAI) was one such paradigm.

John Seely Brown developed SOPHIE (a Sophisticated Instructional Environment) as a new kind of learning environment in which the computer based instruction system literally understands its subject domain and can use its knowledge base to help the student debug and articulate his own ideas and reasoning strategies.

John Anderson of Carnegie University developed a theory of cognition (ACT) and developed ICAI tutors in algebra, geometry and teaching computer programming languages. Anderson's goal was to achieve a one sigma difference in school performance. Results show a one letter-grade improvement for all students.

Intelligent Tools

Another approach was to build the intelligence into the tool. If educators were to raise the entire level of educational performance, merely learning faster or better would not be sufficient. Often the difficulty in problem solving is not inherent in the nature of the problem, but in the tools available to us. Computer aided design and computer aided manufacturing in engineering greatly empowered students to achieve what professional engineers were able to accomplish using the older methods. The aim was to build the intelligence into the tool and let students focus on problem solving and reasoning.

There are at least three essential reasons why intelligent tutoring systems are confirmed as a good "test bed" in realization of the projects for artificial intelligence.

- Applications for wide spectrum of domain knowledge including artificial intelligence itself.
- Open for development because they can easily embody a spectrum of levels of "intelligence", without losing their effectiveness.
- Multifarious functions because it integrates various specific ways of thinking in problem solving area (What? Whom? and How?).

Until this time, projects in computer-based instruction (or computer applications in education, in general) were the domain of large projects that had the funds necessary for expensive computers. With the introduction of microcomputers, it became possible for the individual university researcher, the small public school and even the individual public school teacher to buy one and to start using it for educational purposes. From 1977 to today we have seen phenomenal growth in the educational uses of computers. All colleges and universities have microcomputers and most elementary and secondary schools have them, too.

2
Goals for Computer Technology in Education

After studying this chapter, the reader will be able to: Write the goals for use of computers in education; Comprehend the student goals related to computer technology in education; Differentiate the functional technology literacy goals and independent lifelong learning goals; Identify the educational system goals related to capacity building; List the goals related to assessment and evaluation for computers in education; Describe the goals related to basic technology operations and concepts for teachers; Discuss the goals related to personal and professional use of technology for teachers; Write the goals for teachers related to application of computer technology un instruction

The students of today are the citizens of the future in a word of rapidly changing technology. The daily skills, which were sufficient for our parents are changing rapidly for our children. It is our responsibility to train our students for a work experience in which it is anticipated that they will change occupations several times during their working careers. Computer education develops each individual student for a place in society.

The emphasis in learning has changed from memorizing facts to learning how to acquire information. Our changing technology demands that we provide the tools necessary for our students to be able to access this information. Computer education is a tool, which supports academic instruction and enhances critical thinking skills in a stimulating environment. This education helps the student to achieve objectives of self-realization, social competence and economic efficiency. These skills prepare our students for the workplace and enhance their academic pursuits. With the help of the computer technology in education, we want to:

- to introduce students to computer's role in society, including the past, the present and the future.

- to familiarize students with programming languages, computer operations and terminology.
- to develop a working knowledge of commercially prepared software.
- to promote ethical values pertaining to the use of the computer.
- to prepare students for future technological challenges.
- to enhance problem solving skills.
- to create an environment for interdisciplinary learning.
- to stimulate student potential for creativity.

Goals for Computer Technology in Education

There are 13 goals for computer technology in education. These goals have emerged and evolved during the past 20 years as microcomputers have come into common use in schools and as the information highway has developed. These goals are divided into four major categories:

- Functional Technology Literacy
- Independent Lifelong Learning
- Capacity Building
- Assessment and Evaluation

Student Goals: Functional Technology Literacy

The four goals listed in this chapter serve to define *functional technology literacy* and provide guidelines to curriculum developers. The emphasis of the goals related with the above category is on both basic skills and on higher-order problem-solving skills.

Goal 1: Computer Technology Literacy: Basic Level

All students shall be functionally literate in computer technology. A basic level of computer technology literacy should be achieved at the end of the eighth class. It consists of a relatively broad-based, interdisciplinary, general knowledge of applications, capabilities, limitations, and how they work and societal implications of computers and other information technology. Here are six specific objectives that underlie this computer technology literacy goal.

(a) General Knowledge: Students shall have oral and reading knowledge of computers and other information technology and their effects on our society. More specifically, each discipline that student's study shall include instruction about how electronic aids to information processing and problem solving are affecting that specific discipline.

(b) Procedural Thinking: Students shall have knowledge of the concept of effective procedure, representation of procedures, roles of procedures in problem solving and a broad range of examples of the types of procedures that computers can execute.

(c) Generic Tools: Students shall have basic skills in use of word

processing, database, computer graphics, spreadsheet and other general purpose multidisciplinary application packages. This also includes basic skills in using menu-driven hypermedia software to create hypermedia materials as an aid to communicating.

(d) Telecommunications: Students shall have basic skills in using telecommunications to communicate with people and to make effective use of computerized databases and other sources of information located both locally (for example, in a school library, a school library, a local community library) and throughout the world. They shall have the knowledge and skills to make effective use of the Internet and the World Wide Web.

(e) Hardware: Students shall have basic knowledge of the electronic and other hardware components and how they function. They shall understand the functionality of hardware sufficient to detect and correct common difficulties, such as various components not being plugged in or not receiving power, various components not being connected and printer out of paper.

(f) Computer Input: Students shall have basic skills in use of a variety of computer input devices, including keyboard and mouse, scanner, digital camera, touch screen and probes used to input scientific data. They shall have introductory knowledge of voice input and pen-based systems.

Goal 2: Information Technology Literacy: Intermediate Level

At intermediate level, the students should have the deeper knowledge of computers and other information technology. The computer related knowledge and skills at this level would be as follows:

(a) Skill in Creating Hypermedia Documents: This includes the ability to design effective communications in both print and electronic media, as well as experience in desktop publication and desktop presentation.

(b) Skill in Use of Information Technology: This an aid to problem solving in the various high school disciplines. A student taking advanced math would use computer modeling. A commercial art student would create and manipulate graphics electronically. Industrial arts classes would work with computer-aided design. Science courses would employ microcomputer-based laboratories and computer simulations.

(c) Skill in Computer-Mediated, Collaborative, Interdisciplinary Problem Solving: This includes students gaining the types of communication skills (brainstorming, active listening, consensus-building, etc.) needed for working in a problem-solving environment.

Goal 3: Computer-as-Tool in Curriculum Content

The use of computer applications as a general-purpose aid to problem solving using word processor, database, graphics, spreadsheet and other general purpose application packages shall be integrated throughout the curriculum content. The intent here is that students shall receive specific instruction in each of these tools, probably before completing elementary school. Middle school, junior high school and high school curriculum shall assume a working knowledge of these tools and shall include specific additional instruction in their use. Throughout secondary school and in all higher education, students shall be expected to make regular use of these tools and teachers shall structure their curriculum and assignments to take advantage of and to add to student knowledge of computer-as-tool.

Goal 4: Computer Technology Courses

A high school shall provide both of the following "more advanced" tracks of computer-related coursework.

(a) Computer-related coursework will prepare a student who will seek employment immediately upon leaving school. For example, a high school vocational curriculum shall prepare students for entry-level employment in a computerized business office. A graphic arts curriculum should prepare students to be productive in use of a wide range of computer-based graphic arts facilities. These courses should be the part of the Tech Prep (Technical Preparation) programme of study in a school. For this purposes there is a current need to mould the curriculum according to the need of the students for preparing students IT (Information Technology) literate.

(b) Computer science coursework, including problem solving in a computer programming environment, designed to give students a college-preparation type of solid introduction to the discipline of computer science.

Student Goals: Independent Lifelong Learning

The three goals listed in this section focus on computer technology as an aid to general learning.

Goal 5: Distance Education

Telecommunications and other electronic aids are the foundation for an increasingly sophisticated distance education system. Education shall use distance education, when it is pedagogically and economically sound, to increase student learning and opportunities for student learning.

Note that in many cases distance education may be combined with computer-assisted learning (CAL, *see* Goal 6) and carried out through the WWW (*see* Goal 1D), so that there is not a clear dividing line between these two approaches to education. In both cases students are given an increased range of learning opportunities. The education may take place at a time and place that is convenient for the student, rather than being dictated by the traditional course schedule of a school. The choice and level of topics may be more under student control than in our traditional educational system.

Goal 6: Computer-Assisted Learning (CAL)

Education shall use computer-assisted learning when it is pedagogically and economically sound, to increase student learning and to broaden the range of learning opportunities. CAL includes drill and practice, tutorials, simulations, and microworlds. It also includes computer-managed instruction [*see* Objective (c) below]. These CAL systems may make use of virtual realities technology.

(a) All students shall learn both general ideas of how computers can be used as an aid to learning and specific ideas on how CAL can be useful to them. They shall become experienced users of CAL systems. The intent is to focus on learning to learn, being responsible for one's own learning and being a lifelong learner. Students have their own learning styles, so different types of CAL will fit different students to greater or lesser degrees.

(b) In situations in which CAL is a cost-effective and educationally sound aid to student learning or to overall learning opportunities, it will be an integral component of the educational system. For example, CAL can help some students learn certain types of material significantly faster than can conventional instructional techniques. Such students should have the opportunity to use CAL as an aid to learning. In addition, CAL can be used to provide educational opportunities that might not otherwise be available. A school can expand its curriculum by delivering some courses largely via CAL.

(c) Computer-managed instruction (CMI) includes record keeping, diagnostic testing and prescriptive guides as to what to study and in what order. CMI software is useful to both students and teachers. Students should have the opportunity to track their own progress in school and to see the rationale for the work they are doing. CMI can reduce busywork. When CMI is cost-effective and instructionally sound, staff and students shall have this aid.

Goal 7: Students with Special Needs

Computer-related technology shall be routinely and readily available to students with special needs when research and practice have demonstrated its effectiveness.

(a) Computer-based adaptive technologies shall be made available to students who need such technology for communication with other people and/or for communication with a computer.

(b) When CAL has demonstrated effectiveness in helping students with particular special learning needs, it shall be made available to the students.

(c) All school staff that work with students with special needs shall have the knowledge and experience needed to work with these students who are making use of computer-based adaptive technologies, CAL and computer tools.

Educational System Goals: Capacity Building

The three goals in this section focus on permanent changes in our educational system that is needed to support achievement of Goals 1-7 listed previously.

Goal 8: Staff Development and Support

The professional education staff shall have computers to increase their productivity, to make it easier for them to accomplish their duties and to support their computer-oriented growth. Every school and college shall provide for staff development to accomplish Goals 1-7, including time for practice, planning and peer collaboration. Teacher training institutions shall adequately prepare their teacher education graduates so they can function effectively in a school environment that has Goals 1-7.

This means, for example, that all teachers shall be provided with access to computerized data banks, word processors, presentation graphics software, computerized grade books, telecommunications packages and other application software that teachers have found useful in increasing their productivity and job satisfaction. Computer-based communication is becoming an avenue for teachers to share professional information. Every teacher should have telecommunications and desktop presentation facilities in the classroom. Computer-managed instruction (CMI) can help the teacher by providing diagnostic testing and prescription, access to item data banks and aids to preparing individual education plans.

Goal 9: Facilities

The schools and colleges shall integrate into its ongoing budget adequate resources to provide the hardware, software, curriculum development, curriculum materials, staff development, personnel and time needed to accomplish the goals listed above.

Goal 10: Long-Term Commitment

The schools and colleges shall institutionalize computers in schools through the establishment of appropriate policies, procedures and practices. Instructional computing shall be integrated into job descriptions, ongoing budgets, planning, staff development, work assignments and so on. The educational institutions shall fully accept that "computers are here to stay" as an integral part of an Information Age school system.

Assessment and Evaluation

The three goals listed in this section focus on doing strategic planning and on obtaining information about the effectiveness of programmes for computer technology that are implemented by teachers, schools and colleges.

Goal 11: Strategic Plan

Each school and college shall have a long-range strategic plan for computer technology in education. The plans shall include ongoing formative evaluation and yearly updating.

Goal 12: Student Assessment

Authentic and performance-based assessment shall be used to assess student learning of computer technology. For example, when students are being taught to communicate and to solve problems in an environment that includes routine use of the computer as a tool, they shall be assessed in the same environment.

Goal 13: Formative, Summative, and Residual Impact Evaluation

Implementation plans for information technology shall be evaluated on an ongoing basis, using formative, summative and residual impact evaluation techniques. Formative evaluation provides information for mid-programme corrections. It is conducted as programmes are being implemented. Summative evaluation provides information about the results of a programme after it has been completed, such as a particular staff development programme, a particular programme of loaning computers to students for use at home, and so on. Residual impact evaluation looks at programmes in retrospect, perhaps a year or more after a programme has ended. For example, a year after teachers participated in an in-service programme designed to help them learn to use some specific pieces of software in their classrooms, are they actually using this software or somewhat similar software?

Goals for Teacher Technology Education

In recent years, a great deal of thought has gone into determining what computer knowledge and skills teachers need to have. It is clear that a two-pronged approach is needed in teacher education. One prong is aimed at preserve education. Newly graduated teachers must have the knowledge and skills to help our schools achieve the student Goals 1-7 listed above. The second prong is in-service education. Every school needs to have in place an in-service programme that helps all teachers gain the knowledge and skills to achieve the student goals. The National Council for Teacher Education (NCTE) is the official body in India for accrediting teacher preparation programmes. The NCTE is doing the efforts in the development of teacher preparation standards. The emphasis of NCTE is to equip the teacher trainers with the recent technology. Now there is a need for both in-service teachers and pre-service teachers that know the capabilities of the computer technology in teaching-learning process and how they could use this technology in their classroom. For both pre-service and in-service teachers, the goals listed below are minimal. They provide a starting point, but they are far from the levels of competencies that teachers need if computer technology is going to have a significant positive impact on our educational system.

All candidates seeking initial endorsements in teacher preparation programmes and particularly programmes in educational computing and technology require foundations in:

- Basic Technology Operations and Concepts
- Professional and Personal Use of Technology
- Application of Technology in Instruction

Basic Technology Operations and Concepts

Candidates will use computer operating systems and user interfaces to run programmes; access, generate and manipulate data; and to publish results. They will also evaluate performance of hardware and software components of computer systems and apply basic troubleshooting strategies as needed.

Performance Indicators

Candidates will:

- operate a multimedia computer system with related peripheral devices to successfully install and use a variety of software packages.
- use terminology related to computers and technology appropriately in written and oral communications.
- describe and implement basic troubleshooting techniques related to using a multimedia system with related peripheral devices.
- operate and interface peripheral devices with a computer system supporting imaging including scanner, digital camera and/or video camera.
- observe demonstrations or uses of specific purpose electronic devices and adaptive assistive devices for special needs.
- observe demonstrations or uses of broadcast instruction, audio/video conferencing and other distant learning applications.
- demonstrate knowledge of uses of computers and technology in business, industry and society.

Personal and Professional Use of Technology

Candidates will apply tools for enhancing their own professional growth and productivity. They will use computer technology in communicating, collaborating, conducting research and solving problems. In addition, they will plan and participate in activities that encourage lifelong learning and will promote equitable, ethical and legal use of computer/technology resources.

Performance Indicators

Candidates will:

- use productivity tools for word processing, database management and spreadsheet applications.
- Apply productivity tools for creating basic multimedia presentations.
- use computer-based technologies including telecommunications to access information and enhance personal and professional productivity.

- use computers to support problem-solving, data collection, information management, communications, presentations and decision making.
- demonstrate knowledge of equity, ethics, legal and human issues concerning use of computers and technology.
- Identify computer and related technology resources for facilitating lifelong learning and emerging roles of the learner and the educator.

Application of Computer Technology in Instruction

Candidates will apply computers and related technologies to support instruction in their subject areas. They must plan and deliver instructional units that integrate a variety of software, applications and learning tools.

Performance Indicators

Candidates will:

- explore, evaluate and use computer resources including applications, tools, educational software and associated documentation.
- describe current instructional principles, research and appropriate assessment practices as related to the use of computer technology resources.
- design, deliver and assess student-learning activities that integrate computers for a variety of student grouping strategies and for diverse student populations.
- design student-learning activities that foster equitable, ethical and legal use of technology by students.
- Practice responsible, ethical and legal use of technology, information and software resources.

3
Computers and Pedagogy

After studying this chapter, the reader will be able to: Define the term 'Pedagogy'; Describe 'Pedagogical Thinking'; Application of 'Pedagogical Thinking'; Comprehend the pedagogical thinking about the use of computers in education; Give reasons for 'Why', 'When' and 'How' to use computers in education; Differentiate between 'Behaviourism', 'Cognitivism', 'Constructivism' and 'Connectivism' schools of thoughts on how people learn; Generalize the pedagogies derived from different learning theories; Compare the implications of different learning theories for classroom practices; Tabulate the main characteristics of different learning theories

As a starter to our thinking, it can be useful to explore a few points relating to our current understandings of pedagogy. From the outset it is important not to confuse pedagogy with either curriculum or simply 'teaching'; pedagogy informs both. Pedagogy is the way we teach, the strategies behind our teaching and the focus of our teaching. Pedagogy is also about learning; one cannot teach without being a learner. Understanding what is involved in the process of being a learner is part of pedagogy.

Definition of Pedagogy

Pedagogy is a term that is commonly used in teaching and learning matters, and there are a range of meanings. According to Alexander (2000, 2008a, 2008b), pedagogy is both the act of teaching as well as the thinking behind it. As Alexander (2008a) states, *"Teaching is a practical and observable act. Pedagogy encompasses that act together with the purposes, values, ideas, assumptions, theories and beliefs that informs, shape and seek to justify it"*.

Pedagogical Thinking

Children are central to everything that affects them as citizens and as people with rights and responsibilities. We need an understanding against which the questions 'what?', 'how?', 'why?', 'where?' and 'when?' can be asked in relation to learning and teaching, in order that whatever decisions we make as educators, we have something that guides our actions in the many different situations in which we work.

It is useful to consider the elements at the heart of the pedagogical decisions that we make. We need to consider what we mean when we talk about learning, teaching and development, to be enquiring about the role of interactions and environment as integral features supporting learning, teaching and development and to be aware of the values and principles that underpin all that we do.

For example, when we talk about learning, teaching and development, do we need to consider more deeply:

- our understandings of the many ways in which children learn and the need to add to and extend our own knowledge consistently,
- what we mean by children being central to their own learning, whether we are allowing for personal choice and individual responses,
- whether we are giving children enough time to allow them to deepen and develop their own theories and demonstrate their understandings,
- whether we are recognizing and valuing children's existing capabilities, interests and perspectives, and building on these to ensure valuable, coherent and challenging experiences,
- whether children are actively engaged in their learning, and whether it is purposeful, enjoyable and relevant to them, and
- whether we are giving ourselves enough time to support learning, not just across a variety of contexts, but also in *depth*.

When we talk about interactions, does this provoke further questions about?

- how and why we interact with children in certain ways at certain times,
- how to become more responsive and thoughtful in our interactions.
- whether we give ourselves enough time for interactions and for supporting interactions between children,
- whether our interactions are supported by knowledge of the child that families and others share with us, and
- why the appropriate approach may be not to interact directly.

When we talk about environment, do we need to consider more deeply:

- whether we consider the organisation of learning spaces, both indoors and outdoors, to be one of our priorities when planning for children's learning,
- how we negotiate with staff and children about the intentions for the learning space, both indoors and outdoors,

- whether resources, in terms of how they are presented, make the environment feel cluttered and lacking in space, or promote independence and in-depth exploration,
- whether we need to give more thought to questioning the place of systems and routines within the environment, both indoors and outdoors,
- whether in creating our learning environment, both indoors and outdoors, sufficient consideration has been given to its aesthetic qualities, in terms of colour, lighting, shape and design, and
- whether the wider environment, including family and community, is being taken into account when we plan learning experiences and opportunities.

When we think about the values and principles that underpin all of the above, do we need to be aware of and also reflect on?

- our image of children in twenty first century Scotland and how we value childhood;
- the values that we put on learning, the values that we bring to learning and the impact that these have on children;
- the ways in which we encourage the development of confident, competent individuals with high self-esteem and high aspirations;
- how we value diversity, tolerance and respect for self and others;
- the ways in which we value all that children bring with them, their knowledge and experiences, and important aspects of their lives; and
- the ways in which we value relationships and the contribution of others, children, families, colleagues, and other professionals.

Pedagogical Thinking about the Use of Computers in Education

Computer technology can be useful for the education only when we use it successfully. And the success of the use of computers in teaching-learning process depends on some thoughtful questions that should be asked before the use of computers in education. These questions given below:

1. Why to use computers in education?
2. When to use computers in education?
3. How to use computers in education?
4. What is learning?
5. How learning occurs in the mind of the children
6. How to make computer a learning tool?
7. How to use the computers in teaching-learning process?
8. What is the role of the teacher?
9. What is the role of the learner?

The answers of the above questions can be obtained only through the pedagogical thinking about the use of computers in education. The pedagogical thinking about the use of computers is related to the various fields listed below:

- Learning Theories,
- Pedagogical Strategies,
- Instructional Designs, and
- Computers.

Many alternative conceptual frameworks exist for describing the relationships among learning theories, pedagogical strategies, instructional designs and information and communication technologies. There are three schools of thought that posits basic principles and theories about learning; these inform the goals and models that school of thought has for instruction, which in turn influences the group's perspective on the design of pedagogical media. Many category systems are available to characterize contrasting positions about these issues.

Schools of Thought on How People Learn

Drawing on Ertmer and Newby (1993) and Driscoll (2005), Dabbagh lists three competing schools of thought on how people learn: Objectivism/Behaviorism, Cognitivism/Pragmatism, and Constructivism/Interpretivism.

Objectivism/Behaviourism

Objectivism/Behaviorism posits that reality is external and is objective, and knowledge is gained through experiences. Behaviorists believe that, since learning is based on experience, instruction centers on manipulating environmental factors to create instructional events inculcating content and procedures in ways that alter students' behaviors.

Cognitivism/Pragmatism

Cognitivism/Pragmatism posits that reality is mediated through cognitively developed representations, and knowledge is negotiated through experience and thinking. Cognitivists believe that, since learning involves both experience and thinking, instruction centers on helping learners develop interrelated, symbolic mental constructs that form the basis of knowledge and skills.

Constructivism/Interpretivism

Constructivism/Interpretivism posits that reality is internal, and knowledge is constructed. Constructivists believe that, since learning involves constructing one's own knowledge, instruction centers on helping learners to actively invent individual meaning from experience.

Each school of thought is not a single, unified theory, but rather a collection of theories distinct from each other, but loosely related by a common set of fundamental assumptions.

Connectivism

Connectivism provides insight into the dynamics of networks, environments and ecologies that supports a continual learning process. In this view, learning is strongly a networked process where a learner aggregates external contents into a holistic representation.

The Pedagogies Derived from Learning Theories

This section categorizes the pedagogies distilled from the review of learning theories undertaken in Chapter-4, 5, 6 and 7 and discusses the various essential pedagogical dimensions of learning and support mechanisms derived from these which were made available to learners while engaging in student-centered learning process.

The review of learning theories that was undertaken in Chapter-4, 5 and 6 indicates that the characteristics of these theories varied from more individual and cognitively focused through to an emphasis on social and situative learning. These broad views of learning or schools of thought may be categorized as Behaviourist (learning as observable and measurable behaviour), Cognitive/ Constructivist (learning as the construction of knowledge and meaning) and Situative (learning as social practice). All current approaches to learning, teaching and assessing can be located within these three broad perspectives. The essential difference is that behaviourist approaches rely on the notion that human behaviour is predictable, but the other two consider, according to (Winn and Snyder, 1996), the role of unobservable mental states and introspection, which are part of human behaviour.

The Pedagogy Derived from the Behaviourist Perspective

This pedagogy focuses particularly on tasks and its analysis, drill and practice:

Common Behavioural Approaches to Learning are as Follows:

- The learner takes passive and reactive role;
- Learning is mainly factual recall;
- Instruction is logically sequenced and is systematic;
- Instructional processes are aimed at learners in general and not on the individual learner; yet, learning is assumed to occur at a personal level, not socially;
- It assumes that a well-designed instruction can result in a desired learning outcome;
- Learning can be measured through learners' ability to reproduce;

- Approach to assessment is as scientific measurement at the level of the individual.

Implications of Behaviourism for Practice

- List the learning outcomes (Bloom's Taxonomies show how these can be categorised);
- Assessment must be based on the learning outcomes and nothing else;
- Break the material down into small units;
- Carefully sequence the units according to the desired learning;
- Present the rules for learning the topic;
- Ensure that the learner actively responds (does things);
- Provide opportunities for frequent learner feedback; and
- Reinforce correct behaviour with immediate rewards.

All these have strong influence over learners' attention, perception and memory. Gaining attention is the first step in Gagne's events of instruction. Therefore, it is crucial for educators to recognise and respond to the emotions and moods of their students in order to facilitate engagement and motivation.

The Pedagogy Derived from the Cognitive/Constructivist Perspective

Constructivist Learning Environments

Here the focus is on the learning design guidelines and goals that attempt to incorporate various views of social constructivism in the context of activity theory. Constructivist philosophy can work with a curriculum with the onus on student centred, collaborative, reflective and resource-based learning. The constructivist view of learning can be summarised as below:

- learning is a personal/subjective interpretation of the world;
- learning is an active process of constructing knowledge through understanding rather than acquiring knowledge;
- learning is a self-regulated process in which meaning is developed on the basis of experience and prior knowledge;
- conceptual growth comes from the negotiation of meaning, the sharing of multiple perspectives and the changing of our internal representations through collaborative learning;
- learning should be situated in realistic settings; testing should be integrated with the task and not be a separate activity.

Accordingly, two aspects that are very relevant for active construction of knowledge are:

- Interactions with the environment;
- Collaboration among learners which help them in their development of understanding;

The design principles for constructivist teaching and learning activities can be listed as follows:

- Ownership of the task/personal learning objectives;
- Coaching and modelling of thinking skills;
- Scaffolding;
- Guided discovery;
- Opportunity for reflection and metacognition;
- Cognitive puzzlement through ill-structured problems; and
- Integrated assessment strategies.

Implications of Constructivism for Practice (Carlile, Jordan, and Stack, 2004; Jonassen, Davidson, Collins, Campbell, and Haag, 1995)

- Present an overview of the topic including purpose and objectives;
- Approach material from the learner's perspective and values;
- Acknowledge and accommodate student diversity (ability, age, gender, culture, nationality);
- Encourage reflection through the use of learning journals etc;
- Provide multiple representations of reality - avoid oversimplification of instruction by representing the natural complexity of the world;
- Present authentic tasks;
- Explain the relevance of the topic;
- Build on what is already known;
- Encourage active and discovery and independent learning;
- Give timely feedback on performance;
- Constructively align objectives, strategies and assessment;
- Support collaborative construction of knowledge through social negotiation not competition among learners for recognition.

The Pedagogy Derived from the Situative Perspective: Communities of Practice

The situative perspective to learning represents a shift from cognitive view of learning (as if it were a process contained in the mind of the learner, decontextualised from the world) to a situational orientation to learning—the study of learning as in a specific time, place and social activity—as 'situated learning'; in this view, 'distributed' among person, language, artifacts, activities and environment (Lave and Wenger, 1999).

The pedagogy of learning from a situative perspective focuses on intellectual development through the cycle of learning, moving through the phases of externalisation (of tacit knowledge), sharing, discussion, refinement and then internalisation (Goodyear, 2002). This can occur through 'situatedness' by participating in a community of practice, and learning groups whereby learners can have joint engagement in some activity and share ideas mediated through individual relationships (Mayes and de Freitas, 2004). According to situated learning (Tennant, 1997: 77):

- It makes no sense to talk of knowledge that is decontextualized, abstract or general; and
- New knowledge and learning are properly conceived as being located in communities of practice.

The modern trend is towards more 'situative' approaches to curriculum design, teaching approaches and assessment strategies. Situative view to learning can be summarised as below:

- All learning is 'situated' in the practices of communities;
- Learners construct knowledge and understandings within a social and cultural context;
- A learner will always be influenced by the social and cultural setting in which the learning occurs;
- Shift from a focus on the individual learning to an emphasis on social and collaborative learning;
- Social interaction and collaboration are essential components of situated learning;
- New learning is shaped by prior knowledge and cultural perspectives; and
- Construction of meaning is from authentic activity and experience; Tennant (1997) argues that there is an intimate connection between knowledge and activity.

Herrington (1997) identifies the following characteristics or elements of a situated learning model:

- authentic context that reflects the way knowledge will be used in real life;
- authentic activities and assessment;
- access to expert performances and modelling of processes;
- multiple roles and perspectives;
- collaborative construction of knowledge;
- coaching and scaffolding; and
- articulation and reflection. (p. 44)

Significant Pointers for Practice of Situative Learning

- Learning is in the relationships between people;
- People can become participants in communities of practice; and
- There is an intimate connection between knowledge and activity. Problem solving and learning from experience become central processes.

Common strategies include problem-based learning, anchored instruction and cognitive apprenticeship.

Mapping Pedagogies and Technologies

Given below is a summary of important learning theories, the key characteristics they promoted, and some insight into how they might be realized in the context of online and blended learning.

Table 3.1: Mapping the Main Characteristics of Learning Theories and the Affordances of New Technology

Theories	*Main Characteristics and Pedagogical Strategies*	*Potential online applications*
Behaviourist	• Focuses on stimulus-response and observable and measurable learning outcomes; • Trial and error learning; • Learning through association and reinforcement; • Focus on observable and measurable overt outcomes; • Learning is at a personal level, not social.	• Presentation of appropriately sequenced content online in multiple media formats to convey information; • Online assessments to test individual learner's achievement level using e-assessment; • Teacher provides appropriate feedback so that students can monitor how they are doing and take corrective action if required; • Peer feedback.
Cognitive	• Focuses on the processes by which learners build their own mental structures when interacting with an environment or through engagement in hands-on, self directed tasks; • Views learning as transformations in these cognitive structures; • Pedagogical focus is on the processing of information through communication, negotiations, and problem solving; • Emphasis on interpersonal relationships involving collaborative and cooperative construction of knowledge; • Useful for designing sequences of conceptual material which build on existing information structures;	• Interactive online materials; • Links to different resources at different difficulty levels in order to accommodate learners at different knowledge levels; • Technology-supported strategies to scaffold student's working memory, and to present content in multiple formats; • Provide prerequisite materials or pre-instructional strategies, such as advance organizers to help learners recall prior knowledge or to activate existing cognitive structures as part of the learning process (Ausubel, 1960); • Include various pedagogic strategies in online instruction to accommodate individual differences and learning styles (Cassidy, 2004); • Access to online resources and expertise offers the potential to develop more engaging and student-centred, active and authentic learning environments;

(*Contd.*)

Table 3.1 (*Contd.*)

Theories	*Main Characteristics and Pedagogical Strategies*	*Potential online applications*
	• Pedagogical focus is task orientated, encourages hands-on, self-directed activities orientated towards discovery.	• Different online communication tools — asynchronous and synchronous communication offer the potential for more diverse and richer forms of dialogue and interaction between students and tutors and amongst peers; • The potential for new forms of communities of practice or facilities to support and enhance collaborative knowledge construction; • Archive of materials, and different forms of communication and experiences provide ample opportunity for reflection anytime and to learn at one's own pace; • Microworlds and simulations.
Situative	• All learning is 'situated' in the practices of communities; • A learner will always be influenced by the social and cultural setting in which the learning occurs; • Shift from a focus on the individual learning to an emphasis on social and collaborative learning; • Social interaction and collaboration are essential components of situated learning; • Construction of meaning from authentic activity and experience; • Common strategies include problem-based learning, anchored instruction and cognitive apprenticeship.	• Access to resources and expertise offers the potential to develop more engaging and student centred, active and authentic learning environments; • Different online communication tools — asynchronous and synchronous communication offer the potential for more diverse and richer forms of dialogue and interaction between students and tutors and amongst peers; • The potential for the development of new forms of communities of practice or facilities to support and enhance collaborative knowledge construction; • Application of Laurillard's conversation model to elearning highlights the importance of activities and dialogue, and the need for discursive tools, adaptability, interactivity and reflection. • Networking capabilities of the Web/ Communication tools in WebCT enable more diverse access to different types of learning resources and the potential for the development of different types of communities.

The attributes summarized in the above table as well as many of the aforementioned concepts provide useful heuristics for creating online and blended learning environments.

4
Behaviourist Pedagogy

After studying this chapter, the reader will be able to: Explain the Behaviourism learning theory; Describe the fundamentals of Behaviourism; Define the Behaviourist pedagogy; Tell the name of famous Behaviourist; Comprehend the contribution of some famous Behaviourist in education; Specify the effects of Behaviourism on instructional design; Explain the important instructional designs based on Behaviourist pedagogy

Behaviourism refers to a theory of learning that focuses on behavioural conditioning. As a learning theory, behaviourism can be traced back to Aristotle, whose essay "Memory" focused on associations between events such as lightning and thunder. Other philosophers that followed Aristotelian thought were Hobbs (1650), Hume (1740), Brown (1820), Bain (1855) and Ebbinghause (1885) (Black, 1995). The theory of behaviourism concentrates on the study of overt behaviours that can be observed and measured (Good & Brophy, 1990). It views the mind as a "black box" in that response to a stimulus can be observed quantitatively, totally ignoring the possibility of thought processes occurring in the mind. Some key players in the development of the behaviourist theory were Pavlov, Watson, Thorndike and Skinner.

Rewards and Punishments

This type of learning is based on rewards and punishments or rather the use of positive and negative reinforcement. Behavioural learning strives to create permanent change in observable behaviours by strengthening the relationship between specific stimuli and desired responses. When a learner's response is what the teacher wants "or is correct" the behaviour is positively rewarded. The correct answer-and-rewards model of learning is used in educational settings around the world. While behaviourism is considered by some to be "old hat", there is evidence showing that the learning theory is widely used especially in assessment. Behavioural approaches are well-suited to reinforcing pedagogical objectives particularly when memorization is paramount. Behaviourism is easy to deploy pedagogically online and popular in game design. In gaming, there are many opportunities to reinforce desired behaviours which can be integrated into computer training by repetition. Behaviourism was established as a learning model through the works of Skinner, Watson, Pavlov, Thorndike (connectionism), Bandura, Tolman (moving toward cognitivism).

Classical Conditioning

Learning where an unconditioned stimulus following a neutral stimulus closely causes an unconditioned response. After repetition, the neutral stimulus will cause the unconditioned response without the unconditioned stimulus and will become a conditioned response.

Operant Conditioning

Learning where behaviours are modified by consequences; behaviours may change in form, frequency or strength; in brief, a voluntary response is followed by a reinforcing stimulus.

Major Contributors to the Behavioral Movement and their Contributions

The Table 4.1 clearly shows the major contributors to the behavioural movement and their contributions.

Implications of Behaviorism on Instructional Design

One of the key areas where behaviorism impacts instructional design is in the development of instructional objectives. Morrison, Ross and Kemp (2001, p. 91) define an instructional objective written from a behavioral perspective as "a precise statement that answers the question, 'What behavior can the learner demonstrate to indicate that he or she has mastered the knowledge or skills specified in the instruction?'" Writing "precise" instructional objectives can be challenging but offers instructional designers clear, measurable goals to which to guide their instructional design. Mager (1984, p. 21) determined that performance, conditions, and criterion are the elements of instructional objectives. From a behavioral viewpoint, the conditions element of writing instructional objectives can represent the stimulus/environment and the performance element can represent the response while the criterion element is considered the acceptable level of behavior expected. In all, an implication of behaviorism on instructional design is built upon the concept that learning is based on mastering a set of behaviors that are predictable and therefore reliable. Thorough instructional and learner analyses and precise instruction will lead to desirable and demonstrable skills.

Table 4.1: Major Contributors to the Behavioural Movement

Contributor	*Contribution(s)*
Robert Mager	How to write objectives (1) describe a behavior, (2) the conditions under which the behavior takes place, (3) the desired minimal level of learner proficiency. (1962).
W. James Popham	(1967) Objectives: instructional objective must describe an observable behavior of the learner of a product which is a consequence of observable behaviors.
B.F. Skinner	Programmed instruction, teaching machine, Skinner box (1950s) Operant Conditioning (responses are contrived) – if operant response is followed by a reinforcing stimulus the strength of the response is increased. Studies on animals as well as applications to humans; +/- reinforcement, punishment, extinction, schedules of reinforcement, forgetting.
E.L. Thorndike	S-R studies with cats in box with latch; Classical conditioning (natural responses); Laws of Effect, Readiness and Exercise. Connectionism. Bond-theory. (1900-10s)
Ralph Tyler	Eight Year Study - Educational objectives.
Ivan Pavlov	S-R studies with dogs and salivation: "conditioned reflex", classical conditioning. (1900s)
John Watson	Father of American behaviorism; experiment with Albert; Classical conditioning.
Sidney Pressey	(1920s) Teaching machines: immediate feedback, self-correcting, self-pacing. Believed human learning was different from animal learning.

Behaviourist Pedagogy and Instructional Design

Until the 1960s, behaviourism did not have an impact on educational technology. Given below, there are six areas that demonstrate the impact of behaviourism on educational technology:

I. Behavioural Objectives Movement

A behavioural objective states learning objectives in "specified, quantifiable, terminal behaviours" (Saettler, pp. 288, 1990). Behavioural objectives can be summed up using the mnemonic device ABCD (Schwier, 1998), for example—

After having completed the unit the, student would be able to answer correctly 90 per cent of the questions on the post-test

Here,

- **A** → Audience – the student;
- **B** → Behaviour – answer correctly;
- **C**→ Condition – after having completed the unit, on a post-test; and
- **D** → Degree – 90 per cent correct.

The advent of behavioural objectives can be traced back to the Elder Sophists of ancient Greece, Cicero, Herbart and Spencer.

(i) Taxonomic Analysis of Learning Behaviours

(a) Bloom's Taxonomy of Educational Objectives

Bloom's Taxonomy of Educational Objectives or simply *Bloom's Taxonomy*– is a classification of different skills that educators set for student learning objectives. It was proposed in 1956 by the educational psychologist Benjamin Bloom at the University of Chicago. His taxonomy divides educational objectives into three "domains": affective, psychomotor and cognitive. Like other taxonomies, Bloom's is hierarchical; meaning that learning at the higher levels is dependent on having attained prerequisite knowledge and skills at lower levels. The *cognitive domain* includes those behaviours of objectives dealing with intellectual outcomes such as knowledge, understanding and thinking skills. The *affective domain* includes those objectives that emphasize feelings and emotions such as interest, appreciation, attitudes, etc. The *psychomotor domain* deals with those objectives that emphasize motor skills such as doing, practicing, demonstrating, etc. with each of these three domains, categories or levels for classifying objectives are described in hierarchical order from the simplest to the most complex learning/behavioural outcomes. Below is a description with examples of behaviours and model questions that may be used for each category within each domain. Within each domain, the lowest number indicates the lowest category or level with the highest number indicating the highest category or level. The main goal of Bloom's Taxonomy is to motivate educators to focus on all three domains, creating a holistic approach to education (Table 4.2).

(b) Gagne's Taxonomy of Learning

Robert Gagne developed his taxonomy of learning in 1972. Gagne's taxonomy was comprised of five categories as below:

1. Verbal Information
2. Intellectual Skill
   - 2.1 Discrimination
   - 2.2 Concrete Concept
   - 2.3 Defined Concept
   - 2.4 Rule
   - 2.5 Higher Order Rule
3. Cognitive Strategy
4. Attitude
5. Motor Skill

(ii) Mastery Learning

Mastery learning assumes that all students can master the materials presented in the lesson. Morrison originally developed mastery learning in the 1930s. His formula for mastery was:

Table 4.2: Classification of Instructional Objectives

Code	*Descriptive of Categorize (Ideas)*	*Examples of Behaviour*	*Examples*	*Instructional Strategies*
(1)	(2)	(3)	(4)	(5)
Cognitive Domain				
1.	**Knowledge** Knowledge is defined as the remembering of previously learned material. This may involve the recall of a wide range of material, from specific facts to complete theories but all that is required is the bringing to mind of the appropriate at information. Knowledge represents the lowest level of learning outcomes in the cognitive domain.	Define, Identify, Label, List, Match, Memorize, Name, Outline, Recall, State, Repeat, Relate, Record, Underline, Recite, Select, Choose, Recognize	Who? Where? Which one? What? How? What is the best one? Why? How much? When? What does it mean?	Highlighting Rehearsal Memorizing Mnemonics
2.	**Comprehension** Comprehension is defined as the ability to grasp the meaning of material. This may be shown by translating material from one form to another (words to numbers) by interpreting material (predicting consequences or effects). These learning outcomes go one step beyond the simple remembering of material and represent the lowest level of understanding.	Defend, Describe, Discuss, Explain, Generalize, Give example, Identify, Infer, Locate, Predict, Recognize, Report, Restate, Rewrite, Summarize, Tell, Translate, Interpret, Select	State in your own words? Which are facts? What does this mean? Give an example Select the best definition Explain what is happening	Key examples Emphasize connections Elaborate concepts Summarize Create Visual representations (concept maps, outlines, flow charts).
3	**Application** Application refers to the ability to use learned material in a new and concrete situation. This may include the application of such things as rules, methods, concepts, principles, laws and theories. Learning outcomes in this area requires a higher level of understanding.	Apply, Change, Compute, Demonstrate Discover Dramatize, Employ, Illustrate, Modify, Operate, Practice, Predict, Prepare, Produce, Relate, Solve, Use, Sketch	Predict what would happen if apply	Modeling Cognitive apprenticeships Mindful practice Not just a routine Practice Algorithms Coached practice Case studies

(Contd.)

Table 4.2: (*Contd.*)

(1)	(2)	(3)	(4)	(5)
4	**Analysis** Analysis refers to the ability to break down material into its component parts so that its organizational structure may be understood. This may include the identification of the parts, analysis of the relationships between parts and recognition of the organizational principles involved. Learning outcomes are of higher intellectual level than comprehension and application, as it needs an understanding of both the content and the structural form of the material.	Analyze, Break down Calculate Categorize Compare, Debate Differentiate Distinguish Examine Experiment Identify, Inspect, Inventory, Point out, Relate, Separate, Solve, Subdivide, Test, Relationship	What is the function of—? What's the relationship between---? Make a distinction. What ideas justify the conclusion? Examine the result of --?	Models of thinking Challenging assumptions Retrospective analysis Decision-making situations Debates
5	**Synthesis** Synthesis refers to the ability to put parts together to form a new whole. This may involve the production of a unique communication (theme or speech) a plan of operations (research proposal) or a set of abstract relations (scheme for classifying information). Learning outcomes in this area are stress creative behaviours with major emphasis on the formulation of new patterns of structures.	Arrange, Assemble, Categorize, Collect, Combine, Compare, Compile, Construct, Create, Design, Formulate, Generate	Propose an alternative Modify this theory Relate these things Rewrite the script State a rule How would you test-----? Design a machine to perform a specific task	Modeling Challenging assumptions Reflection through journaling Debates Discussion and other collaborative learning activities Decision-making situations
6	**Evaluation** Evaluation is concerned with the ability to judge the value of material (statement, novel, poem, research report, principle) for a given purpose. The judgments are to be based on definite criteria. These may be internal (organization) or external (relevance to the purpose) and a student may determine the criteria or be given to them. Learning outcomes are highest in the cognitive hierarchy as they contain elements of the other entire categories plus conscious value judgments base on.	Appraise, Assess, Choose, Compare, Conclude, Contract, Criticize, Describe, Discriminate, Estimate, Evaluate, Explain, Interpret, Judge, Justify, Measure, Rate, Relate, Revise, Score, Select, Summarize, Support, Value	Which is more important, moral, better, logical, valid, appropriate Find the errors? Select the most effective solution	Challenging assumptions Debates Discussion Collaborating learning activities Decision-making situations

(*Contd.*)

Table 4.2: (*Contd.*)

(1)	(2)	(3)	(4)	(5)
	Affective Domain (Attitudes)			
7	**Receiving** Receiving refers to the students' willingness to attend particular phenomena or stimuli (classroom activities, text book, etc.). From a teaching standpoint, it is concerned with getting, holding and directing the students' attention. Learning outcomes range from the simple awareness to selective attention on the part of the learner.	Ask, Choose, Describe, Discriminate, Follow, Give, Hold, Identify, Listen, Locate, Names, Observe, Point to, Prefer, Realize, Reply, Select, Use	Listen to others with respect Listen for and remember the name of newly introduced people	Awareness Willingness to hear Selected attention
8	**Responding** Responding refers to active participation on the part of the student. At this level, he not only attends a particular phenomenon but also reacts to it in same way. Learning outcomes in this area may emphasize acquiescence in responding (read assigned material), willingness to respond (voluntarily reads beyond assignment) or satisfaction in responding (reads for pleasure or enjoyment). The higher levels of this category include those instructional objectives that are commonly classified under "interests", that is, those interests that stress enjoyment of particular activities.	Answer, Assist, Assume, Comply, Conform, Consider, Contribute, Cooperate, Discuss, Display, Engage, Enrich, Exhibit, Explore, Extend, Help, Label, Obey, Participate, Perform, Practice, Present, Read, Recite, Report, Respond, Select, Tell, Volunteer, Willing, Write	Participate in classroom Discussions Gives a presentation	Active Participation on the part of the learners Attends and reacts to a particular phenomenon Emphasize learning outcomes Compliance in responding Willingness to respond Satisfaction in responding
9	**Valuing** Valuing is concerned with the worth or values a student attachment to a particular object, phenomenon or behaviour. This ranges in degree from the simpler acceptance of a value (desire to improve group skills) to the more complex level of commitment (assumes responsibility for the effective functioning of the group). Valuing is based on the internalization of a set of specified values but clues to these values are expressed in the student's overt behaviour. Learning outcomes in this area are concern with behaviour that is consistent and stable	Accept, Assume, Responsible, Complete, Continue to desire, Describe, Devote, Differentiate, Enable, Examine, Explain, Feels, Follow, Form, Grow, Influence, Initiate, Invite, Is loyal to, Join, Justify, Participate	Demonstrates belief in the democratic process Proposes a plan to social improvement and follows through with commitment	Attachment Internalization

(*Contd.*)

Table 4.2: (*Contd.*)

(1)	(2)	(3)	(4)	(5)
	enough to make the value clearly identifiable. Instructional objectives that are commonly classified under "attitudes and "appreciation" would fall into this category.	Prefer, Read, Report, Select, Share, Study, Work, Demonstrates, Propose		
10	**Organization** Organization is concerned with bringing together difference values, resolving conflicts between them and beginning the building of an internally consistent value system. Thus, the emphasis is on comparing, relating and synthesizing values. Learning outcomes may be and concerned with the conceptualization of a value (recognizes the responsibility of each individual for improving human relations) or with the organization of a value system (develops a vocational plan that satisfies his need for both economic security and social service). Instructional objective relating to the development of a philosophy of life would fall into this category.	Adhere, Alter, Arrange, Combine, Compare, Complete, Crystallize form, Defend, Explain, Generalize, Identify, Is realistic, Judgment, Judge, Modify, Order, Organize, Prepare, Regulate, Relate, Synthesize, Weigh	Recognizes the need for balance between freedom and responsible behaviour Creates a life plan in harmony with abilities, interests and beliefs	Organizes values into priorities Creation of unique value system Comparing, relating and synthesizing different values
11	**Characterization** At this level of the affective domain, the individual has a value system that has controlled his behaviour for a sufficiently long time for him to develop a characteristic life style. Thus the behaviour is pervasive, consistent and predictable. Learning outcomes at this level cover a broad range of activities but the major emphasis is on the fact that the behaviour is typical or characteristic of the student.	Act, Approach, Arrive, Change, Discriminate Display, Examine, Find, Influence, Is conscientious, Is consistent, Judge, Listen, Modify, Perform, Plan, Practice, Propose, Qualify, Question, Ready, Rely, Revise, Serve, Solve, Use, Verify, View	Shows self-reliance when working independently Cooperates in group Activities Displays a Professional commitment to ethical practice on a daily basis Revises judgments	Value system that controls the student's behaviour

(*Contd.*)

Table 4.2: *(Contd.)*

(1)	(2)	(3)	(4)	(5)
Psychomotor Domain (Skills)				
12	**Perception** The ability to use sensory cues to guide motor activity. This ranges from sensory stimulation, through cue selection to translation.	Choose, Describe, Detect, Differentiate, Distinguish, Identify, Isolate, Relate, Select	Detects non-verbal communication cues Estimate where a ball will fall after it is thrown and moving to the correct location to catch the ball	Meaningful observation Alternative behaviour
13	**Set** Set means readiness to act. It includes mental, physical and emotional sets. These three sets are dispositions that pre-determine a person's response to different situations. It is also called mindsets. This subdivision of psychomotor domain is closely related with the "Responding" subdivision of the affective domain	Begin, Display, Explain, Move, Proceed, React, Shows, State, Volunteer	Knows and acts upon a sequence of steps in a manufacturing process Shows desire to learn a new process	Mental, physical & emotional stability Responses against different situations
14	**Guided response** The early stages in learning a complex skill that includes imitation and trial & error. Adequacy in performance is achieved through practicing.	Copy, Trace, Follow, React, Reproduce, Respond, Perform	Performs a mathematical equation as demonstrated	Steps with conscious awareness of efforts
15	**Mechanism** This is the intermediate stage in learning a complex skill. Learned responses have become habitual and movements can be performed with some confidence and proficiency.	Assemble, Calibrate, Construct, Display, Fastness, Fix, Grind, Manipulate, Measure, Mend, Mixes, Organize, Sketch	Use a personal computer Drive a car	Practicing Little conscious effort
16	**Complex Overt Response** The skillful performance of motor acts that involve complex movement patterns. Proficiency is indicated by a quick, accurate and highly coordinated performance, requiring a minimum of energy. This category includes performing without hesitation and automatic performance. Note: The key words are the same as "Mechanism" but will have adverbs or adjectives that indicate that the performance is quicker, better, more accurate, etc.	Assemble, Build, Calibrate, Construct, Display, Fastens, Fixes, Grind, Manipulate, Measure, Mend, Organize, Sketch	Maneuvers a car into a tight parallel parking spot Operate a computer quickly and accurately Displays competence while playing the piano	Performance without hesitation

(Contd.)

Table 4.2: (*Contd.*)

(1)	(2)	(3)	(4)	(5)
17	**Adaptation** Skills are well developed and the individual can modify movement patterns to fit special requirements.	Adapt, Alter, Change, Rearrange, Reorganize, Revise, Var	Responds effectively to unexpected experiences Modifies instruction to meet the needs of the learners	Improvement & changes in physical patterns
18	**Origination** Creating a new movement patterns to fit a particular situation or specific problem. Learning outcomes emphasize creativity based upon highly developed skills.	Arrange, Build, Combine, Compose, Construct, Create, Design, Initiate, Make, Originate	Constructs a new theory Develops a new and comprehensive training programming Creates a new gymnastic routine	Unique behaviour pattern

- Pre-test
- Teach
- Test the result
- Adapt procedure
- Teach and test again

(iii) Military and Industrial Approach

For military and industrial training, "behavioural objectives were written descriptions of specific terminal behaviours that were manifested in terms of observable, measurable behaviour." (Saettler, 1990). Robert Mager wrote a book on "Preparing Instructional Objectives," in 1962, which promoted interest and use of behavioural objectives among educators. Gagne and Briggs, who also had backgrounds in military and industrial psychology, developed a set of instructions for writing objectives that is based on Mager's work.

II. Teaching Machines and Programmed Instruction Movement

Although the elder Sophists, Comenius, Herbert, and Montessori used the concept of programmed instruction in their repertoire, B.F. Skinner is the most current and probably best known advocate of teaching machines and programmed learning. Contributors to this movement include the following:

Pressey: introduced a multiple-choice teaching machine at the 1925 American Psychological Association meeting.

Peterson: Pressey's former student, who developed "Chemosheets" in which the learner checked their answers with a chemical dipped swab.

Crowder: designed a branched style of programming for the US Air Force in 1950's to train troubleshooters to find malfunctions in electronic equipment.

Skinner: based on operant conditioning skinner's teaching machine required the learner to complete or answer a question and then receive feedback on the correctness of the response. Skinner demonstrated his machine in 1954.

Programmed Instruction

Programmed instruction is an instructional method where learning content is broken down into small sections or short chunks. The behavioural principles devised by Skinner, the famous researcher in behaviourism, are used in many classrooms around the world today. Programmed instruction is a type of instruction that lends itself to computer-based learning. Programmed instruction was adapted by the American psychologist and learning theorist Robert Mills Gagné who described programmed learning as a part of his classroom teaching. The difference between programmed instruction and programmed learning is that the former concept was devised to modify behaviours whereas the latter was devised to teach facts. Skinner's theory is based on the stimulus-response and reinforcement model of learning. Skinner said that positive reinforcement is important in learning but teachers use too little of it. He noted learning can be divided into "very small steps and reinforcement must be contingent on the accomplishment of each" step along the way.

In *"The Science of Learning and the Art of Teaching"*, Skinner said that effective instructional materials, which he called programmed instructional materials, should include small steps, frequent questions, immediate feedback, and allow for self-pacing approaches.

Components of Programmed Instruction

The main components of programmed instruction are as follows:

- Behavioural objectives, clearly stated
- Small frames of instruction, carefully sequenced
- Self-pacing instructional sections, units, modules
- Active learner response to questions
- Immediate feedback and positive reinforcement

Steps in Programmed Instruction Design

The main steps of programmed instruction design are given below:

- Specify the goals of instruction: what is to be learned
- Identify the 'entry skills of the learners', i.e., what is the current level of skills of the learners
- Develop a series of steps that will get the students form where they are to where they should be
- Instruction is programmed in small steps, i.e., successive approximations to the desired behaviour
- Provide appropriate reinforcement

Principles of Skinner's Programmed Instruction

The principles of Skinner's programmed instruction are listed below:

- Shaping refers *"the reinforcement of successive approximations to a goal behavior"* (Driscoll, 2000). This process requires the learner to perform successive approximations of the target behaviour by changing the criterion behaviour for reinforcement to become more like the final performance. In sum, learner's behaviours are shaped by the reinforcement of desired learning behaviours. To begin shaping, learners should be rewarded for each step of the learning sequence, no matter how small.
- Chaining: Skinner proposed that acquiring complex behaviours is a result of chaining. Chaining establishes *"complex behaviors made*

up of discrete, simpler behaviours already known to the learner" (Driscoll, 2000). In programmed instruction, content is arranged in small steps, and progress from simple to complex tasks, and require a response from the learner to proceed. Behavioural chaining occurs when a succession of steps is learned. Learners master each step in sequence until the entire sequence is learned.

III. Individualized Approaches to Instruction

Individualized instruction began in early 1900s and was revived in the 1960s. The Keller Plan, Individually Prescribed Instruction, Programme of Learning in Accordance with Needs and Individually Guided Education, all are examples of individualized instruction in the U.S. (Saettler, 1990).

(i) Keller's Personalized System of Instruction (PSI) (1963)

F.S. Keller, a colleague of Skinner, developed Keller Plan. The Keller Plan was used for university level. The main features of the Keller Plan are as follows:

- Individually paced
- Mastery learning
- Lectures and demonstrations motivational rather than critical information
- Use of proctors, which permitted testing, immediate scoring, tutoring, personal-social aspect of educational process

Keller's Personalized System of Instruction (PSI) is a personalized/ customized system of instruction that promotes the mastery of predetermined sets of objectives for learners. As originally described by Keller in *Good Bye Teacher* in 1968, PSI consists of short self-paced units where study guides are used to help learners navigate content. The units in each module show learners how much mastery they have achieved, and 90 per cent must be attained at each unit level and module in order to proceed to the next. In Keller's system, student proctors assist individual learners with problems as they learn and lectures are delivered by instructors for motivational purposes only. PSI combines mastery learning with the principles of behavioural reinforcement. Mastery learning also requires that the desired performance of learners is precisely outlined in the learning objectives. Burton, Moore and Magliaro have described PSI as an interlocking system of instruction that consists of sequentially, progressive tasks. The teaching method has been shown to be effective in producing significant improvement in student achievement (Burton, Moore and Maliaro, 1996). Aspects of the Keller's system can be seen in other self-pacing systems of instruction.

Five Essential Features of PSI

In his seminal paper "Goodbye, Teacher" (Keller, 1968), Keller describes the five components of PSI as:

1. A personalized system *"permits students to move through a course at a speed commensurate with his/her ability and demands on his time"* i.e., a self-pacing feature
2. It *"lets the student go ahead to new material only after demonstrating mastery of that which preceded"* i.e., progressively sequential units
3. Any lectures and demonstrations do not convey "critical information... but are vehicles of motivation"
4. Teacher-student communication is conveyed via written text
5. The use of proctors, "which permits repeated testing, immediate scoring, almost unavoidable tutoring, and a marked enhancement of the personal-social aspect of the educational process"

According to Keller (1968), instructional design systems should be developed to improve and update the provision of instructional information. He searched for methodical patterns based on previous successes so that students can progress in a systematic manner toward specified outcomes. Keller developed his system appropriately called the *Personalized System of Instruction (PSI)* or the Keller Plan. PSI is an interlocking system of instruction, which consists of sequential, progressive tasks that area designed as highly individualized learning activities. In this design, students determine their own rate and amount of learning, as they progress through a series of instructional tasks.

More Detail towards PSI

The main steps of PSI are given below:

- Identify goal statements
- Break content into chunks
- Develop study guides, including objectives, study procedures, questions, individual works
- Student self pace each
- Test and provide immediate feedback
- Review and retest
- Present more new units

(ii) Individually Prescribed Instruction (IPI) 1964

Learning Research and Development Center of the University of Pitsburgh developed IPI in 1964. The main features of the IPI were:

- prepared units,

- behavioural objectives,
- planned instructional sequences,
- used for reading, mathematics and science,
- included pre-test and post-test for each unit, and
- materials continually evaluated and upgraded to meet behavioural objectives.

(iii) Programme for Learning in accordance with Needs (PLAN) (1967)

PLAN was developed under the sponsorship of American Institutes for Research (AIR). The main features of PLAN are included:

- schools selected items from about 6000 behavioural objectives;
- each instructional module took about two weeks instruction and were made up of approximately five objectives;
- mastery learning; and
- remedial learning plus re-testing.

IV. Computer Assisted Instruction (CAI)

Computer-assisted instruction was first used in education and training during the 1950s. Early work was done by IBM, Gordon Pask, O. M. Moore, etc but CAI grew rapidly in the 1960s when federal funding for research and development in education and industrial laboratories was implemented. The U.S. Government was keen to determine the possible effectiveness of computer-assisted instruction and developed two competing companies (Control Data Corporation and Mitre Corporation) who came up with the PLATO and TICCIT projects. Now a days CAI is the thrust area of the educational research. In developing countries like India, the potential features of CAI are unlimited. There is a need to explore this current area for the upliftment of the traditional teaching-learning process.

V. System Approach to Instruction

The systems approach was developed out of the efforts made during 1950s and 1960s with focus on language laboratories, teaching machines, programmed instruction, multimedia presentations and the use of the computer in instruction. Most systems approaches are similar to computer flow charts with steps that the designer moves through during the development of instruction. Rooted in the military and business world, the systems approach involved setting goals and objectives, analyzing resources, devising a plan of action and continuous evaluation/modification of the programme.

5
Cognitivist Pedagogy

After studying this chapter, the reader will be able to: Explain the Cognitivism learning theory; Define the Cognitivist pedagogy; Give reasons why cognitivist revolution replace Behaviourism; Write the main features of Cognitivist classroom; Tell the name of some famous Cognitivist; Comprehend the contribution of some famous Cognitivist in education; Specify the effects of Cognitivism on instructional design; Explain the important instructional designs based on Cognitivist pedagogy.

As early as the 1920s, educators began to see the limitations of behavioural learning models. For instance, Tolman found that rats used in experiments seemed to be able to retrieve "mental maps" of the mazes that they had used before. Because some parts of a maze were closed off, the rats did not use them for they "knew" through previous existing cognitive schema that certain paths would block their paths. Visually, rats could not see the dead-end pathways but still opted for longer routes due to previous memories.

There were other reasons that the science of learning moved beyond behavioural models. Behaviourists were unable to explain why certain social behaviours in children were not always reinforced through a reward system. So how did these children learn these behaviours? In fact, what researchers learned was that children often imitate appropriate behaviours through observation, and in some instances adopt behaviours without any positive reinforcement or rewards.

Still other researchers extended the principles of behaviourism to include other elements. Bandura and Walters, for example, departed from traditional behavioural conditioning by suggesting children must perform tasks and receive positive reinforcement before they can be said to have learned something. In their book, *Social Learning and Personality Development*, some individuals were seen to adopt social behaviours through observational experiences in the home or school. This finding led to Bandura's social learning theory (Dembo, 1994).

Cognitivism

Cognitivism is a theory and psychology of learning that states human beings process information and meaning through the retrieval of experiences stored as *mental schema.* Cognitive structures help us to think, absorb and retain information and knowledge via previously-experienced events. This process involves access to memories and building mental schema to recognize, recall, apply, understand and reflect on knowledge. Cognitivists do not require outward displays of learning behaviour but only as an indication of the internal cognitive processes taking place. Finally, cognitivists seek to understand how we learn and how cultural differences affect how we perceive cognitive development across the lifespan. Cognitivism uses the metaphor of the mind as computer: information comes in, is processed and ultimately leads to a change in our thoughts and perceptions.

Cognitivists believe that learners process, store and retrieve information from the brain or *the black box.* The learner's ability to create associations and knowledge is part of their skill in processing and assimilating information. This is why a structured set of tasks that teach new skills is favoured by most cognitivists. Cognitivism is also known as the science of human cognitive development. Cognitivism is best described as learning established through continuity, structures and repetition. Observing others in the same situation as well as personal reinforcement are contributors to learning retention. Online learning makes it easy for learners to repeat lessons and to associate sound with text or images with concepts, etc.

Basic Tenets of Cognitivism

> *"Cognitive theorists recognize that much learning involves associations established through contiguity and repetition. They also acknowledge the importance of reinforcement, although they stress its role in providing feedback about the correctness of responses over its role as a motivator. However, even while accepting such behavioristic concepts, cognitive theorists view learning as involving the acquisition or reorganization of the cognitive structures through which humans process and store information."*
>
> — Good and Brophy, 1990, pp. 187

The cognitivist revolution replaced behaviourism as the dominant paradigm. Cognitivism focuses on the inner mental activities – seeing into the "black box" of the human brain (mind) provides insights into how people learn. Mental processes such as thinking, memory, knowing, and problem-solving need to be explored. Knowledge can be seen as schema or symbolic mental constructions. Human beings are not "programmed animals" that respond to stimuli; people are rational beings and require active participation to learn, whose actions are a consequence of thought. Changes in behaviour are observed, but only as an indication of what is occurring within the learner. Cognitivism uses the metaphor of the mind as computer: information comes in, is being processed, and leads to certain outcomes.

Cognitivist Classrooms

The main features of cognitivist classrooms are listed below:

- create an environment where there are many variables;
- provide tools where learners can develop their understanding of something;
- pose many questions to help learners refine their thinking and recognize where they may be needing attention;
- don't be afraid of failure in a cognitivist classroom; it may be a tool to help learners realize they have more to learn;
- instructors are required to monitor their learners' progress; ask many questions;
- instructors manage problem-solving and provide structured activities, especially with group learning; and
- instructors provides opportunities for students to connect new information to *cognitive schema.*

Major Contributors to the Cognitive Movement and their Contributions

The major contributors to the cognitive movement and their contributions are given in Table 5.1.

Implications of Cognitivism on Instructional Design

Implications of cognitivism on the design of instruction are prominent throughout the task analysis and learner analysis phases of instructional design models. Cognitivists believe learners develop learning through receiving, storing and retrieving information. With this notion, it is imperative for instructional designers to thoroughly analyze and consider the appropriate tasks needed in order for learners to effectively and efficiently process the information received. Likewise, designers must consider the relevant learner characteristics that will promote or impede the cognitive processing of information. Blanton (1998, p. 173) further elaborates that the implications of cognitive learning theory on instructional design should bear in mind that "the [instructional] goals should include learner needs and interest, reflect the concerns of society, and make every effort to insure that goals are focused at least toward the present and, hopefully, toward the future needs of the learner." Unlike behaviorism, which is environment-focused, cognitivism

Table 5.1: Major Contributors to the Cognitive Movement

Contributor	*Contribution(s)*
(1)	(2)
Ausubel	(1963, 1968) Cognitive Scaffolding, Advanced organizers, subsumptive theory
Benjamin Bloom	Taxonomy of Educational Objectives in the Cognitive Domain (1956) Mastery Learning Systems Approach
Jerome Bruner	Inquiry thinking and discovery learning. Good thinker not only has knowledge but intuitive rasp of subject. Intuitive thinking obtained though discovery learning. Popularized importance of intuitive thinking in his text Process of Education, 1959 The student who grasps how bits of information within a subject are related is able to continually and independently relate additional information to a field of study. The act of learning consists of three processes: acquisition, transformation and evaluation. Spiraling curriculum (1966): previous learning is the basis of subsequent learning. (1966) Description of an instructional theory: (1) motivational experiences, (2) ways of structuring info., (3) presentation sequences, and (4) nature and pacing of rewards and punishment. Defined Instruction as "an effort to assist or shape growth."
John Carroll	(1963) Model of School Learning: Degree of learning = f (time spent/needed)
Edgar Dale	(1946) Audio-Visual Methods in Teaching, "Cone of Experience "
Fleming and Levie	(1978) Message design, perception, visual literacy (Fleming text: "Picturing Your Mind")
James Finn	Audiovisual movement. Transformation to IT. Article "Professionalizing the Audiovisual Field"
Donald Ely	1968 definition of the field.
Robert Gagne	Domains of Learning Cumulative learning theory Conditions of Learning (1965, 1989) Events of Instruction — a micro-design model
Robert Glaser	Named and elaborated on Instructional Systems (1965). Reiser (1987) credits Glaser with first use of the term Criterion-referenced measures. (1976) Definition of a Psychology of Instruction: (1) process for analyzing component performance, (2) description of initial state of learner, and (3) description of conditions that promote competence.
Robert Heinich	Definition of the field. Along with Galbraith, defined Technology as "the application of science to solve problems"

(*Contd.*)

Table 5.1: (*Contd.*)

(1)	(2)
C.F. Hoban, Sr.	(1937) Visualizing the Curriculum, concrete to abstract materials (like Dale).
David Merrill	Component Display Theory, Component Design Theory, Transaction Theory
Dan Beckwith	Systemic Design, contextual analysis
Hannafin, Hooper and Rieber	ROPES: incorporates cognitive procedures into an ISD framework; techniques for retrieving information, orienting, presenting, encoding, and sequencing instruction within a given context. (1989). Used in message design.
George Miller	Miller's +/- 2 "chunking" (1956)
Charles Reigeluth	Elaboration Theory (1979, 1983)
Rita Richey	Contextual Analysis
	Adult Learning Theory
Edward Tolman	Sign learning (bridged behaviorism and cognitivism).

directs instructional designers to consider the learner as the focus of the design process. This does not inhibit the design of instruction in any way but merely shifts the focus of the design. In fact, a cognitivism learning perspective facilitates instructional design since it is grounded upon an objective view of knowledge transfer.

Cognitivist Pedagogy and Instructional Design

Although cognitive psychology emerged in the late 1950s and began to take over as the dominant theory of learning on instructional design in late 1970s. Cognitive science began a shift from behaviouristic practices, which emphasized external behavior, to a concern with the internal mental processes of the mind and how they could be utilized in promoting effective learning. The design models that had been developed in the behaviorist tradition were not simply tossed out but instead the "task analysis" and "learner analysis" parts of the models were embellished. The new models addressed component processes of learning such as knowledge coding and representation, information storage and retrieval as well as the incorporation and integration of new knowledge with previous information (Saettler, 1990). Because Cognitivism and Behaviorism are both governed by an objective view of the nature of knowledge and what it means to know something, the transition from behavioral instructional design principles to those of a cognitive style was not entirely difficult. The goal of instruction remained the possible communication or transfer of knowledge to learners in the most efficient and effective manner (Bednar *et al.*, in Anglin, 1995). For example, the breaking down of a task into small steps works for a behaviorist who is trying to find the most efficient and full proof method of shaping a learner's behavior. The cognitive scientist would analyze a task, break it down into smaller steps or chunks and use that information to develop instruction that moves from simple to complex building on prior schema.

The influence of cognitive science in instructional design is evidenced by the use of advance organizers, mnemonic devices, metaphors, chunking into meaningful parts and the careful organization of instructional materials from simple to complex. Some important instructional models in the area of cognitivism are given below:

(A) Gagne's Nine Events of Instruction

Robert Mills Gagné (1916–2002) was an American educational psychologist best known for his 1965 monograph *"Conditions of Learning"*. Much of Gagné's research is focused on issues related to the sequencing of learning and instructional events in the classroom and how learning objectives might be better connected to appropriate instructional designs and strategies.

Gagné suggests that learning tasks for intellectual skills can be organized in a hierarchy of *learning events* according to complexity: stimulus recognition, response generation, procedure following, use of terminology, discriminations, concept formation, rule application and problem solving. The primary significance of the hierarchy is to identify prerequisites that should be completed to facilitate learning at each level. Prerequisites are identified by doing a task analysis of a learning/training task. Learning hierarchies provide a basis for the sequencing of instruction. According to Good & Brophy (1990), Gagne's nine events are meant to be *"... taken into account when designing instruction. Although some steps might need to be rearranged (or might be unnecessary) for certain types of lessons, the general set of considerations provide a good checklist of key design steps."*

Steps of Gagné's 9 Events of Instruction

Gagné's 9 events of instruction are given below:

1. Gain attention of learners (reception)
2. Inform learners of learning objectives (expectancy)
3. Stimulate recall of prior learning (retrieval)
4. Present the content (stimulus), and break it down into components to avoid information overload (selective perception)
5. Provide "learning guidance" (semantic encoding)
6. Elicit performance (practice/responding)
7. Provide feedback to learners (reinforcement)
8. Assess their performance (retrieval of information)
9. Enhance knowledge retention and transfer to real-life, authentic work (generalization)

Intellectual Framework of Gagné's 9 Events of Instruction

While Gagné's theoretical framework covers many aspects of learning, the focus is on the development of intellectual skills. The theory can be applied to the design of instruction in many subject areas and domains (Gagner & Driscoll, 1988). In its original form (Gagne, 1962), there was considerable attention given to using the framework in military training. By 1987, Gagné had moved firmly into addressing the multifaceted role of using instructional technologies and their role in learning. Some of Gagné's work is based on cognitive modelling where learning occurs sequentially in the *framework.* Here, instructors and designers can see for themselves how adult learners are led through stimulating content and presented with opportunities to engage in the classroom. Gagné nine instructional events suggest that there are contiguous levels (or events) and that specific instructional approaches are needed to enact them. The cognitive processes in the nine events serve as a foundation for instructional design, even today. Some critics, however, contend that Gagné's models are out of date and no longer speak to the demands of 21st century learners; still others suggest that the nine events of instructional design are timeless and form a foundation for all instructors.

Strengths and Weaknesses of Gagne's Nine Events of Instruction

The main strengths and weaknesses of Gagne's Nine Events of Instruction are given below:

Table 5.2: Strengths and Weaknesses of Gagne's Nine Events of Instruction

Strengths	*Weaknesses*
Gagne's conditions of learning are similar to guidelines; more heuristic than prescriptive	The systematic approach is comprehensive but Gagne does not allow step for planning
The nine events form the background structure to build lessons on; students master one step before moving on to the next; retention and transfer leads to durable learning	With nine steps, the model can feel long and arduous
Gagne explains lessons should follow instructional events but sequence can be changed	Some goals are easy to classify as learning outcomes but many are not
Gagne's events is a process-oriented model; you won't miss any major parts of the process	Repetition may not be well received by learners; may feel inhibited by it

Applying Gagne in the Classroom

The following table suggests how the nine events can be applied to designing different technology-supported learning platforms:

Table 5.3: Applications of Gagne's Nine Events in the Classroom

Gagne's Nine (9) Events	*Online Gaming*	*Learning Modules*	*Course Management System/ CMS/LMS*
1. Gain Attention	• use quality video clips and audio	• use animation, video, audio • tell a story, pose a question	• send an email or social media invitation • provide a space for introductions for learners • use graphics
2. Inform Learner of Objective(s)	• discuss how to 'win'	• give overview, rules and tasks/quests	• give overview of goals
3. Stimulate Recall	• draw on learners' background	• incorporate pre-tests • draw on information from previous module(s)	• relate past module content to new material • provide module reviews • use pre-tests
4. Present Material	• use ideas that encourage yet challenge	• use clear, current and accurate material • put user-controlled, easy to navigate content and information front and centre • provide animation and 3D models	• present material that is clear, up-to-date and accurate • provide paper-based support and link to online articles, videos, audio etc. • consider information literacy and media literacy skills
5. Provide Guidance	• offer hints, pop-ups, alternates, suggestions	• provide "help" guides and tutorials	• provide email contacts • set-up chat-rooms and threaded discussions • offer answers to FAQ • include links to supporting references/glossaries
6. Elicit Performance	• encourage interactivity among learners	• assign tasks/quests/ challenges/problems	• assign meaningful tasks and activities • give clear and concise instructions • incorporate group and 'buddy' work • try social media, Facebook, Twitter • provide a means for posting • include element of individual responsibility
7. Provide Feedback	• add up scores • provide reward for achieving level • plan for written and/or audio feedback	• add up scores • give written and verbal feedback • use animated rewards for correct answers • provide corrective feedback	• include "you've now completed..." messages, • encouragement encourage instructor use of discussion threads • incorporate assignment drop-off box/feedback tools
8. Assess Performance	• ensure achievement is assessed	• track scores/best scores • incorporate score reporting (via email)	• incorporate EPortfolio into process • monitor and track student participation
9. Enhance Retention and Transfer	• ensure skills are transferable between levels • ensure knowledge is transferable across genres	• note transferable information in feedback • suggest websites for further information • provide material sequentially	• suggest further readings • provide real-world examples, optional tasks • make connections with other courses and networks

(B) Anderson's Intelligent Tutors

John Anderson accounts for cognitive performance through the ACT model of information processing. According to this model, declarative knowledge is compiled into procedural skill through repeated practice performing a task. Whereas a novice must keep a procedure's steps in mind while performing, an expert turns several steps into an integrated routine, similar to the way subroutines work together in computer programming. Once knowledge is compiled from declarative to procedural knowledge, it may be performed with a minimum of allocated conscious attention. Anderson and colleagues at Carnegie Mellon University have tested out ACT instructional approach through a series of intelligent tutoring systems aimed at teaching well-defined procedural skills, including programming in LISP (Anderson, Farrell, & Sauers, 1984), generating proofs for geometric theorems (Anderson, Boyle, & Yost, 1985), and solving algebraic equations (Lewis, Milson, & Anderson, 1988).

Based on a cognitive analysis of the task, a model of the ideal student performance is developed for varying stages of competence, including assorted "buggy" procedures. As instruction proceeds, the system fits the learner's response pattern to its performance model, selects problems to minimize errors and optimize learning, and provides feedback as well as remediation accordingly. The technique of comparing learners' performance with a preexisting performance model is termed *model tracing*. The programme does not make available the model's production rules to students directly; rather, the production rules trigger various instructional events, most notably intervention and feedback following incorrect performance. Thus, in intelligent tutoring approach, new knowledge is best learned in the context of solving relevant problems, instruction is centered around problem-solving practice.

(C) Clancey's Intelligent Tutoring Environments

Clancey's (1986) programme GUIDON and its descendents use heuristic classification methods as the basis for an intelligent tutoring environment for medical diagnosis. The programme differs from ACT* model prescriptions in several ways given below:

- it assume that the learner has a basic understanding of terms, concepts and disease processes.
- it assumes that learning is more efficient if the student determines what he/she needs to know next without being explicitly controlled by the system.
- most significantly, it is failure driven; that is, primary instruction occurs in the form of feedback to student errors.

GUIDON requires the student to make a diagnosis, then to justify it with reasons. When the student's diagnosis "fails," he/she must take steps to correct the reasoning that led to it. Thus while the student develops expertise in medical diagnosis in a realistic problem-solving context, he/she also learns to detect and correct buggy procedures and misconceptions. The programme is almost learner-controlled; at any point, the student can choose to browse through the expert taxonomies and tables, examine the expert's reasoning during problem solving, ask questions, or request explanations. But ultimately the student must generate the appropriate links in a solution graph for each case.

(D) Qualitative Mental Models

White and Frederiksen's (1986) programme to teach troubleshooting in electrical circuits emphasizes the relationship between qualitative models and causal explanations. White and Frederiksen believe that mastery of qualitative reasoning should precede quantitative reasoning. Their programme builds on students' intuitive understandings of the domain, carefully sequencing "real-world" problems that require the student to construct increasingly complex qualitative models of the domain. Although the programme encourages students to engage in diverse learning strategies (exploring, requesting explanations, viewing tutorial demonstrations or problem solving), it tries to minimize errors. Thus, like the ACT model, it does not directly address buggy algorithms and misconceptions.

(E) Reciprocal Teaching

Brown and Palincsar (1989; Palincsar & Brown, 1984) have developed a cooperative learning system for the teaching of reading, termed *reciprocal teaching*. The teacher and learners assemble in groups of 2 to 7 and read a paragraph together silently. A person assumes the "teacher" role and formulates a question on the paragraph. The group, whose members are playing roles of producer and critic simultaneously, addresses this question. The "teacher" advances a summary, and makes a prediction or clarification, if any is needed. The role of teacher then rotates, and the group proceeds to the next paragraph in the text. Brown and colleagues have also developed a method of assessment, called *dynamic assessment*, based on successively increasing prompts on a realistic reading task. The reciprocal teaching method uses a combination of modeling, coaching, scaffolding, and fading to achieve impressive results, with learners showing dramatic gains in comprehension, retention, and far transfer over sustained periods.

(F) Schoenfeld's Mathematics Teaching

Schoenfeld (1985) studied methods for teaching math to college students. He developed a set of heuristics that were helpful in solving mathematics problems.

Like the writing and reading systems, Schoenfeld's system includes explicit modeling of problem-solving strategies, and a series of structured exercises affording learner practice in large and small groups, as well as individually. He employs a tactic called "postmortem analysis," retracing the solution of recent problems, abstracting out the generalizable strategies and components. Unlike the writing and reading systems, Schoenfeld carefully selects and sequences practice cases to move learners into higher levels of skill. Another interesting technique is the equivalent to "stump the teacher," with time at the beginning of each class period devoted to learner-generated problems that the teacher is challenged to solve. Learners witnessing occasional false starts and dead ends of the teacher's solution can acquire a more appropriate belief structure about the nature of expert mathematical problem solving. Schoenfeld's positive research findings support a growing body of math research suggesting the importance of acquiring a conceptual or schema-based representation of math problem solving.

(G) Cognitive Flexibility Hypertexts

Spiro and colleagues (Spiro & Jehng, 1990) have developed hypertext programmes to address problems typically associated with acquiring knowledge in complex, ill-structured domains. The programmes utilize videodiscs that construct multiple "texts" (audio/video mini-cases, about 90 seconds each) of a domain. The multiple representations in KANE induce students to restructure their thinking as they grapple with the thematic issues, which are presented through the mini-cases. It relies on the learner to generate the relationships, which are embodied in a set of mini-cases. Spiro's programmes are best thought of as "rich" environments that allow sophisticated learners to pursue their learning goals in a flexible way. They do not typically include skill practice in a traditional sense, but instead rely on learner purposes and externally imposed assignments to give meaning to student browsing. There is an authoring shell, built into the system for teachers or students to use. Students, for example, may construct a series of mini-cases into a "visual essay" illustrating a theme not present on the Theme menu.

(H) Learning through Design Activities: Computer Tools

Harel and Papert (1990) and Lippert (1988, 1990) have examined the effect of learning a content domain while simultaneously learning other domains, particularly software design.

Instructional Software Design Project

Harel and Papert (1990) created a "total learning environment" in which fourth-graders simultaneously learned fractions and Logo programming; the students' goal was to design and develop a Logo programme to teach something about fractions. "The 'experimental treatment' integrated the experimental children's learning of fractions and Logo with the designing and programming of instructional software", four hours a week during a 15-week semester. The students in the first control group spent the same amount of time learning Logo, but with a different purpose. The second control group programmed only once a week. Each group completed a two-month unit on fractions as part of the regular math curriculum.

Expert Systems

Lippert (1988, 1990) describes the way in which an expert system shell can be used as both an instructional and a learning strategy to "facilitate the acquisition of procedural knowledge and problem-solving skills in difficult topics" (1988, p. 22). Again, students learn by designing-developing an expert system individually or in groups, on their own or under the guidance of a teacher. According to Lippert, the strategy can be used with students as young as grade VIth and in any domain whose knowledge base can be expressed in productions.

(I) Learning Coaches and Cognitive Apprenticeship

Learning coaches are teachers, mentors and guides who are knowledgeable about the learning needs of diverse learners; typically, they are skilled at coaching, collaboration and information-sharing. The learning coach works as part of a support team (or close to another teacher) to build learners' capacity to solve their own problems.

The *cognitive apprenticeship model* put forward by Collins *et al.* (1989; 2006) is an excellent starting point in defining the learning coach. Collins proposes six strategies to develop learners' cognitive skills:

- modeling
- coaching
- scaffolding
- articulation
- reflection
- exploration.

Learning coaches can (and should) demonstrate strong collaborative skills and an understanding of changes that occur in learners when given appropriate support (scaffolding) and activities (exploration). Learning coaches typically support learning in a variety of environments, and have the ability to identify, model and share best practices. The coach may draw upon and use diverse models, tools and strategies including the idea of *differentiated instruction* (providing students with different ways to understand material, to process, construct and make sense of ideas; to develop teaching materials so that all students can learn effectively, regardless of differences in skills, knowledge, abilities or experience).

(J) ADDIE Model

ADDIE is a five-step (or stage) model used to systematically design and organize units in training and in workshops. As an instructional design model or IDM, ADDIE was first described in 1975. Similar models include the ASSURE model, Gagne's and Kemp's and Merrill's. ADDIE is one of a number of IDMs and the acronym is used to remind instructors about how to plan their workshops and courses. ADDIE can be applied to decisions that have to be made about learning content, instructional methods and delivery, and is meant to align with an instructor's learning theories and philosophies. The goal of instructional design is to ensure quality, consistency and effectiveness of the learning experience but also to support the philosophical orientation of instructor and learners. One of the challenges of current instructional design is to incorporate forms of social learning and other interactive pedagogies into the classroom. According to Davis (2013), the ADDIE model is helpful in collaborating with instructional designers, faculty and other librarians in higher education.

Development Phases of ADDIE Model

ADDIE consists of five phases of development:

A – *Analysis*
D – *Design*
D – *Develop*
I – *Implement*
E – *Evaluate*

The ADDIE model is an iterative model of instructional design whose aim is to examine the entire design and development process from start to finish. This includes some early consideration of learning objectives such as *"What do the learners need to learn from this course or workshop?"*. However, it comprises the entire middle as well as final stages of course development, and may include when instructors encourage their learners to reflect back on events during their training. Question prompts such as "Did you feel you learned what you wanted to learn?" and "Did the participants learn what the instructors wanted them to learn?" can provide some possible directions to pursue this important line of questioning. Keep in mind that learning how to do something is different from learning about how to do something...

(K) ASSURE Model

The ASSURE model is a six-step instructional design model whose intent is to help teachers systematically develop the most appropriate approach to teaching for their students. ASSURE emphasizes an instructional approach with an appreciation of students' learning styles and drawing on constructivism where learners interact with others in their environment to build on previous knowledge. Some instructional designers see ASSURE as an enriched version of ADDIE, given its additional step and emphasis on multimedia. In any case, ASSURE is designed to help teachers in their teaching by considering the use of multimedia and technology and, ultimately, to "assure" themselves that their students will be learning. The model is based on Gagne's Nine Events of Instruction, and is a useful acronym for any instructor who wants to design online courses in a systematic fashion.

Steps of ASSURE Design Model

The six steps of ASSURE design model are given below:

A – Analyze Learners

- The first step in using ASSURE is to analyze who your learners are, whether they are librarians, undergraduates, medical students or faculty.
- What sorts of knowledge, skills and abilities will they bring to the classroom? Do you know anything about their preferred learning stylcs?
- A pre-test can be administered to your learners, when possible, or you can discuss the group with one of the leaders in the class.

S – State Objectives

- After you develop a clearer view of who your students are, state your learning objectives for your class or workshop;
- A statement of what students will be able to do as a result of the instruction;
- Learning objectives or learning outcomes provide insight for your students and what you hope they will get out of the activities in the classroom;
- The ABCD's of writing good learning objectives are audience (who are your teaching?); behaviours that will be demonstrated; conditions under which desirable behaviours will be observed and the degree to which new skills will be mastered.

S – Select Media and Materials

- Now that you have some idea of your audience's present knowledge, skills, and attitudes, and your objectives worked out, proceed to build an instructional bridge to connect these two;
- Select available materials, modify existing materials or design new materials to help accomplish this task;

- Select different media to use. Any of the media or technologies that have been deemed appropriate should enhance classroom

U – Utilize Materials

- As an instructor, preview all teaching materials before you use them with students, including any media or equipment
- Be sure the room works for what you have planned. If you are using video or sound, computers or projects, ensure that everything is working well, and make sure you have a backup
- Hardware and software are created by human beings, and mistakes can be made
- Don't get discouraged if your equipment lets you down. Ensure your instructional materials are suitable and current

R – Require Learners' Performance

- First, require the active intellectual engagement of your learners
- At some point in your classroom activities, your learners will need to practice what they have learned from you
- As an instructor, you will need to describe how they will use the materials you have provided. Any responses that are correct should be positively reinforced. Classroom activities should allow learners to receive feedback before any evaluation or test is administered.

E – Evaluate and Revise

- Teachers should reflect on their workshop, its objectives, instructional strategy, learning materials and the assessment to determine whether these elements were effective or not.
- Obtain feedback from peers, people who were in the classroom or from the learners themselves. When teaching students, some things may simply not work.
- Use group discussion, exit interviews, assessments, and other types of student feedback to evaluate your work.
- Manage your expectations. Perhaps your learning materials were not useful enough; your instructional strategies ineffective.
- Your assessment of students may reveal they didn't learn what you wanted them to learn. Perhaps your class was not long enough for the students to master the learning objectives.

(L) Reigeluth's Elaboration Theory

Reigeluth's elaboration theory is a cognitivist learning theory that proposes instruction should be organized for optimal learning in tiers of increasing complexity. These tiers of complexity are what Reigeluth calls *"hierarchical task analysis"* (1979). Reiguluth's macroprescriptive framework aids in the selection, sequencing, synthesis and summarizing of content for instructional designers from the most basic skill (small, fragmented pieces of the whole) to the most sophisticated or complex (larger more detailed pieces of the whole). Reigeluth believes instructional layers of meaning can be organized so that each successive layer will literally elaborate on any previous layers already covered by the instructional design of the workshop or course. Through elaboration, knowledge retention of the learners is improved. Information layering is a sequencing approach that runs from simple to complex and can repeat again from the most general-to-specific.

Elaboration Theory's Macro Strategies

Reigeluth (1979) said that elaboration theory deals primarily with overall "macro" strategies for organizing instructional content such as:

- Instructional content should be organized in order of increasing complexity
- Sequencing should take a holistic approach to foster meaning-making and motivation; whole-tasks are broken down to manageable part-tasks (components)
- Examples and elaborations should be embedded within activities and lessons
- Reigeluth uses the analogy of a zoom lens to explain the nature of elaboration
- Learners begin with a wide angle view to see the whole picture and major relationships within it (e.g. composition or balance of picture) but with no detail
- Zooming in at one level on a given part of the picture allows the person to see the major parts
- After studying its parts, learners can go back to wide-angle views to examine other parts of the whole
- Learners continue with this elaborative pattern of zooming in at one level to see the major parts and zooming back out for context until the whole has been seen
- Learners follow the zoom-in/zoom-out pattern for second levels of detail, third levels, and so on
- Once a high level of detail is reached, learning can proceed to the next learning module or *tier*

Two Sequencing Strategies

- *Topical sequencing*: a topic or task is taught to whatever depth of understanding or competence is required before moving to the next topic

- *Spiral sequencing*: learners master topics or tasks over several iterations, i.e. the basics of one topic are learned, then another and another before returning to learn more about each

Assimilation Process

Elaboration theory is an extension of the work of Ausubel (advance organizers) and Bruner (spiral curriculum). Learners need to develop meaningful contexts into which ideas and skills can be assimilated:

- Sequencing strategies may be topical or spiral-like in approach
- Organizing structure: an elaborative sequence.
- Organizing structure may be one of three types: conceptual, procedural or theoretical.
- Simple to complex: choose something which contains simplest most fundamental idea in first lesson, and elaborate in subsequent lesson.
- Within sequence, move from general to detailed, simple to complex, abstract to concrete.
- Summarizers are content reviews.
- Synthesizers are presentation devices designed to help learners integrate content into meaningful whole and assimilate into prior knowledge.
- Analogies relate content to learners' prior knowledge.
- Cognitive strategies: variety of cues—pictures, diagrams, mnemonics, etc.—trigger cognitive strategies to process material.
- Learners are encouraged to exercise control over content and instruction; labeling and separation of components facilitate effective learner control.

Wilson and Cole (1992)

Wilson and Cole make four recommendations for restructuring Reigeluth's elaboration theory:

- Deproceduralize the theory: in its current form, explicit steps are provided for designing and sequencing instruction. Elaboration theory should be reformulated into a set of guiding principles referenced more clearly to learning processes. A principle-based formulation will allow designers to adapt the concepts to a greater variety of situations.
- Remove unnecessary design constraints: ET may constrain designers without any demonstrable return in instructional effectiveness. Examples include: the use of three primary structures (conceptual, procedural, and theoretical); tying together the primary course goal and primary organizing structure; and using a single structure as a basis for organizing a course. These prescriptions make ET's application more standardized and parsimonious.

- Base organization and sequencing decisions on learners' understanding and the logic of the subject matter.
- Assume a more constructivist stance toward content structure and sequencing.

(M) Merrill's Component Display Theory

Component display theory is a form of instruction that looks at components of the teaching process, at a *microlevel*, especially single ideas and methods for teaching small sections or chunks. The theory stands as a contrast with Reigeluth's Elaboration Theory which can be conceived as a macrolearning design system. According to Merrill, learning has two dimensions: content and performance. Content encompasses facts, concepts, procedures and principles. Performance consists of memory, utilization, generalizing.

CDT is an analytical framework that can be used to identify components of instruction to achieve instructional goals. As such, it describes instructional strategies in terms of components: primary and secondary presentation forms and interdisplay relationships. The underlying principle of the theory is based on Gagné's Conditions of Learning (1965, 1985). As Gagné said, different kinds of learning outcomes require unique conditions. CDT extends Gagne's classification by separating content types from performance. Content and performance are two dimensions that are typically used to classify learning. Another way to consider content and performance is, in order for librarians to teach online searching, they first need to know how to search a database for themselves. The performance of that skill (and its teaching) is separate.

Taxonomy of Presentation Types

Component display theory provides a detailed taxonomy of presentation types and prescriptions for different kinds of learning outcomes. The prescribed conditions for learning are described in terms of different types of presentation, practice and learner guidance. There are four primary presentation forms: rules (expository presentation of a generality), examples (expository presentation of instances), recall (inquisitory generality) and practice (inquisitory instance). The secondary presentation forms include: prerequisites, objectives, helps, mnemonics and feedback. It's a good idea for librarian instructors to understand that a progressive use of these tools will help learners acquire the skills and knowledge that we are trying to teach them in the workshop.

The Limitations of CDT

Merrill described a number of limitations of CDT (Merrill, Li, & Jones, 1991):

- Content analysis can seem to focus on components of instruction not integrated them into a larger whole.

- There are limited or no prescriptions for knowledge acquisition.
- Prescriptions for course organization strategies can seem superficial.
- Theories such as CDT can seem to be closed; its principles can seem to be based on subsets of available knowledge, but it may not account for or be able to accommodate new knowledge as it presented.
- In CDT, each phase of instructional development is performed independently, and provide no real means for integration or sharing
- The resulting instruction teaches components but not integrated knowledge or competencies.
- The resulting instruction is often passive rather than interactive.
- These theories are inefficient to use because instructional designers must build every presentation from fundamental components.

While CDT provides a systematic way of dissecting instructional material and matching various components to instructional methods, there is a danger of paralysis through analysis. Instructional designers should be aware that the flow of courses and how components make up the whole bind together. Instructors should allow learners to observe and reflect on relationships between components; i.e., learners should be able to identify the big picture and relate learning back to real-world problems.

Instructional Transaction Theory (ITT)

Instructional transaction theory is a cognitive learning theory that aims to identify patterns of instructional transactions through the use of computer programmes. Patterns are then used to develop instructional algorithms to generate improvement in instructional transactions. Merrill believed that building particular programmes as instructional development tools would "*...enable automating certain steps of the instructional design process and increase efficiency*". Instructional algorithms operate on a set of 'knowledge objects' that incorporate three types of instructional strategies: presentations, practices and learner guidance. ITT identifies what knowledge components are required for a given type of instruction and what instructional strategies are needed to facilitate design (Merrill, 1999).

ITT is concerned with two primary considerations: What to teach? and how to teach? Knowledge representation is a critical part of the theory. ITT attempts to provide a detailed, prescriptive instructional design theory to enable the development of an automated instructional design expert system. Merrill introduced it to provide more precision to design for specific instructional outcomes. As a synthesis-oriented theory, ITT emphasizes the integration of the component display theory into instructional transactions. An instructional transaction is all of the interactions necessary for a student to acquire a particular kind of knowledge or skill.

Merrill's 'Knowledge Representation'

Instructional strategies in ITT are described as algorithms for manipulating the elements of knowledge objects. But what are knowledge objects? According to Merrill, knowledge objects are containers that consist of compartments or slots for different but related elements of knowledge. The content of knowledge objects typically consist of:

- *Name*: one or more symbols or terms that reference the knowledge.
- Portrayal: one or more multimedia objects that will show or represent the knowledge object.
- *Description*: an open compartment into which an author can place desired information about the knowledge object.

Jones, Li, and Merrill (1990) identified four types of knowledge objects:

- *Entities*: objects in the world, such as device, persons, creatures, places and symbols.
- *Properties*: quantitative or qualitative attributes of entities.
- *Activities*: actions that the learner can take to act on objects in the world.
- *Processes*: events that occur in the world that change the values of properties of an entity.

ITT for Automated Design

Instructional transaction theory provides precise ways to describe knowledge representation, instructional strategies and instructional-design prescriptions; in short, it makes automated instructional design a real possibility for the designer. The goals of ITT can be summarized as the development of the following:

- *Effective Instruction*: ITT provides a more precise description of different kinds of instructional transactions required for different kinds of instructional outcomes (goals or objectives).
- *Efficient Instructional Development*: ITT builds appropriate instructional transactions into instructional development tools which enable automating portions of the design process.
- *Instructional Learning Environments*: ITT represents knowledge as knowledge objects, which enables the building of a general-purpose simulation engine; this makes a learning environment builder possible to enable efficient development of more effective instructional interactions.
- *Adaptive Instruction*: The representation of knowledge in the form of knowledge objects and representation of instructional transactions as algorithms makes possible instructional strategies that can be

adapted to individual learners in real time as they interact with the instructional materials.

ITT's Learning Environment

According to ITT, the learning environment is built on the following elements:

- The instructional goal it is designed to promote.
- The knowledge structure required by the knowledge environment: structure is determined by the relationship among processes, entities, and activities from the knowledge objects.
- The general simulation engine operates on the knowledge structure to present activities and processes that occur.
- The learning activities of exploration by which students interact with the learning environment: the learning activities are carried out under the instructional strategies of presentation, practice and learning control. An instructional strategy incorporates all of the conditions for teaching a given type of learning an instructional transaction.

Merrill, Jones and Li (1992) previously identified 13 classes of instructional transactions (Merrill, Jones, & Li, 1992) in three categories: component, abstraction and association. These instructional transactions include: IDENTIFY (component or naming or parts-of; related to "facts" in CDT); EXECUTE (activity or procedures or how-to; "procedures" in CDT), and INTERPRET (process or what-happens; "principles" in CDT).

Scandura's Structural Learning Theory

Scandura's structural learning theory may be defined as "a rule-based learning theory of human problem-solving" which assumes that "working memory follows a cognitive process that involves holding both rules and data". In other words, structural learning theory says that "what is learned" are rules that comprise a domain, range and procedure. In a sense, SLT represents a comprehensive meta-theory, which accommodates a large number of more specific cognitivist and behavioural theories.

As one of the cognitivist perspectives, the structural learning theory was developed by Joseph Scandura in the 1970s. Other information processing theories of cognition and memory share one common feature: that the structure (state-space) of memory is fixed and retrieval from memory involves searching through that established structure. Cognitivists suggest that learning involves transforming cognitive structures from one type into another. However, this form of representation is questioned by Scandura, and he proposes his structural learing theory to take its place. By comparison, his theory argues that human knowledge has a more flexible structure, particularly regarding individual differences and learning.

Used in Mathematics and Engineering

Structural learning theory argues that human knowledge consists of simple rules or pathways which must first be learned or mastered. The rules of a domain are composed of the minimum capabilities possessed by the learners. Used mostly in mathematics and engineering, SLT assumes that "working memory" holds both rules and data, and that the memory load associated with a set of tasks depends on rule(s) that govern them. Alternative rules may indeed exist for a subset of tasks, and problem-solving may be easier when a higher order rule is mastered. For example, higher order rules account for creative behaviours and "unanticipated outcomes" by making it possible to generate and learn new rules. In addition to mathematics and engineering, SLT has been applied in artificial intelligence and computer-assisted instruction. The theory aims to help learners develop their own background knowledge and encourage learner processing.

Major Steps in Structural Learning and Analysis

Structural learning theory identifies rules for a set of tasks, and breaks them down into components. Its major steps are: 1) selecting a representative sample of problems, 2) identifying solution rules for each, 3) converting each into a higher order problem whose solutions = the rule, 4) identifying a higher order solution for solving a new problem, 5) eliminating redundant solutions from a rule set (i.e., those derived from other rules), and (6) notice steps 3 and 4 = 1 and 2. The result of repeating higher order rules, and eliminating redundant ones, is a succession of rule sets, each consisting of rules which are simpler individually but collectively more powerful. SLT prescribes teaching the simplest solution for problems and teaching more complex paths until the entire rule is mastered. The theory proposes that we should teach as many higher-order rules as possible as replacements for lower order rules. SLT suggests a strategy for individualizing instruction by analyzing which rules a student has/has not mastered and teaching only the rules, or portions thereof, that have not been mastered.

6
Constructivist Pedagogy

After studying this chapter, the reader will be able to: Explain the Constructivism learning theory; Differentiate between cognitive constructivism and social constructivism; Define the Constructivist pedagogy; Explain why Constructivism is important; Distinguish between Accommodation and Assimilation; Tell the name of some famous Constructivist; Comprehend the contribution of some famous Constructivist in education; Specify the effects of Constructivism on instructional design; Explain the important instructional designs based on Constructivist pedagogy.

Constructivism may be considered an epistemology (a philosophical framework or theory of learning) which argues humans construct meaning from current knowledge structures. These arguments about the nature of human learning guide constructivist learning theories and teaching methods of education. Constructivism values developmentally-appropriate facilitator-supported learning that is initiated and directed by the learner. This is the path through which educators (facilitators) wish to approach students in constructing meaning of new concepts."

Constructivism is a popular learning theory (or perspective) that says learners actively build new knowledge by accessing past experiences, which are then used for new information and situations. Implied in this perspective is the initiative shown by learners to ask questions as new information is incorporated into their understanding of something. Put another way, knowledge is not passively received by listening or reading but is more of an active, experiential process. As a theory of learning, constructivism was originally described by Swiss psychologist Jean Piaget who said that learners construct their sense or understanding of something by building on their previous or existing mental models. Learners then actively incorporate new ideas and adapt them for their own understanding. Understanding is subjective in constructivism because it is created by the learner using new information and previous knowledge rather than the new information just being absorbed.

The theory suggests that knowledge is always cumulative and a sum total of all experience.

Cognitive Constructivism and Social Constructivism

There are two main schools of constructivism: cognitive and social constructivism.

Cognitive Constructivism

Cognitive constructivism focuses on how learners come to understand something based on their learning style and cognitive development. It implies that teachers, in their efforts to understand a learner's existing cognitive abilities, can guide their discovery and understanding of something but that students must take some personal responsibility for the process.

Social Constructivism

Social constructivism, a concept pioneered by Russian psychologist Lev Vygotsky, focuses on how social interactions help learners construct understanding. The learner engages in a collaborative process to construct new meaning. Social constructivism is illustrated in the use of social networks to create new meaning and understanding through peer-to-peer collaboration and the incorporation of previous knowledge from multiple sources.

In constructivism, past experience is critical to the learner for encounters with new ideas and information are used as a foundation. Each new experience is approached with pre-existing "mental models" or the sum total of one's knowledge. This provides a basis from which to accommodate new information and build new knowledge. The philosophy is currently popular in medical education due to problem-based learning which mirrors some of the real-life problems that arise in the practice of medicine. In online learning, PBL is well-suited to the sharing of case-studies and scenarios which can then be solved through discussion and debate. Key learning theorists in this area are Vygotsky, Piaget, Dewey and Bruner. Constructivism is not a new concept; its roots can be traced back to the work of 18th century philosopher Giambattista Vico.

Why Constructivism is Important?

Teaching methods in higher education are changing. One component of curriculum redevelopment is a change in focus from transmitting information onto students (literally "downloading" information online and during lectures) to something more interesting and interactive. In traditional classes, instructors transmit information to students who listen passively and their understanding of this content is later tested. In interactive classes, students are more involved in their learning and reach new levels of understanding through discussion, debate and negotiation of complex ideas. Constructivism is important because it places responsibility on the learner to ask questions and seek assistance if they do not understand something.

In addition, constructivist teaching fosters more critical thinking and aims to motivate learners so they are more actively involved in class. Zemelman tells us that learning in all subject areas involves inventing and constructing new ideas. Constructivist theories and activities should be incorporated into all classrooms, and instructors should work to create a learning environment where learners can construct their own understanding. Fosnot recommends that a constructivist approach can be used to create learners who are autonomous and inquisitive. A constructivist approach frees teachers from the burden of teaching everything so that students can make some of their own decisions.

Accommodation and Assimilation

Accommodation is the reframing of new experiences into the mental capacity of the individual. Individuals conceive how the world operates; when things do not operate as expected, these new perceptions must reframe expectations with outcomes. Assimilating is about incorporating new experiences into the old. This causes an individual to develop a new perspective on something, to rethink what was once understood and to evaluate what is new. Ultimately, the goal is to alter one's perception in new and expected ways.

Major Contributors to the Constructivism Movement and their Contributions

Table 6.1 clearly shows the major contributors to the constructivism movement and their contributions.

Implications of Constructivism on Instructional Design

Instructional designs considerations within a framework of constructivism begin with taking into account the learner's prior knowledge, understandings, and interests. Boethel and Dimock (2000, p. 17) state, "Teachers must understand what learners bring to the learning situation and begin there in helping students build new knowledge." Therefore, like cognitivism, constructivism begins with a thorough learner analysis and determination of appropriate tasks to promote constructivist learning.

As opposed to an objective approach to learning, constructivism is more open-ended in expectation where the results and even the methods of learning themselves are not easily measured and may not be consistent with each learner. Thus, heavy attention must be paid to the context of the learning situation. Spector (2000, p.7) notes that when from the perspective of constructivism, "context must be taken into explicit consideration when

Table 6.1: Major Contributors to the Constructivism Movement

Contributor	*Contribution(s)*
Piaget	Piaget's theory is fundamental to cognitivism and to constructivism. His central idea is that "knowledge proceeds neither solely from the experience of objects nor from an innate programming performed in the subject but from successive constructions" (Fosnot, 1996). Piaget (1985) proposed that the mechanism of learning is the process of equilibration, in which cognitive structure assimilates and accommodates to generate new possibilities when it is disturbed based on human's self-organizing tendency.
Lev Vygotsky	Vygotsky's sociohistorical development psychology focuses on the dialectic between the individual and society, and the effect of social interaction, language, and culture on learning. To Vygosky (1978), learning is a continual movement from the current intellectual level to a higher level which more closely approximates the learner's potential. This movement occurs in the so-called "zone of proximal development" as a result of social interaction. Thus, an understanding of human thinking depends in turn on an understanding of the mechanism of social experience; the force of the cognitive process deriving from the social interaction is emphasized. Also, the role of the adult and the learners' peers as they conversed, questioned, explained, and negotiated meaning is emphasized.
Bruner	A major theme of Bruner's construction theory is that learning is an active process in which learners construct new ideas or concepts based upon their current/past knowledge. The learner selects and transforms information, constructs hypotheses, and makes decisions, relying on a cognitive structure, e.g. schema and mental models, to do so. The interconnection of the new experience with the prior knowledge results in the reorganization of the cognitive structure, which creates meaning and allows the individual to "go beyond the information given".
vonGlasersfeld	Von Glasersfeld development of the epistemological basis of the psychological variant incorporates both the Piagetian notion of assimilation and accommodation and the cybernetic concept of viability (Cobb, 1994). The value of knowledge no longer lies in its conveyance of truth, but its viability in individual experience. Von Glasersfeld (1992) stated that "Truths are replaced by viable models, and viability is always relative to a chosen goal." Similar to Piaget, von Glasersfeld sees learning as an active process of self-organization in which the individual eliminate 'perturbation' (disequlibrium in Piaget's term) from the interaction with others as well as an active construction of viable knowledge adapted from the interaction with others. Individuals' construction of their ways of knowing is the focus of von Glaserfeld. But, he also recognizes the importance of social interaction as a process of meaning negotiation in this subjective construction of knowing.

planning instruction." Addressing types of context in which the learning takes place is necessary in the scope of constructivism because it not only addresses instructional context but also learner context. Within the context of the learner, attention must be paid to the "goals of the learner...the learner's perceived utility of the instruction... and the learner's perception of accountability (Morrison, Ross, and Kemp, 2001, p. 55-56). These address directly the fundamental assumptions of constructivism.

Constructivist Pedagogy and Instructional Design

Constructivism explains learning as a process where an active and self-regulated learner who resolves conflicts between ideas and reflects on theoretical explanation constructs personal knowledge. Sources of meaning are context and experience. It professes that there is a real world, which we experience and that meaning is imposed on the world by us. As a result, there are many meanings or perspectives for any given event or concept. There is not absolute, ultimate, shared reality. Rather, reality is an outcome of a constructive process. The goal of instruction is not assure individuals know particular things, but to construct plausible interpretations of their own.

Constructivist learning can take place in the classroom, in computer micro worlds or in open, virtual environments. Among the concerns some have about constructivism are:

- is constructivism a theory, a philosophy or a strategy for achieving particular type of learning outcomes?
- is there adequate recognition of the impact of entry behaviors?
- is constructivist instruction efficient? Is it instruction?
- is constructivism too extreme?

Some important instructional models in the area of constructivism are given below:

(A) Anchored Instruction

John Bransford and colleagues at Vanderbilt University have developed several instructional products using video settings. *Young Sherlock Holmes* or *Indiana Jones* may provide *macrocontexts* within which problems of various kinds may be addressed. For example, when Indiana Jones quickly replaces a bag of sand in place of the gold idol, the booby trap is tricked into thinking the idol is still there. This scene opens up questions of mass and density: If the idol were solid gold, how big must a sand bag be to weigh the same, and could Indy have escaped as he did carrying a solid-gold idol of that size? Based on a single macrocontext, learners may approach a variety of problems that draw on science, math, language, and history. Bransford and colleagues have applied the name *anchored instruction* to this approach of grounding instruction in information-rich situations, and have reported favourable findings in field-based and laboratory studies (The Cognition and Technology

Group at Vanderbilt, 1990). Recently, several videodisc-based macrocontexts called the Jasper Series have been developed as a basis for research and classroom instruction (The Cognition and Technology Group at Vanderbilt, in press; Sherwood and The Cognition and Technology Group at Vanderbilt, 1991; Van Haneghan *et al.*, in press).

Anchored instruction is a form of *situated instruction* one which is *anchored* through the use of real problems and real contexts so that learners can explore possible (even real) solutions. Anchored instruction is a form of social constructivism and related to situated learning and problem-based learning. However, AI differs somewhat because the information needed to solve anchored problems is generally made available to learners through the use of short video segments (8 to 12 minutes). In classrooms using AI, students work together to formulate strategies to solve problems embedded in the anchor. As the problem is of interest to students, they work together to solve it. Although anchored instruction resembles problem-based methods, it is less open-ended, and more prescriptive. However, it is useful in directing students through specific tasks.

Anchored instruction should be viewed as a major paradigm for technology-based learning. Original work on this model was conducted by the Cognition and Technology Group at Vanderbilt which found that anchored instruction is *"...(situated) in video-based, problem-solving environments that teachers and students can explore. Its goal is to foster problem-solving and to help students become independent thinkers"*. Its initial focus was the development of interactive videodiscs that encouraged students and teachers to pose and solve complex problems. The videos serve as "anchors" to generate problem-solving and learning. AI was also developed to remedy *inert knowledge,* i.e., knowledge that is inflexible, or applicable only to a few situations. In 2012, multimedia, web-media and other interactive technologies can be used for AI.

One of the goals of anchored instruction is for students to become autonomous. It is essential that instructional designers and teachers interact with students in order to build that autonomy. Students should therefore work on problems in small groups, and eventually report their solutions to the entire class. During their reports, students can discuss the pros and cons of various. One of the benefits of AI is that students are able to understand problems more deeply by exploring the relationship among pertinent variables. AI helps students to learn more about the issues that subject or domain experts typically encounter and get to see how they might identify, represent and solve problems. Most groups will struggle in using AI. The instructor must also learn through experience when to provide strategic support to their students and when to let them find their own way.

***Features of Anchored Instruction*:** The main features of Anchored Instruction are given below:

- Anchored instruction situates instruction in the rich context of meaningful authentic problem solving environments
- Further it provides examples of problems and opportunities that experts encounter and helps students to explore knowledge that experts use
- Simulation of apprenticeship that comprises authentic tasks
- Video formats are used because they help students to develop pattern recognition skills; allow students to explore dynamic, visual and spatial representations of the problem and information to inform their mental models of the problem situation
- Videodisc has random-access capabilities that enable students to explore the information from different perspectives
- Goal-oriented problem solving process: Students are challenged to engage in problem finding and problem solving activities. Students must identify major goals, generate the sub-problem that represent obstacles to the goal, and devise strategies to deal with various subproblems

***Design Principles of Anchored Instruction*:** The instructional design principles underlying the anchored instruction are:

- Instruction highlights the use of knowledge to help students to see the needs of learning the new information and set up the learning goals.
- Students are encouraged to identify their own questions to the problem, to set up their own goals, and issues when they explore the anchors, a problem solving environment in a videodisc format, to identify relevant information and to come up with solutions.
- Teachers need to learn to give control to students letting students to establish their learning goals. Teachers are no longer authoritative sources of knowledge, but facilitators and guides to support students' problem solving process, such as helping them to identify their goals.

Anchors are macro-contexts that consist of rich information, and differ from micro-contexts which are individual examples used to illustrate a particular learning dimension. It is ultimately more manageable for teachers to organize instruction around anchors than to find all the resources necessary to accomplish community-based projects. Anchors equalize the preparation of the students, and provide common ground of shared knowledge to facilitate participation.

(B) Case-based Reasoning

Case-based reasoning is a constructivist learning theory that argues we draw on previous experiences to make sense of the world. The assumption is that when cases are introduced and indexed cognitively in the human brain (where other experiences are "indexed") reminders are sent to us and the potential for generalization occurs (Kolodner & Kolodner, 1987). Compared to expert systems, and storing past experiences as a set of rules, CBR seeks to store past experiences as instances of problem-solving (Kolodner, 1992; Maher, Balachandran, & Zhang, 1995). Further, CBR aims to generate solutions based on previously-solved problems and the principle that people solve new problems by remembering similar episodes and situations.

According to Schank (1990), human memory is story-based, and human beings typically index knowledge as stories (and even stories as knowledge). This is particularly true in medicine which is based on patient stories or histories. Medical students and residents (i.e., problem-solvers) are reminded of their past experiences with patients, and use those experiences to guide themselves through new experiences. Kolodner defines a case as "a contextualized piece of knowledge representing an experience that teach a lesson fundamental to achieving the goal of the reasoner." In CBR, problem-solving is a process of remembered problem-solving steps which may be adapted to fit new circumstances. Here, too, adapted solutions are indexed as new cases are moved into learner memory banks for future use.

Studies on the nature of expertise show that experts differ from novices in the amount of knowledge they store and its organization and accessibility (Chase & Simon, 1973; Chi, Feltovich, & Glaser, 1981; Gobbo & Chi, 1986). A critical factor here is the ability to deal with new situations by recalling and reusing experience. It is thought to be valuable to use CBR to teach novices, who do not have a lot of problem-solving experience, by presenting stories of others in problem-solving contexts.

***Analogies in Case-based Reasoning*:** In order to assist learning from prior problem-solving episodes, the problem-solver should be able to execute the basic process of retrieving, adapting and storing stories. Montazemi & Gupta (1997) elaborate on the process between adapting and storing, i.e., evaluating the adapted solution and predicting success or failure of the solution. In tandem with Leake's concept of analogy (1996), a process model of CBR might be proposed.

The proposed process emphasizes the performance of reasoning through analogy, and the feedback of evaluation to learn lessons about success or failure. Leake says that case-base reasoning is fundamentally analogical. Didierjean and Cauzinille-Marmeche (1998) say that there are two processes that support reasoning through analogy: one is to use abstract knowledge, the other is to use case-based reasoning. Psychological experiments show that human reasoners do use both processes of reasoning by analogy simultaneously (Goldin-Meadow *et al.*, 1993; Didierjean & Canzinille-Marmeche, 1998).

In case-based reasoning, the degree of relevance of the retrieved case to the new situation is crucial. Research into CBR focuses on the issue of indexing to form correspondence between the new experience and the previous. An index allows a reminder to be sent as patterns are recognized and where cases seem relevant. Kolodner makes clear the importance of this, and defines a case as "a contextualized piece of knowledge representing an experience that teaches a lesson fundamental to achieving the goal of the reasoner". The key for learners is to remember how to apply the previous case knowledge, and how much information is applicable so that the situations can be resolved even when they appear, at first glance, to be rather different.

***Benefits of Cases*:** The main benefits of cases are as follows:

- To retrieve in memory the experience closest to the new situation
- To locate a solution based on experience and adapted to meet demands of new situation
- To evaluating use of solutions
- To storing problem-solving as part of memory system

Case-based reasoning originated in the field of artificial intelligence. As such, it promotes higher-ordered thinking through cases. Support for teaching with cases comes from the research in cognitive science. Situated cognition emphasizes the importance of context. Learning should therefore be situated in practitioners' culture (Brown, Collins, & Duguid). Cases that consist of actors, goals and a sequence of events (Kolodner & Guzia, 2000) are useful as instructional tools because they involve learners in analyzing authentic, real-life problems.

This model derives its theoretical support from memory organization and reminding in cognitive science (Shank, 1982; 1990). It uses prior experiences in the process of problem solving. As a learning model, it shows that the acquisition of expertise is an accumulation of experiences and a cognitive indexing of experiences for retrieval (Koschmann *et al.*, 1997). The power of reasoning through access to old cases provides instructional practices. Kolodner, Hmelo, and Narayanan (1996) suggest incorporating CBR with PBL to enhance learning; they suggest that a library of cases should provide a variety of problem-solving experiences to augment memory and enhance learners' problem solving and reasoning skills. The theoretical support for learning in CBR comes from the ability of reasoning the old problem solving to navigate new ones.

(C) Cognitive Flexibility Theory

Cognitive flexibility theory is a conceptual model for designing learning environments based on cognitive learning theory. As such, it focuses on the nature of learning in complex and unstructured domains of knowledge. CFT is used in learning environments that support interactive technologies and emphasizes advanced knowledge acquisition. CFT allows for "flexible reassembly of preexisting knowledge to adaptively fit to the needs of a new situation." (Spiro *et al.*, 1991). CFT embodies fundamental concepts of both cognitivism and constructivism; its emphasis is on presentation of information from multiple perspectives and the use of case studies to present diverse examples. Founded by Spiro with Feltovich and Coulson, CFT is intended to be applied to new approaches of learning in the design of hypermedia. Their research includes knowledge acquisition in complex domains, hypermedia learning environments, multimedia case-based methods in education, biomedical cognition, and constructive processes in comprehension and recall. CFT research deals with trying to find out ways to avoid over simplifying instruction while designing platforms.

***Principles of Cognitive Flexibility Theory (CFT)*:** This theory aims to foster learners' ability to spontaneously reconstruct their knowledge to adopt different situational demands (Spiro & Jehng, 1990). The means to achieve cognitive flexibility is to manipulate knowledge representation, and the processes that operate those representations. The major principles of doing this are:

- Reflecting knowledge complexity to provide opportunities for learners to establish interconnections of concepts and principles
- CFT avoids presenting problems as simple, linear sequences of decision-making
- Providing multiple representations of content: students should access content at different times and contexts for different purposes and perspectives
- Multiple thematic organization of content, multiple perspectives of content help learners to construct multiple rcpresentations of content
- A variety of cases can be used to illustrate different themes and perspectives and to support a variety of contexts for learning
- Supporting context-dependent knowledge: knowledge cannot be oversimplified
- Oversimplification isolates knowledge from its context, segments knowledge into discrete components and represents interrelationships of components into a single unifying dimension. It is essential to provide contextual variability for different multiple knowledge

representations and multiple interconnectedness of knowledge components (Sprio, Feltovich, Jacobson & Coulson, 1991).

- In addition, the use of CFT should seek to reduce cognitive loading. Online course designers suggest that the amount of text on a computer screen should never exceed 150 words; alternatively, text can be presented in small meaningful chunks.

Examples or Cases Where CFT is used

Below are some examples where CFT is used:

Jonassen *et al.* describe the use of CFT to the design of a hypertext programme on transfusion medicine. The programme presents different complex clinical cases which students can use to diagnose and treat patients using various sources of information (including advice from experts). The learning environment is ill-defined and complex, presents multiple perspectives and emphasizes construction of knowledge. Feltovich *et al.* found that medical students had some difficulties in transferring knowledge that was previously learned in one context, such as in medical school, to new situations such as problem-solving in the clinic. They argued that students' deficiencies in learning (i.e., inert knowledge) at this advanced stage was as a result of oversimplification (reductive bias) of complexity.

Cunningham describes a method of teacher education, which involves case-based learning that encourages the pre-service teacher to begin thinking like an expert teacher. Cunningham states that a case-study approach to teacher education "bridges the gap between theory and practice" (p. 1) by getting students actively involved in analyzing and interpreting scenarios that they can revisit numerous times. Instead of presenting tidy scenarios with only one right answer, the proposed instruction provides more authentic, "messy", complex problems that, upon analysis, present multiple solutions.

(D) Jonassen's Constructivist Learning Environments (CLE)

Jonassen's constructivist learning environments is a learning model used to design constructivist learning environments. In the digital age, these environments are typically (and often) technology-enabled. Jonassen proposes a model for developing a suitable interactive environment through the use of authentic problems which can take one of several forms from the simple to complex. According to Jonassen, learners should be presented with interesting, relevant and meaningful tasks and activities in order to trigger learning. Activities in the learning environment should promote exploration, experimentation, construction, collaboration and reflection. How might teachers help to trigger learning? Through the introduction of cases (multiple cases and projects integrated at curriculum level) and problems taken from the real world. Jonassen recommends making learning goals and objectives engaging and relevant but not overly-structured; teachers should build on foundational knowledge of students. It is important to use learning experiences that facilitate knowledge-creation and meaning-making; further, information should not be downloaded onto learners. Reigeluth says that the major contribution of Jonassen's CLEs is that the model provides a coherent framework that can be used with other pedagogical approaches. The careful scaffolding of learning and how learners build on previous knowledge are both important considerations in this theory.

***Essential Components in a Jonassen CLE*:** Jonassen and Duffy moved towards a proper design model of CLEs by evaluating projects said to be defined as constructivist. Three common elements were deemed to be fundamental: namely, *context, collaboration and construction.* Depending on a student's prior learning, various case studies and scaffolding are necessary for providing the support necessary within CLEs. Instructors need to provide authentic contexts for tasks, plus information resources, cognitive tools, and collaborative tools in order for learners to be successful within CLEs.

- The problem, question or project is the focus or trigger in the environment
- The focus on problem, question or project constitutes a learning goal that drives process
- The desired quality of the learning environment is for it to be interesting, relevant and authentic

Three major components need to be included in the problem design:

> *Context*: a description of the physical, organization, and sociocultural context in which the problem occur should be presented
>
> *Representation or simulation*: the principle of representing the problem is to make it interesting, appealing and engaging; representation of the problem needs to be authentic to "present the same types of cognitive challenges as those in the real world as well as to be interesting and relevant to the learners so that they can engage in solving the problems
>
> *Manipulation*: meaningful learning needs to be a mindful activity where learners are given opportunities to interact with the environment (and with each other "collaboratively").

Problem manipulation provide such opportunities; they can be causal models for students to test the effects of the manipulation by receiving feedback or students' argumentation to support their solutions to problems

The Internet or the web offers learners a useful interface to information resources. However, the web should be used to fit the requirements of goals in order to be effective within the constructivist learning environment. As the web provides immediate access to all kinds of resources, Jonassen refers to it as gaining multiple perspectives, one that allows learners to take different approaches to problems, especially as they often have inadequate prior knowledge to solve problems.

***Goals and Pre-conditions*:** Primary goal of the theory is to design for a learning environment to foster problem solving and conceptual development in ill-defined or ill-structured domains

***Principles of CLE*:** The main principles of CLE are as follows:

1. Key to meaningful learning is authentic problems or tasks, and ownership of problem learners attempt to solve
2. Students are required to complete learning activities that include exploration, articulation and reflection
3. CLEs require appropriate instructional supports including modeling, coaching and scaffolding

***Condition of Learning*:** Primary learning setting focuses on problem solving and conceptual development in ill-defined, ill-structured domains

***Required Media*:** Computer-based programmes and multimedia are used to support problem presentation and to scaffold cognitive processes, including knowledge-representation, knowledge-modelling, information-gathering and problem-solving performance

***Role of Facilitator*:** A facilitator can be an instructor or computer or web tool (e.g., database, multimedia, Internet). Facilitator should take the instructional roles including modeling, coaching and scaffolding

***Instructional Strategies*:** Select and provide the following support:

1. appropriate problem, question, case or project
2. related cases or worked examples
3. leaner-selectable information
4. cognitive tools
5. conversation and collaboration tools
6. social/contextual support

***Assessment Method*:** Project- or problem-based task

(E) Problem-based Learning (PBL)

Problem-based learning (or PBL as medical students call it) is a *student-centered* pedagogical theory of classroom learning where small groups of students study (and discuss) complex problems, and work together to formulate suitable solutions to cases. By working with others in groups, medical students can identify what they know, what they need to know and where to find "best evidence" to understand pertinent issues. It is a widely-used teaching-learning method in medical education and increasingly in other areas of health education also. Its main tenets are to help learners develop problem-solving skills, improve self-directed learning and build peer-to-peer collaboration skills.

The instructor or tutor's role in PBL is to facilitate and mentor students during the learning process. He or she provides intellectual and emotional support while modelling best medical practices. Sometimes the practices can be as disparate as understanding basic science concepts, how they apply to clinical work, and bioethics and professionalism. Acting as role models and mentors, tutors are charged with building confidence in students and encouraging them to find their own solutions to clinical problems.

The PBL model began at McMaster University in Hamilton, Ontario in the late 1960s. The curriculum was developed to stimulate learners, assist them to work with peers and sustain high *intrinsic* motivation (Barrows, 1996). In the last few decades, the PBL model has been adopted by medical school programmes around the world, and subsequently adapted for a number of undergraduate programmes (Boud and Feletti, 1997; Duch, 2001; Amador, 2006) and college programmes (Barrows, 1996). The use of PBL has expanded outside medicine to law, education, economics, business and engineering (Barrows 1996). Like other student-centered pedagogies, PBL acknowledges the limitations of traditional didactic teaching, and the value of constructivist interactive approaches to learning.

Process of PBL: PBL is Student-centered. PBL actively engages the student in building their own understanding of complex issues, which places it in the tradition of constructivism. The use of PBL techniques means that how a problem is approached will likely result in a variety of viable solutions; its premise is that some complex problems will in fact have more than one solution.

Characteristics of PBL: The main characteristics of PBL are that:

- it is student-centered and begins with a case or problem,
- interrogation of ideas results in knowledge; learning occurs in small groups,
- tutors act as facilitators and guides to help learners,
- problems stimulate development and use of problem-solving skills,
- new knowledge is obtained through self-directed questioning and information-seeking,
- finally, a reasonable course of action is developed in order to "solve" the problem(s)

(F) Situated Learning Theory

Situated learning theory is a theory developed by Jean Lave and Etienne Wenger and owes much to the work of John Dewey and Lev Vygotsky who believed students were more likely to learn by actively participating in their learning as opposed to listening to lecturers. Situated learning is a matter of creating meaning from the real activities of daily living where learning occurs in a pro-social but informal setting. This notion suggests that learning takes place through social relationships, within a cultural milieu, and by connecting prior knowledge to new contexts. The situated model of learning is part of Lave and Wenger's theory of communities of practice which states that learning should not be viewed as mere transmission of knowledge but as a distinctly embedded and active process. They argue that this type of learning is stimulated by specific contexts (where learning is socially-situated) and within authentic social and physical environments.

***Key Concepts of Situated Learning*:** Key concepts of situated learning are as follows:

- Knowledge is not an object and memory is not a location; knowledge is socially-constructed
- Knowledge is thus located in the actions of people and groups of people; it evolves naturally as a result of individuals participating in and negotiating their way through new situations
- Knowing, learning and cognition are socially-constructed, expressed and reified in the actions of people, and people interacting
- Construction of meaning is tied to specific contexts and purposes
- Mediation artifacts: cultural models are not held by individuals but live in the practices of a community and how people engage with each other, as well as any tools they use, and the specific cultural context
- As situations shape individual cognition, individual thinking and action shape the situation; the reciprocal influence constitutes an alternative conception of systemic causality to the more commonly assumed linear object causality (Wilson and Myers, 2000).

***Importance of Authenticity in Situated Learning*:** The importance of authenticity in situated learning is:

- Knowledge, as a product of a meaning-making process, cannot be separated from its context
- Learning is a continuous, lifelong process from acting within (and reacting to) situations
- The tools of learning, and their usage "reflect the particular accumulated insights of communities of practice"
- Learning is a process of enculturation: "...given the chance to observe and practice in situ the behaviours of members of a culture, people pick up relevant jargon, imitate behaviours"... and start to act in accordance with norms of that culture

(I) Lave's Situated Learning (1988)

Lave discusses the problem of *knowledge transfer* and argues that learning in natural settings occurs as a function of activities, context and culture in which it is situated. He examines cognition in everyday situations and provides descriptions for them:

- Cognition is socially defined, interpreted and supported
- Social contexts can both constrain and assist cognition: research should examine cognition to determine the generality of cognitive skills and articulate culture's role in developing skills
- People devise satisfactory opportunistic *in situ* solutions to problems; they don't employ formal approaches to problem-solving in everyday thinking
- Participation in interaction results in adaptive "survival" skills, as well as successful reasoning and learning

(II) Brown, Collins and Duguid (1989)

According to Brown, Collins and Duguid (1989), different instructional goals such as 'knowing what' and 'knowing how' result in different practices in education. As a kind of decontextualized learning, it separates out the learning from the doing. They suggest that "activity and situations are integral to cognition and learning" and cognitive apprenticeship provides an "authentic place to engage in activity and social interactions".

(III) Gibson's Affordance

Affordance is an ecological concept i.e., *how human beings perceive what something is or does within their environment.* The implications are that "affordance" is a term characterizing the impact of the environment on an organism's behaviour, and how it lives in its environment. Affordance emerges with the action of the organism, i.e., hence, its direct perception of environmental affordances controls its behaviour. The idea of affordances suggests a reciprocal relationship between organism and environment. It is thus important to analyze behaviours in relation to environments. When affordances is considered by humans, our perception of affordance extends beyond the physical environment to conceptual states. Any theory of learning must therefore start with the cultural environment in which learners learn. If knowledge is co-produced within cultures, then the position of learners is a critical variable. Teachers need to respect knowledge communities and help learners to negotiate multiple worldviews.

(IV) Cognitive Apprenticeship

Cognitive apprenticeship is an important practical concept in *situated learning.* This type of learning apprenticeship engages learners to participate in communities of practice, and provides several advantages:

- The legitimacy of apprenticing, and availability of community resources, is important to learners
- Learners have strong goals and motivation in situated contexts
- Learners develop an understanding of the enterprise through an engagement in practice
- Communication among peers and near-peers also facilitates learning

Process of Cognitive Apprenticeship

The process of cognitive apprenticeship is given below:

1. By beginning with a task embedded in a familiar activity, instructors show students the legitimacy of their implicit knowledge and its availability as scaffolding in unfamiliar tasks.
2. By pointing to different decompositions, instructors stress heuristics are not absolute but assessed with respect to particular tasks; even algorithms can he assessed in this way.
3. By allowing students to generate their own solutions, instructors help them to be conscious creative members of the culture of problem-solving.
4. A cognitive apprenticeship helps students' enculturation; acquiring culture's tools or a shared vocabulary and the means to discuss, reflect on, evaluate and validate community procedures is a collaborative process.

(V) Legitimate Peripheral Participation (Lave, 1988, Lave & Wenger, 1991)

Legitimate peripheral participation refers to how learners engage in activities of socio-cultural practice, and how they become increasingly competent in this practice. Participation provides students with ways to belong to a community of practice. Legitimate peripheral participation refers to the social organization of and control over resources. To get full access to resources takes time and experience. The word peripheral is used to "distinguish between new comers and old timers" (Driscoll, 2000) which "encompasses multiple, varied, more-or-less engaged and inclusive ways of being located in the fields of participation defined by a community". Brown, Collins and Dugid (1989) support their propositions about situated learning and cognitive apprenticeship by addressing the following:

- There is a mismatch between the formal learning situations and real world situations
- There is a failure of knowledge to transfer
- Training by abstraction is of little use
- Learning is inherently a social phenomenon

In a nutshell, it can be said that Situated learning emphasizes the idea that what is learned is specific to the situation (context) in which it is learned.

Wilson and Myers (2000) describe it as cognition that "emphasizes the web of social and activity systems within which authentic practice takes place."

(G) Social Learning Theory

Social learning theory argues that learning "...occurs within social situations and contexts. Social learning theory also considers how people learn from each other and includes related concepts such as observational learning, imitation and behavioural modeling. Albert Bandura is considered one of the leading proponents of social learning theory" — Ormond, 1999.

Alfred Bandura's view of social learning emphasizes the value of observing and modeling behaviours, attitudes and emotional reactions of others. In 1977, he said that "...learning would be exceedingly laborious, not to mention hazardous, if [we] had to rely solely on the effects of [our] own actions to inform [our own understanding of something]... fortunately, most human behavior is learned observationally through modeling: from observing others one forms an idea of how new behaviors are performed, and on later occasions this coded information serves as a guide for action..." Bandura improves on the behavioural interpretations of modeling articulated by Miller & Dollard in the 1940s. Bandura's work is related to the theories of Vygotsky and Lave which emphasize the central role of social learning in the developing the intellectual and the social capacity of learners.

***General Principles of Social Learning Theory*:** General principles of social learning theory are as listed below:

1. People learn by observing the behaviours of others, and by observing the outcome of those behaviours
2. Learning occurs without changes in behaviour; on the one hand, behaviourists contend that learning must be represented by a permanent change in behaviour; social learning theorists say, however, that because people are able to learn through observation alone
3. Cognition plays a certain role in learning; in the past 30 years, social learning theory has become increasingly cognitive in its interpretation of human learning. Awareness and expectations of future reinforcements or punishments have an impact on the behaviours people exhibit
4. Social learning theory is a type of bridge or transition between behaviourist learning theories and cognitive theories

***How the Environment Reinforces and Punishes Modeling*:** People are often reinforced to model the behaviours of others. Bandura says that the environment reinforces modeling in several ways:

1. The observer is reinforced by the model; a student who changes how he behaves to fit in with a certain group has a strong likelihood of being accepted into and reinforced by the group
2. The observer is reinforced by a third person; an observer might model the actions of someone else such as an outstanding student. The teacher praises the observer for modeling the behaviours of a good student thereby reinforcing those behaviours
3. Imitated behaviours lead to reinforcing consequences; behaviours we learn from others produce satisfying or reinforcing results. For example, a student in a social media class can observe how extra work done by a peer can be fun. This student in turn would do the same extra work and receive similar satisfaction
4. Consequences of the model's behaviour affect observers vicariously. This is known as vicarious reinforcement. This is where a model is reinforced and an observer demonstrates an increase in the same response. By having students watch a film of a model hitting an inflated clown doll, Bandura showed how a group of children who saw the model were praised for the action. Without being reinforced, the group of children also hit the doll

***Cognitive Factors in Social Learning*:** Social learning theory has cognitive factors as well as behaviourist or operant factors:

Learning without Performance: Bandura makes a distinction between learning through observation and imitation of what has been learned

Cognitive Processing During Learning: social learning theorists argue that attention is a critical factor in learning

Expectations: as a result of being reinforced, people form expectations about the consequences that their behaviours are likely to bring. They expect certain behaviours to bring reinforcements and others to bring punishments. The learner needs to be aware of response reinforcements and response punishments. Reinforcement increases the response when the learner is aware of that connection.

Reciprocal Causation: Bandura proposed that behaviour can influence both the environment and the person. In fact each of these variables, person, behaviour and environment influence each other

Modeling: there are different models; a live model, and an actual person demonstrating the behaviour. There is a symbolic model which puts a person or action in some other medium such as television, videotape, computer programmes.

***Behaviours that Can be Learned through Modeling*:** Many behaviours can be learned through modeling. Examples are students who watch their parents reading, students who watch demonstrations of mathematics problems or someone acting bravely. Aggression can also be learned through modelling. Research shows that children are more aggressive when observing aggressive or violent modeling. Moral thinking and behaviours are also influenced by modeling and observing. This includes moral judgments regarding right and wrong.

***Conditions Necessary for Effective Modeling*:** Bandura mentions four conditions necessary for individuals to model:

1. *Attention*: the person must first pay attention to the model
2. *Retention*: the observer must be able to remember what is observed; one way of increasing this is using the technique of rehearsal
3. *Motor Reproduction*: the third condition is the ability to replicate behaviours the model demonstrates; this means that observers must be able to replicate the action, which may pose a problem for learners who are not developmentally ready
4. *Motivation*: the final ingredient for modeling is motivation; learners must want to demonstrate what they have learned; because the four conditions vary, different people will reproduce the same behaviour differently

***Educational Implications of Social Learning Theory*:** Social learning theory has numerous implications for classrooms:

1. Students learn a great deal simply by observing others
2. Describing the consequences of behaviour increases appropriate behaviours, decreasing inappropriate ones; this includes discussing the rewards of various behaviours
3. Modeling provides an alternative to teaching new behaviours. Instead of using shaping, an operant conditioning, modeling is a faster, more efficient means of teaching. To promote effective modeling, teachers must ensure the four essential conditions exist; attention, retention, motor reproduction and motivation
4. Teachers must model appropriate behavioursand take care they do not model inappropriate behaviours
5. Teachers should expose students to a variety of models; this is important to break down stereotypes
6. Students must believe that they are capable of accomplishing a task; it is important to develop a sense of self-efficacy for students. Teachers can promote such self-efficacy by having students receive confidence-building messages, watch others be successful, and experience success on their own
7. Teachers should help students set realistic expectations; ensuring

that expectations are realistically challenging. Sometimes a task is beyond a student's ability

8. Self-regulation techniques provide an effective method for improving student behaviours

(H) Transformative Learning (TL)

Transformative learning is a term used in educational theory to describe a process which leads the learner to re-evaluate past beliefs and experience…in transformational learning, the student is able to critically reflect on his or her own assumptions about how the world works and sees the world with a new perspective.

Transformational learning is a "constructivist" perspective and theory of deep learning that goes beyond content knowledge acquisition. TL is a process for adults to learn to think for themselves based on critical reflection or assessment of events in their lives. In fact, the way we interpret and reinterpret our experiences in the world is central to transformative learning (Jack Mezirow, 1995). In organizations, for example, professional development is a major form of transformative learning and may dwell on activities that are reflective in nature. Often, these activities embrace transformation of professional identity and work practices. Jack Mezirow, the major theorist in the area, says that critical reflection on our assumptions (particularly about ourselves) leads to "transformation". Mezirow's work is part of a critical tradition in adult education that extends back through Freire, Dewey and Habermas. Mezirow described transformative learning environments where learners have full information, are free from coercion, have equal opportunity to assume roles in class, and can become critically reflective. Moreover, learners are empathetic and willing to search for common ground with others or a synthesis of different points of view in the classroom.

***Goal of Transformative Learning*:** The goal of transformational learning is to change one's "frame of reference". Mezirow says that the frame of reference is the collective assumptions through which we interpret and understand something. A frame of reference includes two elements: habits of mind and points of view. Habits of mind are shaped by the many assumptions which build on cultural, social, educational and political codes. Specific points of view originate from habits of mind. When people begin to examine predetermined assumptions and beliefs, they tend to be more open, inclusive, reflective and willing to change (Choy, 2010). However, not every experience will be transformative; thus reflection is central to it (Mezirow, 1997).

***Aspects of Transformative Learning*:** The theory of transformative learning comprises two aspects: instrumental (or instructional) learning and communicative learning. As Mezirow says, "…a key proposition of transformative learning recognizes the validity of Habermas's fundamental distinction between instructional and communicative learning". Further, instructional learning focuses on "learning through task-oriented problem-solving" and may include an examination of cause and effect (Taylor, 1998). Instructional learning aims to achieve short term objectives such as improved performance; often, the adult learner will ask what the most direct route is to learn something. In communicative learning, how adults communicate their needs, especially how needs link up with feelings, encourages the learner to be self-critical, autonomous and ultimately responsible for their learning path (Mezirow, 1991).

***Phases of Transformative Learning*:** Ten phases of transformative learning are given below:

1. A disorienting dilemma
2. A self-examination with feelings of guilt or shame
3. A critical assessment of epistemic, sociocultural, or psychic assumptions
4. Recognition that one's discontent and the process of transformation are shared and that others have negotiated a similar change
5. Exploration of options for new roles, relationships, and actions
6. Planning of a course of action
7. Acquisition of knowledge and skills for implementing one's plans
8. Provisional trying of new roles
9. Building of competence and self-confidence in new roles and relationships
10. A reintegration into one's life on the basis of conditions dictated by one's perspective

7
Connectivist Pedagogy

After studying this chapter, the reader will be able to: Explore some important questions in relation to learning theories; Know the limitations of traditional learning theories (Behaviourism, Cognitivism and Constructivism); Explain the Connectivism; Define the Connectivist pedagogy; Judge that Connectivism is a learning theory; Enumerate the major ideas of Connectivism; Describe the principles of Connectivism; Apply Connectivism in instructional design; Apply the Connectivist approach in school practices; Know the consideration for pedagogic activities; Explain some important instructional designs in the area of Connectivism; Enumerate the principles of Connectivist instructional designs

There are many questions to be explored in relation to learning theories and the actual impact of the new technologies on learning processes (Siemens, 2005):

- How are learning theories impacted when knowledge is no longer acquired in the linear manner?
- What adjustments need to made with learning theories when technology performs many of the cognitive operations previously performed by learners (information storage and retrieval).
- How can we continue to stay current in rapidly evolving information ecology?
- How do learning theories address moments where performance is needed in the absence of complete understanding?
- With increased recognition of interconnections in differing fields of knowledge, how are systems and ecology theories perceived in light of learning tasks?

Limitations of Traditional Learning Theories

George Siemens (2004) points out that some traditional learning theories such as behaviourism, cognitivism, and constructivism have limitations, because these theories were developed in a time when technology had not impacted learning to the degree it does today. These theories were developed when knowledge was growing more slowly. Nowadays, knowledge is growing at a dramatically greater rate. Siemens (2004) identifies some trends in learning. Many learners move through different fields during their life time, and learning occurs in different ways. Learning is a process, and there is a relationship between learning and work-related tasks. Organizations and individuals are both learning identities.

The traditional learning theories present some limitations. For instance, learning theories do not consider the learning process that takes place outside of people and also the learning that occurs within organizations. Siemens considers some questions exploring how impact the technology and new sciences (chaos and networks) on learning. Chaos is a new reality that is unpredictable and considers that meaning exists. On the other hand, Constructivism assumes learners build understanding through tasks that develop meaning. Another important concept that Siemens includes in his Connectivism framework is Self-Organization. Rocha (1998) in Siemens (2004) defines self-organization as the spontaneous formation of well organized structures, patterns or behaviours from random initial conditions. Learning as a self-organized process requires that the learning systems, both personal and organizational, be open to information, and able to classify its own interaction with an environment. Consequently, the systems must be able and flexible to change. The Self-organization on a personal level is a micro-process of the larger self-organization knowledge constructs created within corporate or institutional environments (Siemens, 2004).

What is Connectivism

George Siemens (2004, 2005) proposes *connectivism* as a theory of learning that takes into account the way how learning is influenced by the new learning technologies. He starts from the observations that previous theories of learning—behaviourism, cognitivism or constructivism—were created during a time when learning was happening in different technological contexts. It is therefore compulsory that learning models that have served previous generations are replaced for greater relevance to present's needs, which include technology and connection making as learning activities. As a learning theory, connectivism provides insight into the dynamics of networks, environments, and ecologies that supports a continual learning process. In this view, learning is strongly a networked process where a learner aggregates external contents into a holistic representation.

Is Connectivism a Learning Theory?

Connectivism is a learning theory for the digital age. Learning has changed over the last several decades. The theories of behaviourism, cognitivism and constructivism provide an effect view of learning in many environments. They fall short, however, when learning moves into informal, networked, technology-enabled arena.

Connectivism is a learning theory, in which knowledge exists outside of the learner and the learner makes connections between information to build knowledge. The connections that learners make help them create their own learning network. Through this connected web, learners will be able to stay up-to-date with content as it changes. It is important for the learner to be able to identify credible resources.

Major Ideas of Connectivism

Siemens outlines the major ideas of connectivism as:

- Learning and knowledge rests in diversity of opinions.
- Learning is the process of connecting specialized nodes or information sources.
- Learning may reside in non-human appliances.
- Capacity to know more is more critical than what is currently known.
- Nurturing and maintaining connections is needed to facilitate learning
- The ability to identify connections between concepts is important.
- Maintaining current and accurate knowledge is the purpose in connectivist activities.
- Decision-making is a learning process as information can change and what is viewed as correct one day may be incorrect the next (Siemens, 2004).

Principles of Connectivism

Some principles of connectivism are given below:

1. The integration of cognition and emotions in meaning-making is important. Thinking and emotions influence each other. A theory of learning that only considers one dimension excludes a large part of how learning happens.
2. Learning has an end goal—namely the increased ability to "do something". This increased competence might be in a practical sense (i.e. developing the ability to use a new software tool or learning how to skate) or in the ability to function more effectively in a knowledge era (self-awareness, personal information management, etc.). The "whole of learning" is not only gaining skill and

understanding—actuation is a needed element. Principles of motivation and rapid decision making often determine whether or not a learner will actuate known principles.

3. Learning is a process of connecting specialized nodes or information sources. A learner can exponentially improve their own learning by plugging into an existing network.
4. Learning may reside in non-human appliances. Learning (in the sense that something is known, but not necessarily actuated) can rest in a community, a network, or a database.
5. The capacity to know more is more critical that what is currently known. Knowing where to find information is more important than knowing information.
6. Nurturing and maintaining connections is needed to facilitate learning. Connection making provides far greater returns on effort than simply seeking to understand a single concept.
7. Learning and knowledge rest in diversity of opinions.
8. Learning happens in many different ways. Courses, email, communities, conversations, web search, email lists, reading blogs, etc. Courses are not the primary conduit for learning.
9. Different approaches and personal skills are needed to learn effectively in today's society. For example, the ability to see connections between fields, ideas, and concepts is a core skill.
10. Organizational and personal learning are integrated tasks. Personal knowledge is comprised of a network, which feeds into organizations and institutions, which in turn feed back into the network and continue to provide learning for the individual. Connectivism attempts to provide an understanding of how both learners and organizations learn.
11. Currency (accurate, up-to-date knowledge) is the intent of all connectivist learning.
12. Decision-making is itself a learning process. Choosing what to learn and the meaning of incoming information is seen through the lens of shifting reality. While there is a right answer now, it may be wrong tomorrow due to alterations in the information climate impacting the decision.
13. Learning is a knowledge creation process...not only knowledge consumption. Learning tools and design methodologies should seek to capitalize on this trait of learning.

Implications of Connectivism on Instructional Design

Constructivism provides different views of learning. Learners are no longer passive recipients and reproducers of information. Learners are active constructors of their own conceptual understanding, and active meaning makers interacting with the physical and social world. The design of learning environment based on constructivist view of learning emphasizes the integration of three types of human experiences (Vygotsky, 1978): historical experience, e.g. the traditions and practices of a culture, social experience, and adaptation experience, in which people engage in active adaptation, changing the environment.

Below are some general principles of learning derived from constructivism (Smith and Ragan, 2000; Driscoll, 2001; Duffy & Jonassen, 1992):

- Learning requires invention and self-organization on the part of learners
- *Disequilibrium facilitates learning*: Errors need to be perceived as a result of learners' conceptions and therefore not minimized or avoided. Thus, challenge students with open-ended investigations in realistic, meaningful contexts need to be offered; allow learners to explore and generate many possibilities, both affirming and contradictory.
- *Reflective abstraction is the driving force of learning*: As meaning-makers, humans seek to organize and generalize across experiences in a representational form.
- *Dialogue within a community engenders further thinking*: the learners are responsible for defending, proving, justifying, and communicating their ideas to the classroom community.

Connectivist Pedagogical Approach

Giesbrecht (2007) indicates that Connectivism presents itself as a pedagogical approach that affords learners the ability to connect to each other via social networking or collaboration tools. Siemens (2003) in Giesbrecht (2007) states that the role of the educator is to create learning ecologies, shape communities, and release learners into the environment. Giesbrecht (2007) which based on Siemens, characterized some limitations about course environments which are represented as one point of view of a subject and presented in isolation. Courses are developed under the assumption that learning only occurs in a certain time frame. Consequently, learning is not dynamic, social or complex. In this view, traditional learning environments are not developed beyond the classroom. Giesbrecht (2007) points out that Connectivism is founded in connections which require that learners interact with elements that extend the learning practice beyond the classroom and allow real life experiences. Under the Connectivism principles education is holistic, where balance between learner needs and institutional needs is essential. During the last decades the technological advanced have facilitated the development of the new scenarios for learning experiences. Online learning is an example of how people both individual and in group are participating in learning experiences from different places through the Internet which is called the network of the networks.

Spencer (2004) describes some positive aspect of using technology for instance; ideas and discussions among students can continue beyond the classroom meeting time, dialogical participation is encouraged, students gain new options for participating, among others.

Consideration for Pedagogic Activities

William (2008) considers allowing students to connect to the internet in the classroom, and encourages sharing information in the network, connecting with other and using methods for critical evaluation of the information available.

Siemens (2006) points out that a learner must be able to see relevance which is defined as the degree to which a resource matches an individuals needs. Relevance is crucial, because if the relevance determined by a learner motivation will increase. The relationship between the course content and the learner needs should be closely tied, and then the learning process is more effective. Also, in this social process, community and collaborative approaches are as important as exposure to the subject matter. Another challenge related to relevance is current content as knowledge is a dynamic experience. Individual's relationship to content has to change as content creation is augmented (Siemens, 2006).

Connectivist Pedagogy and Instructional Design (Ecologies Design)

The exponential increase and ever changing nature of information through hyper-connectivity means that we are required to engage in lifelong learning to stay up to date in our fields of expertise or employment. This learning and professional development needs to be self-sustaining and traditional linear learning design models do not always provide this.

Designing learning around web 2.0 principles can provide individuals with a means of staying current whilst catering for their intuitive 'what's in it for mean' mentality. There are number of models by which learning design can be built around using the structure of social networking sites, as "sharing is a fundamental human activity" and "social networks consist of people who are connected by a shared object.

Social object as: "something (it can be real or virtual) that facilitate conversation, and thus social interaction", and is the basis of popular web 2.0 sites like Flickr, Delicious, Facebook and Twitter, by making activities such as uploading, viewing and sharing as easy as possible, and recognizing that an individual's profile on these sites are also 'social objects', as they are a "constructed representation around which interaction takes place" and are social objects in their own right.

Learning Ecologies

Connectivism suggests that designing ecologies should replace designing instruction. Siemens defines ecology as a continuously evolving system. This system gives the learner the control to explore objectives defined by that learner (Giesbrecht, 2007). In order to facilitate the interaction within ecologies, both synchronous and asynchronous tools are essential as extensions of course environments. These tools are Blogs, Wiki, RSS, among others. William (2008) considers that blogs on-line social networking tool which allows for the exchange of information between individuals. They can be collaborative spaces where people negotiate and construct meaning and text (Richardson 2006). This social networking tool encourages a way of thinking beyond each learners isolated experience. The online tools before mentioned are currently belong to the domain of the so called web 2.0 which facilitate a more socially connected Web where everyone is able to add to and edit the information space (Anderson, 2007). In addition, Mason and Renie (2007) point out about the web 2.0 that "users are less passive receivers of information and more active co-creators of content".

Some important connectivist designing ecologies (instructional models/ designs) are listed below:

(1) *Blogs*: Blog websites such as Blogger.com or Wordpress can be used as individual paperless student learning journals. These could replace traditional paper-based journals but could be made visible to other students to create a collaborative learning environment. Students may be given the opportunity to provide each other with constructive comments and feedback. Blogs could be used as course websites where classroom supporting content (course information, assignment criteria, and homework tasks) is delivered. Students may also be given access to post and share information with their classmates. Blogs can also be used by students (individual or groups) to host project presentation materials and content. Textual information and media could be combined into effective web-based presentations. Importantly, these presentations are not singular events, thus may be viewed and reviewed by other students as resource materials at later times.

(2) *Wikis*: A Wiki is a website that can be used as a gathering point for the collaboration of ideas, thoughts, assignments, topics, etc. for a collective group. Classes can collaboratively create wikis on a given subject or topic that may later be used as an information resource.

(3) *Podcasting*: Podcasting is a way of making audio or video files available on the internet that can either be listened to or viewed on a PC or downloaded to a hand-held device such as an iPod or mp3 player. A podcast

will be treated as a sound recording (audio podcasts) or a film (video podcasts, as known as vodcasts). Podcasts may also include images, including PowerPoint presentations.

(4) *Social Networking*: Social Networking refers to systems that allow members of a specific site to learn about other members' skills, talents, knowledge or preferences. Commercial examples include www.Facebook.com and www.LinkedIn.com. Some companies use these systems internally to help identify experts. Other examples include www.MySpace.com and www.bebo.com.

(5) *Microblogging*: These are similar to blogs, except that posts are intended to be as condensed as possible. The most prominent of these services is arguably Twitter (http://twitter.com/), where users are encouraged to answer the question "What are you doing?" in 160 characters or less (i.e. the length of an SMS text message—one means of posting to the service).

(6) *RSS*: Really Simple Syndication (RSS) allows people to subscribe to online distributions of news, blogs, podcasts and other information.

(7) *Discussion Forums*: A Discussion Forum may be used to extend class discussions and topics or as supplemental enrichment dialogues, outside the classroom environment. They may be designed as spaces for students to share common interests, problems or concerns about course materials so that they may assist each other in the learning process and allowing a greater number of students to participate.

(8) *Chat Room Forums*: Chat forums allow for students and teachers to interact and discuss course content outside of the classroom setting (synchronous conferencing). Students could potentially use chat forums to collaborate on course activities, assignments and projects without having to meet in the same physical space.

(9) *ePortfolios*: An ePortfolio (electronic portfolio) is similar to a traditional portfolio except in electronic form. It is usually in the form of a website and is used to manage and collect documents, files, images, etc. ePortfolios serve many purposes ranging from education (evidence of learning) to presentations and applications. They are particularly useful to display summative work.

(10) *Concept Maps*: Concept Maps are visual tools used often to show how ideas, topics and themes are interconnected. The visual organization of the ideas, topics and themes are done in such a way that the creator(s) can easily recall important and meaningful information without having to read long documents. Can help students recall information easily when studying for tests.

(11) *Social Bookmarking*: Social bookmarking is a way for users to share bookmarks for web resources. It allows users to tag web resources and organize them in such a way that others will be able to benefit from their prior research.

It is beneficial for students doing any project where research is required as students will be able to share the links to web resources already discovered by classmates.

(12) *Web Syndication, Web Feed Management*: Web syndication is a form of syndication in which a section of a website is made available for other sites to use through to making Web feeds available from a site in order to provide other people an updated list of content from it (for example one's latest forum postings, etc.).

(13) *Tag Clouds*: A list of tags used in the site with some kind of visual indication of each tag's relative popularity (ex. large font). Web sites that implement tag clouds functions allow both finding a tag by alphabet and by popularity. Selecting a single tag within a tag cloud will generally lead to a collection of items that are associated with that tag.

(14) *Instant Messaging*: A form of real-time communication between two or more people based on typed text.

(15) *Mash-ups*: Mash-ups are aggregations of content and functionalities from different online sources/applications to create a new service, i.e. mashing-up existing technologies for an entirely new purpose. For example, www.WikiMapia.org takes the functions of a wiki and overlays it with Google Maps for an entirely new kind of map. Similarly, Google Maps can also process RSS feeds from photo-sharing sites which can include positioning data where available (e.g. Flickr), to show photos and the locations where they were taken.

(16) *Content Hosting Services*: Content hosting or content sharing sites allow users to upload content that they have created for others to view. Two of the most popular of these sites are YouTube (www.youtube.com) for videos and Flickr (www.flickr.com) for photographs. Users can also create an individual profile and list their favourite photos or videos. Users are able to rate and comment on the videos or photos posted and provide feedback to the creator and other users.

(17) *Elluminate Live!®*: Elluminate Live!® is a powerful tool that allows teachers to display information in a virtual environment to student users. Students and teachers can communicate online and collaborate on projects. This tool allow for the potential to bring in guest speakers or field experts to speak with students in a virtual environment. Prospectively, appropriate speakers could be found from distant geographical locations thus opening the possibilities and opportunities for students to interact with experts in other parts of the world.

Principles of Connectivist Instructional Designs

Engeström (2008) describes five principles for connectivist instructional designs:

1. Clearly **define the social object** your service is built around. i.e. designs, resources, tools and user profiles.
2. Define the verbs that **users perform** on the objects, so that is it clear what the site is for i.e. 'finding' and 'sharing'.
3. Make the **objects shareable** and easy to use; they encourage users to input social objects, link to other related social networking sites, have interactive design widgets, and runnable learning design sequences, allow social objects to be virally spread through different communication channels and to different communities, offer deep-level integration with a number of other sites/communities and dynamic sharing across the sites appropriate objects, tagging.
4. Turn invitations into **gifts**. Provide fun interactive sessions, acknowledge, user generated favourite designs and linking to other events and activities, prizes for the best entries, will add dynamically to the user's profile.
5. **Charge the publishers**, not the spectators (may have less relevance in educationally social learning design).

8
Computers and Models of Instructional Designs

After studying this chapter, the reader will be able to: Know the curriculum theory; Define then instructional design; List the objectives of instructional design; Know the applications of instructional design; Discuss the types of evaluation in instructional design; Define instructional technology; Understand the role of instructional design in education; Discuss some important models of instructional design

Education and training worldwide is changing from standardization to customization, from educator-centered or teacher-centered to learner-centered and from memorization to understanding. Learners are expected to direct their own learning, pace their learning activities and to become life long learners. The country needs citizens, who can take initiative, think critically and solve problems.

This requires a paradigm shift in education and instruction. Educators become facilitators and only one of many resources available to learners. It also implies that educators have to change their method of instruction. A multitude of instructional design theories are being developed to assist educators in their new roles.

Learning-focused instructional design theory must offer guidelines for the design of learning environments that provide appropriate combination of challenge and guidance, empowerment and support, self-direction and structure (Reigeluth, 1999). Instructional design theories take into account the findings of both learning theories and curriculum theory. These three theories in turn influence the actual design process. Because of the close relationship between instructional design theory, learning theory, curriculum theory and the design process, instructional designers should be familiar with these theories and the design process.

Curriculum Theory

Curriculum theories are concerned with the content of instruction, i.e. with 'what to teach'. Content is closely linked to the goal of the instruction, with defined outcomes to be achieved and identified skills to be mastered. Curriculum theory explores areas such as the social construction of knowledge, the influence of technology on learning and the effect of politics on curricula. It examines ideological orientations towards the curriculum and provides guidelines for curriculum design and development. According to Schubert (1986)—"The character of curriculum shapes and is shaped by its external relationships with knowledge, perspectives and practices in other educational domains: administration, supervision, foundations, policy, studies, evaluation, research methodology, subject areas, educational levels, teaching or instruction, special education, educational psychology and so on."

Instructional Design

Instructional Design is defined as *"a systematic process that is employed to develop education and training programmes in a consistent and reliable fashion"* (Reiser and Dempsey, 2007). In addition, Instructional Design models or theories may be thought of as frameworks for developing modules or lessons that 1) increase and/or enhance the possibility of learning and 2) encourage the engagement of learners so that they learn faster and gain deeper levels of understanding.

Instructional Design (ID) models differ from Instructional System Design (ISD) models in that ISD models have a broad scope and typically divide the instruction design process into five phases (van Merriënboer, 1997, pp 2-3):

- Analysis;
- Design;
- Development;
- Implementation or Delivery; and
- Evaluation.

In addition, ISD models use formative evaluations in all the phases and a summative evaluation at the end of the process. ID models are less broad in nature and mostly focus on analysis and design, thus they normally go into much more detail, especially in the design portion. ID models are normally employed in conjunction with ISD models. The ISD process keeps the entire training, development or educational process on the correct path or objective, while one or more ID models are used that best supports the learning process being designed. There are three types of strategies within Instruction Design theories (Reigeluth, 1983):

Organizational Strategies: Organizational strategies are broken down on the micro or macro level so that the lesson may be properly arranged and sequenced.

Delivery Strategies: Delivery strategies are concerned with the decisions that affect the way in which information is carried to the student, particularly, the selection of instructional media.

Management Strategies: Management strategies involve the decisions that help the learners interact with the learning activities in order that they may increase their knowledge and skills.

Definitions of Instructional Design

The Various definitions of Instructional Design are given below:

Instructional Design as Instructional Systems: Instructional design, also known as instructional systems design, is the analysis of learning needs and systematic development of instruction. Instructional designers often use Instructional technology as a method for developing instruction. Instructional design models typically specify a method, that if followed will facilitate the transfer of knowledge, skills and attitude to the recipient or acquirer of the instruction (Source: www.wikipedia.org).

Instructional Design as a Process: Instructional Design is the systematic development of instructional specifications using learning and instructional theory to ensure the quality of instruction. It is the entire process of analysis of learning needs and goals and the development of a delivery system to meet those needs. It includes development of instructional materials and activities; and tryout and evaluation of all instruction and learner activities.

Instructional Design as a Discipline: Instructional Design is that branch of knowledge concerned with research and theory about instructional strategies and the process for developing and implementing those strategies.

Instructional Design as a Science: Instructional design is the science of creating detailed specifications for the development, implementation, evaluation, and maintenance of situations that facilitate the learning of both large and small units of subject matter at all levels of complexity.

***Instructional** Design as Reality*: Instructional design can start at any point in the design process. Often a glimmer of an idea is developed to give the core of an instruction situation. By the time the entire process is done the designer looks back and her or him checks to see that all parts of the "science" have been taken into account. Then the entire process is written up as if it occurred in a systematic fashion.

Instructional Design as Systematic Development: Instructional Design is the systematic development of instructional specifications using learning and instructional theory to ensure the quality of instruction. It is the entire process of analysis of learning needs and goals and the development of a delivery system to meet those needs. It includes development of instructional materials and activities; and tryout and evaluation of all instruction and learner activities (*Source*: www.umich.edu).

Objectives of Instructional Design

Learning is an active process in which learners construct new ideas or concepts based upon their current/past knowledge. The learner selects and transforms information, constructs hypotheses, and makes decisions, relying on a cognitive structure to do so (Miller, 1956). Cognitive structure (i.e., schema, mental models) provides meaning and organization to experiences and allows the individual to "go beyond the information given".

Thus,

1. Instruction must be concerned with the experiences and contexts that make the student willing and able to learn (readiness).
2. Instruction must be structured so that it can be easily grasped by the student (spiral organization).
3. Instruction should be designed to facilitate extrapolation and or fill in the gaps (going beyond the information given).

Assumptions Underlying Instructional Design

Here are some assumptions underlying instructional design (Smith & Ragan, 1999).

1. In order to design instruction, the designer must have a clear idea of what the learner should learn as a result of the instruction.
2. The "best" instruction is that which is effective (facilitates learners' acquisition of the prescribed knowledge and skills), efficient (requires the least possible amount of time necessary for the learners to achieve the objectives), and appealing (motivates and interests learners, encouraging them to persevere in the learning task).
3. Students may learn from many different media: A "live teacher" is not always essential for instruction.
4. There are principles of instruction that apply across all age groups and all content areas. An example is: Students must participate actively, interacting mentally as well as physically with material to be learned.
5. Evaluation should include the evaluation of the instruction as well as the evaluation of the learner's

Types of Evaluations in Instructional Design

Evaluations are normally divided into two broad categories: *formative* and *summative:*

Formative Evaluation: A *formative evaluation* (sometimes referred to as internal) is a method for judging the worth of a programme while the programme activities are *forming* (in progress). This part of the evaluation focuses on the process. Thus, formative evaluations are basically done on the fly. They permit the designers, learners, and instructors to monitor how well the instructional goals and objectives are being met. Its main purpose is to catch deficiencies so that the proper learning interventions can take place that allows the learners to master the required skills and knowledge.

Formative evaluation is also useful in analyzing learning materials, student learning and achievements and teacher effectiveness. Formative evaluation is primarily a building process which accumulates a series of components of new materials, skills, and problems into an ultimate meaningful whole (Wally Guyot (1978).

Summative Evaluation: A *summative evaluation* (sometimes referred to as external) is a method of judging the worth of a programme at the end of the programme activities (summation). The focus is on the outcome. All assessments can be summative (i.e., have the potential to serve a summative function) but only some have the additional capability of serving formative functions (Scriven, 1967).

The various instruments used to collect the data are questionnaires, surveys, interviews, observations, and testing. The model or methodology used to gather the data should be a specified step-by-step procedure. It should be carefully designed and executed to ensure the data is accurate and valid.

Questionnaires are the least expensive procedure for external evaluations and can be used to collect large samples of graduate information. The questionnaires should be trialed (tested) before using to ensure the recipients understand their operation the way the designer intended. When designing questionnaires, keep in mind the most important feature is the guidance given for its completion. All instructions should be clearly stated...let nothing be taken for granted.

Instructional System

An instructional system is an arrangement of resources and procedures to promote learning. Instructional design is the systematic process of developing instructional systems and instructional development is the process of implementing the system or plan.

Instructional Technology

Instructional technology is the systemic and systematic application of strategies and techniques derived from behavioral, cognitive, and constructivist theories to the solution of instructional problems. Instructional technology is the systematic application of theory and other organized knowledge to the task of instructional design and development.

Instructional Technology = Instructional Design + Instructional Development

Instructional Development

The process of implementing the design plans.

Instructional Design Theory

An instructional design theory is a theory that offers explicit guidance on how to better help people learn and develop. These kinds of learning and development may include cognitive, emotional, social, physical and spiritual learning. Instructional design theories are goal-oriented and identify methods of instruction for specific situations. These methods have sets of components, which make them flexible and adaptable. ID models have the ambition to provide a link between learning theories and the practice of building instructional systems. Some instructional design theories are:

- Cognitive Education
- Teaching and Learning for Understanding
- Constructivist Learning
- Collaborative Problem Solving
- Merrill's First Principles of Instruction
- Multiple Approaches to understanding
- Open Learning Environments
- Learning by Doing
- Problem-Based Learning (PBL)

These theories are not mutually exclusive but overlap and often have a number of common elements.

Role of Instructional Design

Theories of instructional design are prescriptive in nature, specifying how instruction can effect learning, in contrast to theories of learning which are descriptive, focusing on the behaviour and capabilities of the learner (Wagner, 1994). The shift in emphasis from behaviourism and cognitive psychology to constructivism has led to the questioning of the role of instructional design theory in informing the design and use of learning environments. The concept of instructional design, which depends on the belief of an objective reality for the specification of instructional sequences, is firmly based on behaviourism and on a branch of cognitive psychology. There are several critical ways in which the aims of instructional design can be seen to conflict with those of constructivism. These will now be considered to establish their relevance to this thesis.

Instruction can be defined as "purposeful interaction to increase learners' knowledge or skills in specific, pre-determined ways" (p.135) (Ritchie & Hoffman, 1997). Instructional design is concerned with specifying how these interactions occur through the structuring and sequencing of teaching material and experiences. Instructional design theories provide postulates upon which to base these designs. The instructional designer uses information about learning context and objectives to design instructional methods. Instructional material is typically presented with predefined interrelationships and sequences. It is largely a reductionist process in which there is an assumption of a preferred learning model for the students that can be determined and achieved by the instructors (Winn, 1999). This is in direct contrast to constructivism, which emphasises learning as individually constructed by the student as a consequence of personal experience, activity and reflection.

Instructional design theories are premised upon the instructional designer being able to anticipate learning behaviour within the learning environment. A difficulty is that the nature of learning is idiosyncratic and dynamic (Lowyck & Elen, 1993). Learners are individual and complex, and are influenced by many factors (Winn, 1999). Furthermore, a learning environment designed according to constructivist principles will allow multiple ways of progressing to a learning goal. Learning behaviour within constructivist environments is unpredictable, suggesting that instructional design theories do not have a firm basis for application to the design of these environments.

Models of Instructional Design

There has been significant research into the design of educational resources over the years. This research focuses on design within a variety of different educational settings, ranging for example, from a description of the process of designing a curriculum for a particular subject area for all schools across a state, to a description of the process of designing a series of text based learning resources. Depending on the educational context, either the term "curriculum design" or the term "instructional design" is used to refer to this design process. The instructional design process is concerned with the processes used to design or plan the instruction. The term curriculum design has typically been used more often within the context of the design of the school curriculums, with instructional design being used more often within the context of industry training and in particular the design of self- paced learning resources.

Instructional design is the systematic approach to the Analysis, Design, Development, Implementation and Evaluation of learning materials and activities. Instructional design aims for a learner-centered rather than the traditional teacher-centered approach to instruction, so that effective learning can take place. This means that every component of the instruction is governed by the learning outcomes, which have been determined after a through analysis of the learner's needs.

Models for instructional design provide procedural frameworks for the systematic production of instruction. They incorporate fundamental elements of the instructional design process including analysis of the intended audience or determining goals and objectives. An instructional design model gives structure and meaning to an instructional design problem, enabling the designers to negotiate their design task with a semblance of conscious understanding. Models help to visualize the problem, to break it down into discrete, manageable units. A model should be judged by how it mediates the designer's intention, how well it can share a work load and how effectively it shifts focus away from itself toward the object of the design activity. Instructional models prescribe how combinations of instructional strategy components should be integrated to produce a course of instruction (Braxton *et al.,* 1995).

According to Braxton *et al.* (1995), instructional design (ID) models are guidelines or sets of strategies on which the approaches to teaching by instructors are based. Effective instructional models are based on learning theories. Instructional design research has proposed various models of the design process. Braxton *et al.*, cited the following ID models as the most important ones among the specific ID models:

Dick and Carey Design Model

Another well-known instructional design model is The Dick and Carey Systems Approach Model. The model was originally published in 1978 by Walter Dick and Lou Carey in their book entitled *The Systematic Design of Instruction.* The Dick and Carey design model uses a systems approach for designing instruction. The design model describes all the phases of an iterative process that starts by identifying instructional goals and ends with summative evaluation. It is a learner-centered model. The fact that it is a systems model implies that it is more involved with instructional development than design. One of the limitations of this model is that in this model behaviour is not considered.

Dick and Carey made a significant contribution to the instructional design field by championing a systems view of instruction as opposed to viewing instruction as a sum of isolated parts. The model addresses instruction as an entire system, focusing on the interrelationship between context, content, learning and instruction. According to Dick and Carey, "Components such as the instructor, learners, materials, instructional activities, delivery system, and learning and performance environments interact with each other and work together to bring about the desired student learning outcomes". The components of the Systems Approach Model, also known as the Dick and

Carey Model, are as follows (*Source*: http://en.wikipedia.org/wiki/Instructional_design#Dick_and_Carey):

- *Identify Instructional Goal(s)*: goal statement describes a skill, knowledge or attitude (SKA) that a learner will be expected to acquire
- *Conduct Instructional Analysis*: Identify what a learner must recall and identify what learner must be able to do to perform particular task
- *Analyze Learners and Contexts*: Identify general characteristics of the target audience including prior skills, prior experience, and basic demographics; identify characteristics directly related to the skill to be taught; and perform analysis of the performance and learning settings.
- *Write Performance Objectives*: Objectives consists of a description of the behavior, the condition and criteria. The component of an objective that describes the criteria that will be used to judge the learner's performance.
- *Develop Assessment Instruments*: Purpose of entry behavior testing, purpose of pre-testing, purpose of post-testing, purpose of practice items/practice problems
- *Develop Instructional Strategy*: Pre-instructional activities, content presentation, Learner participation, assessment
- Develop and Select Instructional Materials
- *Design and Conduct Formative Evaluation of Instruction*: Designer try to identify areas of the instructional materials that are in need of improvement.
- *Revise Instruction*: To identify poor test items and to identify poor instruction
- *Design and Conduct Summative Evaluation*

Some critics feel that the systems approach is too focused on specific objectives to be successfully applied to the development of instruction, which supports higher-level thinking and the active construction of knowledge by learners. However, advocates of the systems approach dispute this and believe the systems approach can be effectively employed to set appropriate goals and construct learning environments that facilitate the attainment of those goals. The Figure 8.1 illustrates this model—

As shown in the figure, the process of design involves a set of sequential tasks, with a degree of iteration or cycling through the stages. The cycling back through earlier stages occurs primarily in response to the results of the formative evaluation.

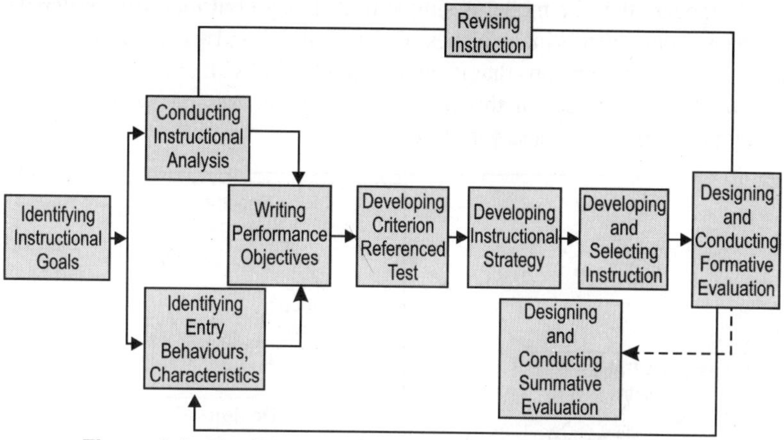

Figure 8.1: The Dick and Carey Instructional Design Model

Hannifin and Peck Design Model

The Hannifin Peck (1987) design model is a three-phase process. In the first phase, a needs assessment is performed. The second phase is followed by a design phase. In the third phase, instruction is developed and implemented. In this model, all of the phases involve a process of evaluation and revision. The Hannafin Peck's design model is simple but elegant in the way in which all the three phases are connected to "evaluate and revise".

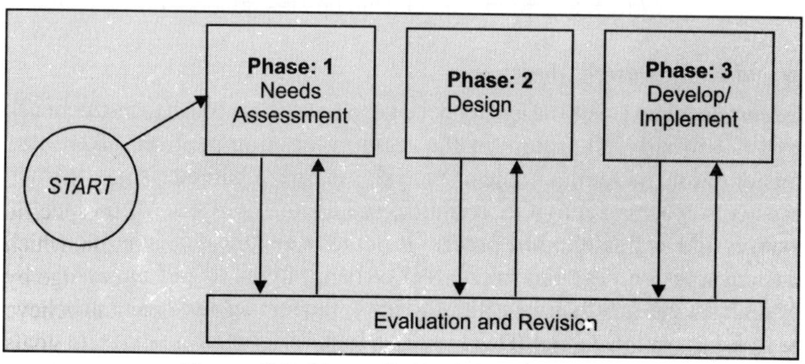

Figure 8.2: Hannafin Peck Design Model

Knirk and Gustafson Design Model

The Knirk and Gustafson (1986) design model is a three-stage process, which includes problem determination, design and development. The problem determination stage involves identifying the problem and setting instructional goals. The design stage includes developing objectives and specifying strategies. Finally, in the development stage, materials are developed.

It appears that the model is simple in its design but inclusive of details and tries to convey this inclusiveness through circles and arrows. It is a small-scale model, which means that it can be used for individual lessons or units. One of the weaknesses of this model is that it focuses on evaluation and development in the process very late

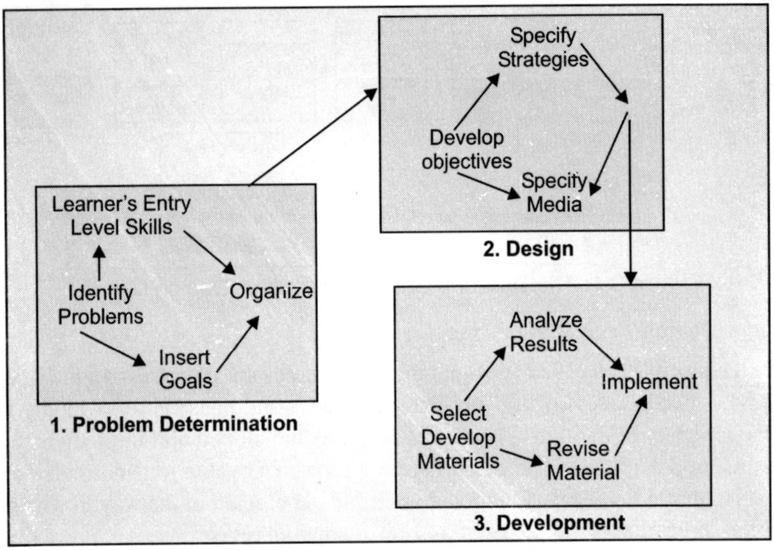

Figure 8.3: Knirk and Gustafson Design Model

Jerrold Kemp Design Model

The Jerrold kemp (1994) design model takes a holistic approach to instructional design. Virtually all factors in the learning environment are taken into consideration including subject analysis, learner characteristics, learner objectives, teaching activities, resources (computer, books, etc.) and support survives and evaluation. The process is iterative and the design is subject to constant revision. The immediate feel of being iterative and inclusive and particularly the fact that the central focus is the learner needs and goals are the strengths of this model. There is also a focus on content analysis, as there would be in any educational design and a focus on support and service, which is not present in other ID models. Much link the Knirk and Gustafson's (1986) design model, Kemp's model is also small scale and can be used for individual lessons.

The model is particularly useful for developing instructional programmes that blend technology, pedagogy and content to deliver effective, inclusive (reliable) and efficient learning.

According to McGriff, Kemp identifies nine key elements (Source: http://edutechwiki.unige.ch/en/Kemp_design_model):

Identify instructional problems, and specify goals for designing an instructional programme.

1. Examine learner characteristics that should receive attention during planning.
2. Identify subject content, and analyze task components related to stated goals and purposes.
3. State instructional objectives for the learner.
4. Sequence content within each instructional unit for logical learning.
5. Design instructional strategies so that each learner can master the objectives.
6. Plan the instructional message and delivery.
7. Develop evaluation instruments to assess objectives.
8. Select resources to support instruction and learning activities.

Figure 8.4 below illustrates the Kemp instructional design model:

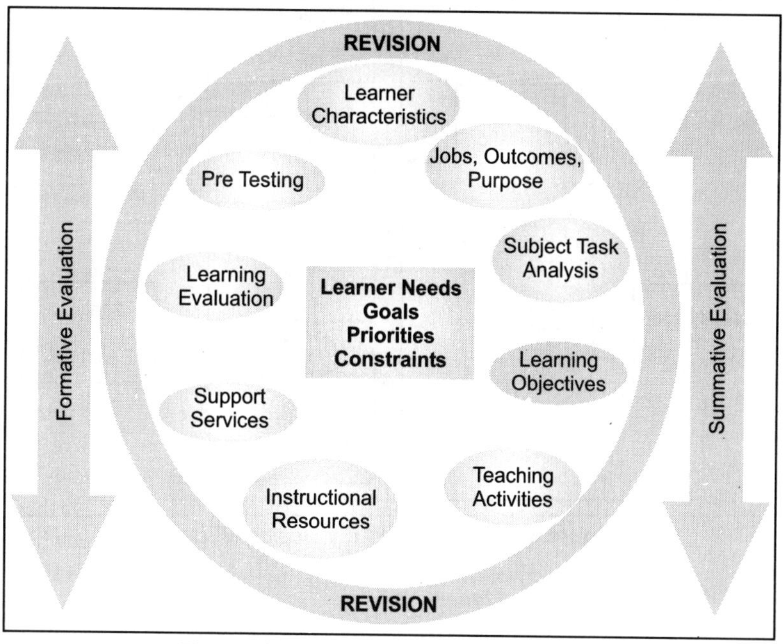

Figure 8.4: Jerrold Kemp Design Model

Gerlach and Ely Design Model

The Gerlach-Ely (1980) design model is a prescriptive model that is well suited to secondary and higher education. It is for novice instructional designers who have knowledge and expertise in a specific context. The model includes strategies for selecting and including media within instruction. It also addresses the allocation of resources. The main strength of this model is that practicing classroom teachers can identify with the process it suggests. The objectives classification taxonomy, for example, is appropriately stated for teachers' use. The taxonomy is also easily related to specific instructional strategies. The weakness of this model is that it may unintentionally reinforce the existing organization of learning and teaching is schools, rather than promoting a re-examination of best practices in classrooms. Gerlach and Ely had a good thought regarding "assessment of entering behaviors" as a precursor to needs analysis, but their approach defined no concrete way of doing this.

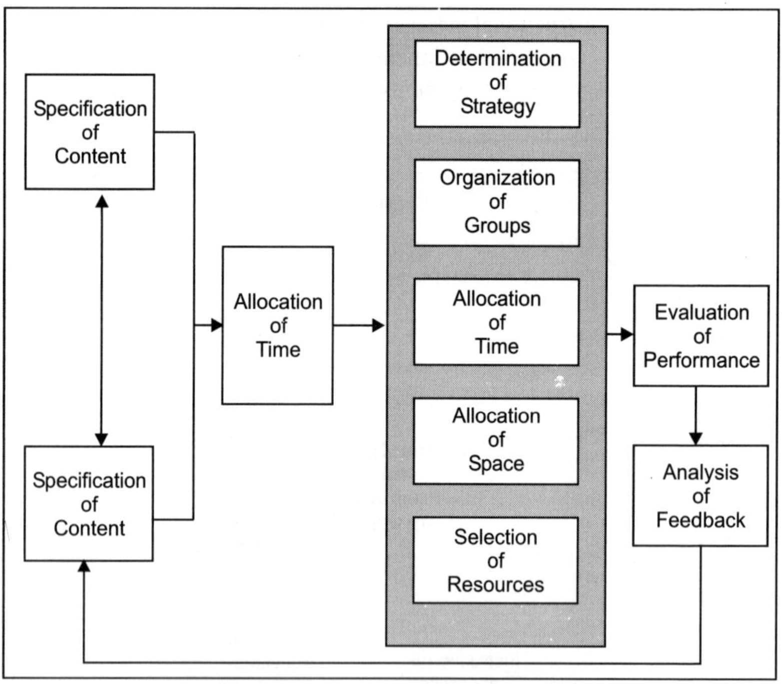

Figure 8.5: Gerlach and Ely Design Model

Rapid Prototyping Design Model

Tripp and Bichelmeyer's (1990) Rapid Prototyping Design Model is a four level process that is intended to create instruction for lessons as opposed to entire curricula. The process stages include performing a needs analysis, constructing a prototype, utilizing the prototype to perform research and installing the final system. This model relies on expert instructional designers to utilize heuristics as well as past experience and intuition to guide the design. One of the strengths of this model is that it is all-inclusive and leaves the processes up to the designers as they see fit. It also has the appeal of having extended involvement with the intended user something that is missing in many models.

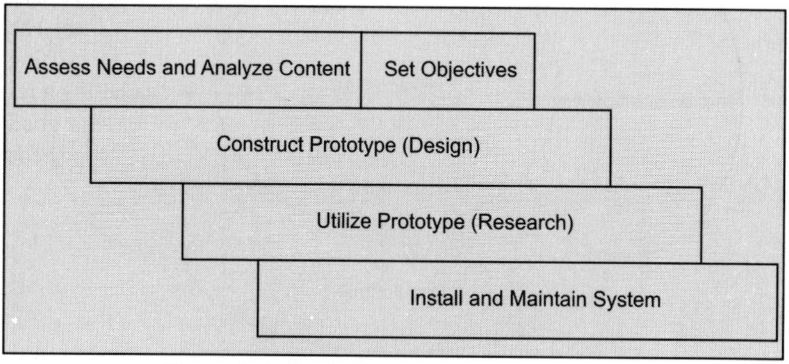

Figure 8.6: Rapid Prototyping Design Model

The ADDIE Design Model

The most familiar instructional design model is the Analysis, Design, Development Implementation and Evaluation (ADDIE) model. Depending on the situation, the five steps of this model are reduced to three or even expended to seventeen. In other words, we can say that these phases sometimes overlap and can be interrelated; however, they provide a dynamic, flexible guideline for developing effective and efficient instruction. It can be shown in the Figure 8.7

The five steps of the ADDIE model give a clear picture to a teacher or a courseware developer that how he can make his instruction fruitful for the learners. It can be seen easily from the Table 8.1.

The ADDIE model is an iterative instructional design process, where the results of the formative evaluation of each phase may lead the instructional designer back to any previous phase. The end product of one phase is the starting product of the next phase.

Now, we are explaining in short the five steps of the model:

Analysis: The analysis phase is the foundation for all other phases of instructional design. During this phase, you must define the problem, identify the source of the problem and determine possible solutions. The phase may include specific research techniques such as needs analysis, job analysis and task analysis. The outputs of this phase often include the instructional goals and a list of tasks to be instructed. These outputs will be the inputs for the design phase.

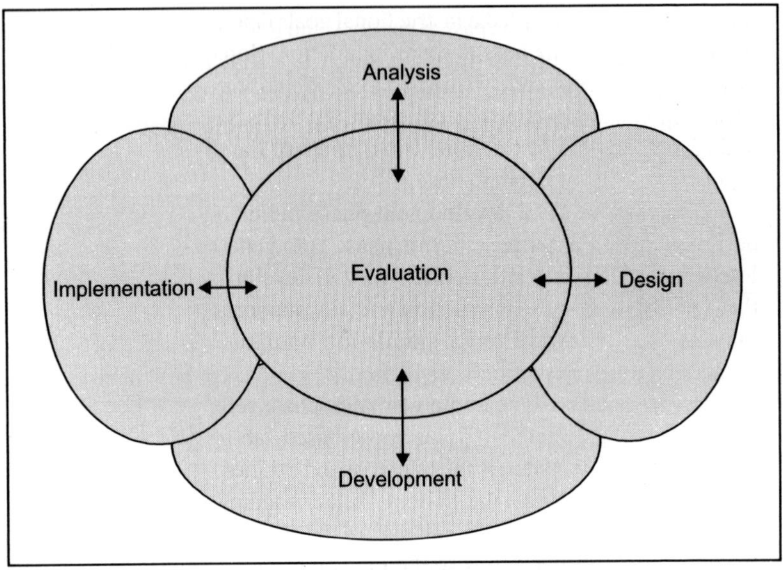

Figure 8.7: The ADDIE Model

Table 8.1: ADDIE Steps

	Sample Tasks	*Sample Output*
Analysis The process of defining what is to be learned	▪ Needs Assessment ▪ Problem Identification ▪ Task Analysis	▪ Learner Profile ▪ Description of Constraints ▪ Needs, Problem Statement ▪ Task Analysis
Design The process of specifying how it is to be learned	▪ Write Objectives ▪ Develop Test Items ▪ Plan Instruction ▪ Identify Resources	▪ Measurable Objectives ▪ Instructional Strategy ▪ Prototype Specifications
Development The process of authoring and producing the materials	▪ Work with Producers ▪ Develop Workbook, Flowchart, Programme	▪ Storyboard ▪ Script ▪ Exercises ▪ Computer Assisted Instruction
Implementation The process of installing the courseware in the real world context	▪ Teacher Training ▪ Tryout	▪ Student Comments, Data
Evaluation The process of determining the adequacy of the instruction	▪ Record Time Data ▪ Interpret Test Results ▪ Survey Graduates ▪ Revise Activities	▪ Recommendations ▪ Project Report ▪ Revised Prototype

Design: The design phase involves using the outputs from the analyze phase to plan a strategy for developing the instruction. During this phase, you must outline how to reach the instructional goals determined during the analyze phase and expand the instructional foundation. Some of the elements of the design phase may include writing a target population description, conducting a learning analysis, writing objectives and test items, selecting a delivery system and sequencing the instruction. The outputs of the design phase will be the inputs for the development phase.

Development: The development phase builds on both the analysis and design phases. The purpose of this phase is to generate the lesson plans and lesson materials. During this phase you will develop the instruction, all media that will be used in the instruction and any supporting documentation. This may include hardware (e.g., simulation equipment) and software (e.g., computer based instruction).

Implementation: The implementation phase refers to the actual delivery of the instruction, whether it's classroom-based, lab-based or computer-based. The purpose of this phase is the effective and efficient delivery of instruction. This phase must promote the students' understanding of material, support the students' mastery of subjects and ensure the students' transfer of knowledge from the instructional setting to the job.

Evaluation: This phase measures the effectiveness and efficiency of the instruction. Evaluation should actually occur throughout the entire instructional design process- within phases, between phases and after implementation. Evaluation may be formative or summative.

Formative Evaluation: Formative evaluation is ongoing during and between phases. The purpose of this type of evaluation is to improve the instruction before the final version is implemented.

Summative Evaluation: Summative evaluation is usually occurs after the final version of instruction is implemented. This type of evaluation assesses the overall effectiveness of the instruction. Data from the summative evaluation is often used to make a decision about the instruction.

The DADI Design Model

The DADI (Definition, Architecture, Design and Implementation) design model is similar to the waterfall model but differ in that:

- You cannot proceed to the next step until the previous step is understood.
- You may however, return to the previous section whenever changes (Fig. 8.8).

The four phases in the DADI design model are:

Definition: During the definition phase, objectives are defined, logistics examined and the scope and depth, the budget and time frame are determined.

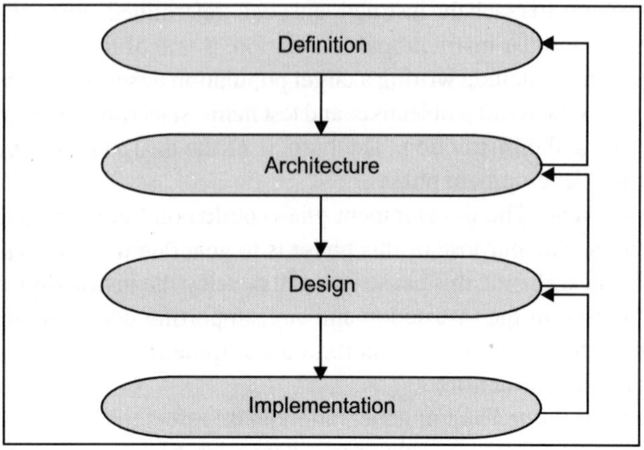

Figure 8.8: The DADI Model

Architecture: During the architecture phase, the major content areas are identified and decisions about navigation and media types are made.

Design: The design phase determines what the product will actually look like.

Implementation: In the implementation phase, content is subjugated to a process, as stated by Pajak, "This stage is strictly: Build, Test, Fix and Repeat."

The Object-Oriented Model

Shorts (1996, online) explains the origins of this models, "This model comes from the push in the software industry to move away from older coding approaches toward an object-oriented approach".

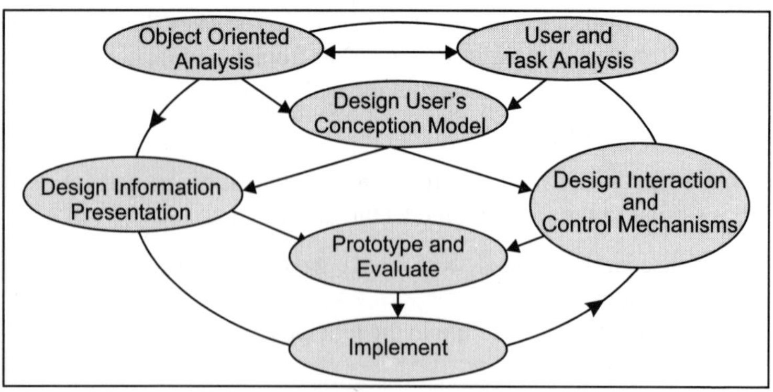

Figure 8.9: Object Oriented Model

The phases in the object-oriented model are:

> *Object-Oriented Analysis:* Its presence in the model preempts an object- oriented perspective.

User and Task Analysis: The user and the task are analyzed and the scope of the project is determined.

Design User's Conceptional Model: The concepts required during the use of the programme are developed.

Design Information Presentation: During this phase the manner in which information will be presented is decided.

Design Interaction and Control Mechanisms: The controls for the programme are developed during this phase.

Prototype and Evaluate: The prototype is developed and tested during this phase.

Implement: The developed and tested object piece is combined with the rest of the programme.

The Waterfall Model

The waterfall model was derived from an engineering and makes use of a strictly linear approach. The idea is that the outputs of one stage flow into the next stage. This implies that each step has to be completed before the next step can be started. The rigidity of this model is not suited to all applications, but it is easier to manage than more flexible models. Some developers add continuous evaluation to this model, using it like the "snakes and ladders" in the game, either to skip steps or slide back to the start.

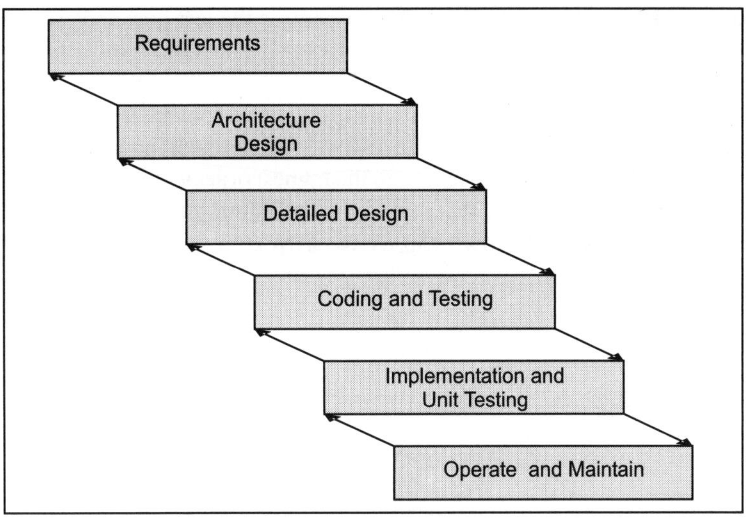

Figure 8.10: Waterfall Design Model

Gagné's 9 Events of Instruction

Robert Gagné is considered to be the foremost contributor to the systematic approach to instructional design and training. Gagne and his followers are known as behaviorists, and their focus is on the outcomes (or behaviors) resulting from training.

Gagné's book, *The Conditions of Learning*, identified the mental conditions for learning. Gagné created a nine-step process called the events of instruction, which correlate to and address the conditions of learning. See the nine events of instruction below (Source: http://edutechwiki.unige.ch/en/Nine_events_of_instruction):

1. Gain attention
2. Inform learner of objectives
3. Stimulate recall of prior learning
4. Present stimulus material
5. Provide learner guidance
6. Elicit performance
7. Provide feedback
8. Assess performance
9. Enhance retention transfer

Bloom's Learning Taxonomy

In 1956, Benjamin Bloom headed a group of educational psychologists who developed a classification of levels of intellectual behavior important in learning. Bloom found that over 95 per cent of the test questions students encounter require them to think only at the lowest possible level...the recall of information.

Bloom identified six levels within the cognitive domain, from the simple recall or recognition of facts, as the lowest level, through increasingly more complex and abstract mental levels, to the highest order which is classified as evaluation. Verb examples that represent intellectual activity on each level are listed given below (*Source*: http://en.wikipedia.org/wiki/Bloom's_Taxonomy):

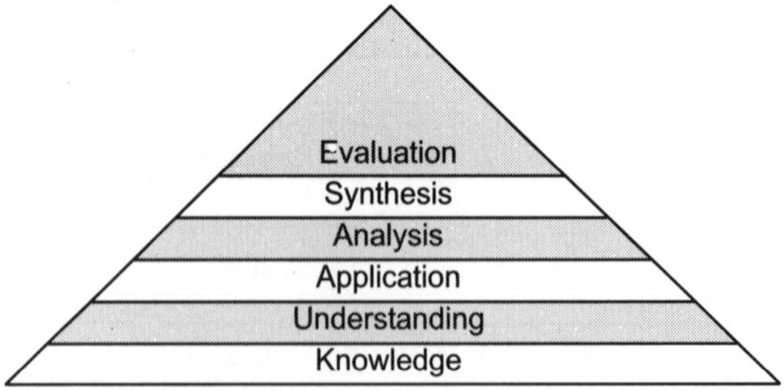

Figure 8.11: Bloom's Taxonomy

1. *Knowledge*: arrange, define, duplicate, label, list, memorize, name, order, recognize, relate, recall, repeat, reproduce state.
2. *Comprehension*: classify, describe, discuss, explain, express, identify, indicate, locate, recognize, report, restate, review, select, translate.
3. *Application*: apply, choose, demonstrate, dramatize, employ, illustrate, interpret, operate, practice, schedule, sketch, solve, use, write.
4. *Analysis*: analyze, appraise, calculate, categorize, compare, contrast, criticize, differentiate, discriminate, distinguish, examine, experiment, question, test.
5. *Synthesis*: arrange, assemble, collect, compose, construct, create, design, develop, formulate, manage, organize, plan, prepare, propose, set up, write.
6. *Evaluation*: appraise, argue, assess, attach, choose compare, defend estimate, judge, predict, rate, core, select, support, value, evaluate.
   During the 1990's a new group of cognitive psychologists, lead by Lorin Anderson (a former student of Bloom), updated the taxonomy to reflect relevance to 21st century work. The new taxonomy includes a higher level cognitive performance titled "Create" (Source: http://ww2.odu.edu)
7. *Create*: design, construct, plan, produce, invent, devise, make.

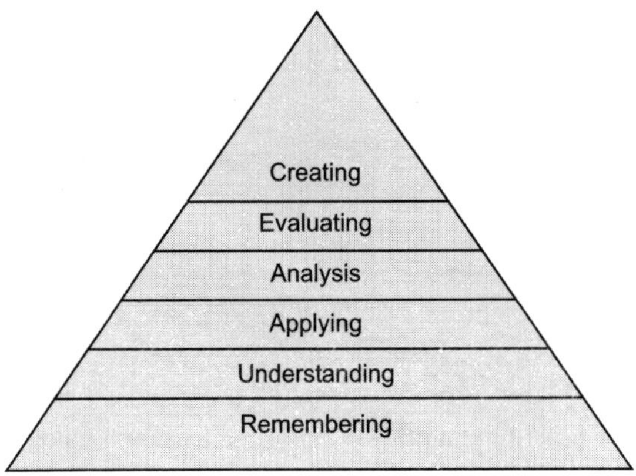

Figure 8.12: Bloom's Revised Taxonomy

Kirkpatrick's 4 Levels of Training Evaluation

Donald L Kirkpatrick, Professor Emeritus, University Of Wisconsin (where he achieved his BBA, MBA and PhD), first published his ideas in 1959, in a series of articles in the Journal of American Society of Training Directors. The articles were subsequently included in Kirkpatrick's book Evaluating

Training Programmes (originally published in 1994; now in its 3rd edition - Berrett-Koehler Publishers).

Donald Kirkpatrick's 1994 book Evaluating Training Programmes defined his originally published ideas of 1959, thereby further increasing awareness of them, so that his theory has now become arguably the most widely used and popular model for the evaluation of training and learning. Kirkpatrick's four-level model is now considered an industry standard across the HR and training communities.

The four levels of Kirkpatrick's evaluation model essentially measure (*Source:* http://www.businessballs.com/kirkpatricklearningevaluationmodel.htm):

- *Reactions*: What they thought and felt about the training;
- *Learning*: The resulting increase in knowledge or capability;
- *Transfer*: Extent of behaviour and capability improvement and implementation/application; and
- *Results*: The effects on the business or environment resulting from the trainee's performance.

All these measures are recommended for full and meaningful evaluation of learning in organizations, although their application broadly increases in complexity, and usually cost, through the levels from level 1-4.

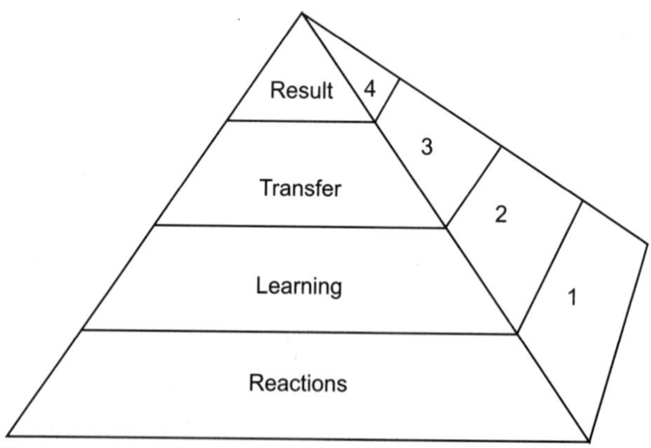

Figure 8.13: Kirkpatrick's 4 Levels of Training Evaluation

Iterative Design

Iterative design is an approach of incrementally developing and refining a design based on feedback and evaluation. Iterative design can apply to a learning experience, the creation of media or the development of learning systems. Some practical examples of iterative design:

Wiki: A wiki is a natural repository for iterative design. The 'Page History' facility allows tracking back to prior versions. Modifications are mostly incremental, and leave substantial parts of the text unchanged.

Common Law: The principle of legal precedent builds on past experience. This makes law a form of iterative design where there should be a clear audit trail of the development of legal thought.

Evolution: There is a parallel between iterative and the theory of Natural Selection. Both involve a trial and error process in which the most suitable design advances to the next generation, while less suitable designs perish by the wayside. Subsequent versions of a product should also get progressively better as its producers learn what works and what doesn't in a process of refinement and continuous improvement.

There are several instructional design models based on the principle of iterative design:

• Rapid Prototyping and • Spiral Model.

Rapid Prototyping

The idea of rapid prototyping as it applies to instructional design, is to develop learning experiences in a continual design-evaluation cycle that continues throughout the life of the project. This cycle, known as the spiral cycle or layered approach, is considered to be iterative, meaning that products are continually improved as they cycle continues. This can be seen more clearly by comparing Rapid Prototyping with a traditional development model:

Classic Design (Waterfall) Model	*Rapid Prototyping (Spiral) Model*
1. Concept definition	1. Concept definition
2. Requirements definition	2. Implementation of a skeletal system
3. Preliminary design	3. User evaluation and concept refinement
4. Detailed design	4. Implementation of refined requirements
5. Code implementation	5. User evaluation and concept refinement
6. Test and acceptance	6. implementation of refined requirements
7. [griping because you now realize that there was something that got left out back in step 2]	7. [etc., etc., in a continuous cycle].

Rapid prototyping allows the designer to start with a low fidelity medium (such as paper and pen) and move to increasingly higher fidelity prototypes as time goes on. There are two types of prototypes that can be developed:

Vertical Prototypes – in-depth functionality for a few features
Horizontal Prototypes – entire screen with no underlying functionality

In addition, there are multiple approached to prototyping:

- Paper prototypes (example: portal.acm.org) – easy to change. Users perceive that it is easier to change. Often throwing in colour or artwork make a use thing that they cannot suggest changes.

- Post-it Prototypes (example: Wizard of Oz Prototyping.
- Wireframe Prototypes/Wireframing – nothing visual, just shaded blocks explaining what will be there.
- Storyboarding.
- Electronic prototypes (inspiration).

Spiral Model

The spiral model was originally conceived as a software development process combining elements of both design and prototyping-in-stages, in an effort to combine advantages of top-down and bottom-up concepts. The spiral model was defined by Barry Boehm in his 1988 article A Spiral Model of Software Development and Enhancement. This model was not the first model to discuss iterative development but it was the first model to explain why the iteration matters. Design and development efforts are applied at each phase of the project, with an eye toward the end goal of the project. This model of development combines the features of the prototyping model and the ADDIE model.

The original spiral model, also known as the spiral lifecycle model, is comprised of 10 iterative steps which move software development to a higher and higher fidelity until it is completed. For the purposes of applying this model to instructional design, Cenammo and Kalk simplify the process into 5 steps:

• Define, • Design, • Demonstrate, • Develop, and • Deliver

Advantages of Spiral Model

- Estimates (i.e. budget, schedule, etc.) become more realistic as work progresses, because important issues are discovered earlier.
- The model is designed to cope with the inevitable changes to the learning experience that will happen over the course of design and delivery.
- Multimedia producers can get their hands in and start working on a project earlier, and therefore shape the design process as well.

Transactional Distance

The concept of Transactional Distance is established by Michael Moore in his paper "Theory of Transactional Distance" (link to full article below). This theory articulates the idea that "distance education is not simply a geographic separation of learners and teachers, but, more importantly, is a pedagogical concept." Even in face-to-face teaching there is some element of transactional distance (Rumble 1986). Still, Moore points out that when talking about distance education we are typically talking about a teaching environment where the separation between the teacher and learner is significant enough that special teaching-learning strategies and techniques must be used.

9

Roles of Computer for Instructional Purposes

After studying this chapter, the reader will be able to: Explain the different roles of computer for instructional purposes; Describe the roles of computer as a learning environment for instructional purposes; Describe the roles of computer as a help tool for instructional purposes; Describe the roles of computer as an object for instructional purposes; Describe the roles of computer as an instrument for instructional purposes

According to Alessi and Trollip (1991: 17) four activities should take place for successful teaching:

- Information should be presented and skills modeled;
- The student should be guided through initial use of the information and skills;
- The student should practice for retention and fluency; and
- The learning should be assessed

For effective teaching and meaningful learning, the above four activities or phases of the given model is important. As we discussed earlier, that in traditional classroom settings, it is very difficult to follow this cyclic process. The computer can follow this cyclic process very effectively. In the present chapter we will discuss that how a computer can be helpful in education.

The role of the computer in the classroom was probably best clarified by the distinction made in Robert Taylor's book "The Computer in the School: Tutor, Tool, Tutee", in which it is suggested that a computer might be used in a classroom in three different ways: (1) as an aid for instruction by a tutor, (2) as a medium of instruction, a tool or (3) as something to be instructed or programmed to, a tutee. This classification scheme has been very useful in making it clear to teacher that computer applications have to be viewed in terms of outcomes and that different outcomes necessitate different approaches to using computers.

From the Taylor's classification, it is clear that computer can play a lot of different roles in education. In the present chapter first of all we will discuss role of computer for instructional purposes than we will see the role of computer school administration. For a clear understanding about the computer applications in instruction, we are given a new model given in figure-9.1 that will clarify you that in how many ways a computer can be use for instructions. In this model there are four classes and a lot of sub-classes of use of the computer in education.

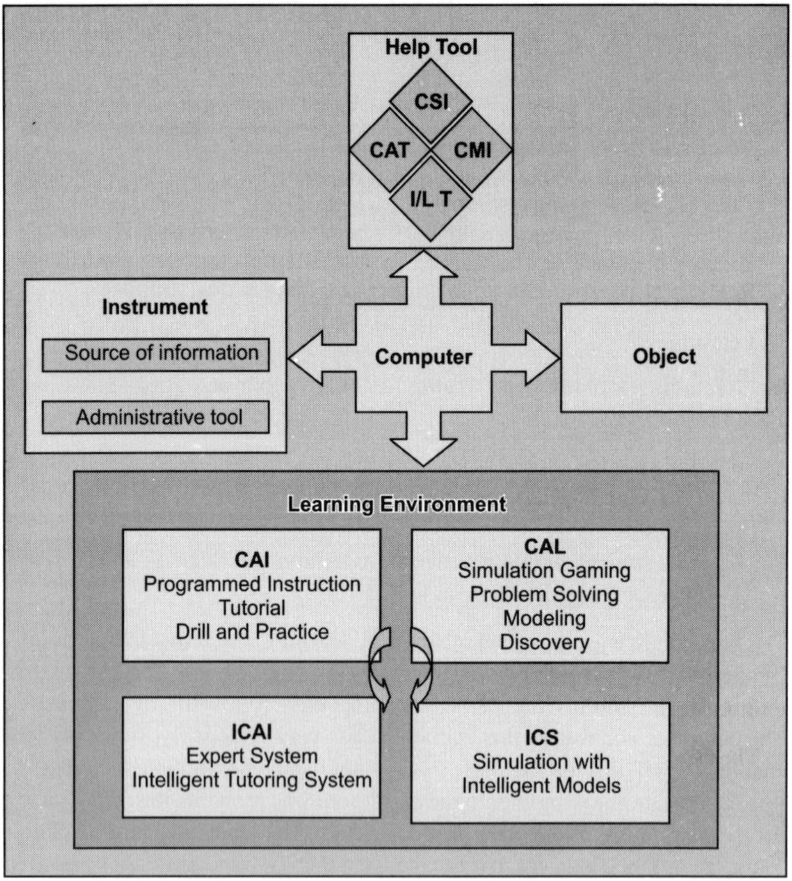

Figure 9.1: A Conceptual Model of Use of Computers in Education

1. Learning Environment

Environments for learning (CAL) or instruction (CAI):

I. *CAI* (Computer-Assisted Instruction)
   (a) Programmed Instruction (simple frame based)
   (b) Tutorial
   (c) Drill and Practice

II. *CAL* (Computer-Assisted Learning)
   (a) Dialogue and Socratic Dialogue
   (b) Discovery
   (c) Simulation
   (d) Modeling
   (e) Gaming
   (f) Problem Solving

III. *ICAI* (Intelligent Computer-Assisted Instruction)
   (a) Expert System
   (b) Intelligent Tutoring System (ITS)

IV. *ICS* (Intelligent Computer Simulation)
   (a) Simulation with intelligent models

2. Help Tool

Learning with the help of the computer. Computer and images support the instruction as a help tool in education:

I. Instructional/Learning Tool
   (a) Word Processing
   (b) Spreadsheets
   (c) Database Management Programmes
   (d) Presentation Tools
   (e) Internet

II. CSI (Computer Supported Instruction)

III. CAT (Computer Assisted Testing)

IV. CMI (Computer Managed Instruction)

3. Object

The computer as an object of study

I. in informatics/computer science

II. in electronics

4. Instrument

The computer as an instrument

I. as a source of information

II. for administration

(1) Computer as Learning Environment

(I) Computer Assisted Instruction (CAI)

Computer system can deliver instruction directly to students by allowing them to interact with lessons programmed into the system; this is referred to as computer-assisted instruction. On the basis of the objectives and interactive nature of the programme or courseware, we can divide CAI into three types:

(a) CAI: Programmed Instruction (Simple Frame Based)

This type of CAI instructions is simple in nature just like Skinner's linear programmed instruction. In this type of CAI, subject matter is divided into simple frames followed by one or two questions. These types of programmes gives limited deviations to the users. In other words we can say that these CAI programmes presents restricted learning environment for the learners.

(b) CAI: Tutorial

In CAI, the tutorial style is an attempt to give to the computer the total responsibility for teaching. The computer-assisted tutorial presents the students with new or previously presented material in an individualized manner. It presents information in an organized fashion with frequent reinforcement for correct responses. Thus, tutorial lessons can be perceived as simulation of interaction between an ideal expert teacher (computer) and a student on a one-to-one basis. This interaction tends to be a dialogue, called '*Socratic Mode*' and is the aim of all tutorial courseware (lesson). The identification of all parameters of '*good teaching*' and incorporating them in a teaching system is a difficult task. Tutorial programmes are characterized by their ability to handle *'unexpected events'* either in dialogue or in the subject matter. Existing tutorial lessons vary in a strategy from limited Programmed Instruction (PI) type interaction to sophisticated Socratic Dialogue (SD). In general tutorial instruction consists of sequences of information text, questions, responses, analysis of responses, feedback and remedial instructions. The path of instruction is determined by either performance based decision rules leading to PI type dialogue or adaptive decision rules leading to Socratic dialogue generally, tutorial programmes teach a concept or skill, then assess the student's understanding of that concept by asking the questions. If the student's response demonstrates an understanding of the concept, the computer reinforces the student and moves on to a new concept. If the student's response demonstrates that the skill or concept has not been understood, the computer will reteach the concept at a more appropriate level, presenting it in small steps or through a different approach.

CAI tutorials can be used with students at all ages and functioning levels. This style of instruction is especially useful for students who do not grasp concepts or skills quickly and who need additional instruction on a specific topic. One of the most obvious applications of the CAI tutorial is with students with special needs. CAI tutorials hold great promise for providing these students with the extra instruction they often need but do not receive because of the regular classroom teacher's time constraints.

The CAI tutorial is ideal for the resource teacher expected to re-mediate the skill deficiencies of a large number of students in a wide array of subjects. If setup correctly, often the student can use a computer tutorial to re-mediate a skill deficiency with little or no adult intervention and the teacher is free to work with other students. It is important that the computer not provide the only source of instruction in skill development. Again, the computer should serve as an adjunct to the teacher. Research has shown that when the teacher is the primary provider of instruction with the computer in an adjunct role, learning increases and student attitudes are more positive.

(c) CAI: Drill and Practice

As the name implies, computer-assisted drill and practice is designed to reinforce previously learned information and to provide the student with practice in using this information. The nature of the computer makes it ideal for providing endless practice in almost any curricular area. For example, the computer can generate limitless numbers of math problems according to the student's mental-level provide spelling practice on an individualized list of words or drill on states and capitals. During these individualized drill and practice sessions, the computer can record student responses and summarize student progress in each skill area.

The following example typifies a drill and practice programme providing practice in capitalization. The computer monitor shows the student a sentence with the first word underlined as follows:

> <u>he</u> saw Shyam in Allahabad

By pressing the C or U keys, students can either capitalize or un-capitalize the first letter in the underlined word. Pressing the space bar can move the underlining from word to word. When the student has finished the sentence and pressed the return key, the student can proceed to the next sentence if the capitalization are correct. If the capitalization of the sentence is wrong, the computer provides the student with an example of a correct sentence, as follows:

> He saw Shyam in Allahabad.

The drill and practice programme also provides the student with a summary of the number of correct and incorrect responses and a listing of the incorrectly capitalized words.

(II) Computer Assisted Learning (CAL)

Computer-assisted instruction (CAI) is a narrower term and most often refers to tutorial and drill-and-practice activities offered either by themselves or as supplements to traditional, teacher-directed instruction. Many authors do not make a difference between CAI and CAL. But in my opinion there is a big difference between the two. From the researches conducted on the computer based tutorials and drill-and-practice shows that from these type of programmes we can achieve only lower level of cognitive objectives such as knowledge and understanding, higher order level of cognitive objectives remains. The reason behind this fact is that these types of programmes give a restricted environment to the learners. For achieving these objectives, the student participation is important. Hence in CAI, the central point is teacher on the other hand in CAL the central point is student participation and student learning. This is clear-cut difference between CAI & CAL. CAL can be divided into five type:

(a) CAL: Simulation

CAI Simulation is one of the most powerful computer applications in education. Simulations provide the feeling of working with models. It models the real or imaginary world. Simulation is a one-to-one representation of some aspects of a dynamic system or situation of real world by a model. Simulations allow the students to experience vicariously such real-life events as space-travel, circulation of blood in human body, science experiments, etc. A CAI simulation models or recreates a real-life event not easily shown in a traditional teaching-learning environment.

Simulations are recommended in teaching of students with special needs for number of reason as follows:

- Simulations can introduce a more concrete foundation and sense of realism into what are often frustratingly abstract subjects for the learners.
- Computer simulations force the learner to participate actively rather than passively.
- They can eliminate dangers associated with many real-life experiences.
- When students are placed in pairs or teams, computer simulation can improve socialization among students who have not mastered the skills of co-operative interaction.
- Real-life time periods can be compressed or expended to meet learning requirements.
- Simulations reduce costs substantially over many real-life experiences.

- CAI simulations also allow the learner to make low-risk decisions and receive feedback in the form of simulated consequences.
- Students can experience the same event more than once with the details slightly changed, thus allowing the learner to develop more effective strategies over a series of attempts.

Here we are giving instances in which simulations are most appropriate as a substitute for real-life experiences:

- When the learning objectives are complex and students are unlikely to develop the needed skills in a real-life environment (e.g., work skills).
- When the time scale of the real-life event is too long or too short to allow efficient learning.
- When the real-life experience involves danger and/or high cost.
- When the real-life event cannot be carried out in a normal teaching environment.

Thus, computer simulation can extend the boundaries of the traditional teaching-learning environment in a safe and cost-effective manner. While computer simulations provide the student with learning opportunities often not possible in traditional learning environment, teachers must observe some caution. Simulation alone is not sufficient for the learner to master a skill. Simulated activities should precede the real-life experience and when possible, the skills learned in the simulated environment should be generalized to a real-life environment. Students must understand that the simulation is only a representation of the real-life activity.

(b) CAL: Gaming

Computer-assisted gaming is one of the most popular styles of CAI. Gaming combines learning and enjoyment. Students can carryout it individually or in groups. Many of the popular computer games require the learners to use logic and skill in ways that other learning takes do not. Computer-assisted gaming has several instructional features such as:

- Games can be played in groups or teams requiring co-operation and participant's socialization.
- Games can help in developing decision-making and problem-solving skills without imposing serious consequences for wrong decisions.
- Games can help in developing attention span and other attentional skills in a student who normally cannot focus on a task for an extended period of time.

(c) CAL: Problem Solving

In problem solving, the learner uses previously mastered skills to resolve a challenging problem. The student must examine the data or information presented, clearly define the problem, perhaps state hypotheses, examine the data and generate a solution. The computer may present the problem. It can manipulate the data at the student's command, maintain a database and provide feedback when appropriate.

As the learner faces a problem and attempts to solve it, the computer can be used to do the necessary calculations or manipulation of the data or information. During problem-solving activities student will not only learn about the content under study but will learn to improve their logical thinking skills. These higher-level cognitive processes include reasoning skills, logical and critical thinking. The primary reason for teaching elementary computer languages, such as Logo, is not for the students to learn programming itself but to enable them to use the computer for problem solving.

The problem-solving approach to computer-assisted learning is based on the hypothesis that the thought required to write a computer programme aids the development of general problem-solving skills. It differs from simulation in that the activity of programming, rather than the specific subject of the programme, is considered central. In simulation, the student is given the programmed model to use, not asked to write or change this programme. The underlying educational philosophy of the problem-solving approach is a belief in what may be summarized as '*learning by during*' as opposed to simulation's '*learning by seeing*'.

In this style of CAI, the student learns to make programmes on computer in a language, and then teaches the computer to solve some real-life problems. This form of computer use has several uses. First, because a student can't develop a programme on computer without having the knowledge how to solve the problem? Thus, CAI helps the student to gain a clear concept and understanding of the problem through the programming process. Second, the programming process teaches students how computers work as well as how their own thinking works. Third, students learn logical thinking and problem solving. As a result, using the computer for problem solving can shift the locus of education from end product to process, from simply acquiring facts to manipulating and understanding them. Problem solving is necessary part of any student education. Hence, teachers may want to introduce their students to a programming language called LOGO. LOGO language presents a computer-based learning environment in which children can learn computer programming, problem solving and mathematical thinking. The LOGO learning environment is based on Piaget's developmental psychology. One feature of the LOGO language that seems to be especially advantageous for the students is *"turtle graphics"*. With " turtle graphics", the student programmes the turtle (a small triangular object) to move around the screen and construct geometric and graphic designs. Weir and Watt (1981) believe that this use of the computer has specific positive outcomes on the students. They suggest that:

- Fine motor skills are improved (through the typing).
- Short-term memory is developed (while students learn to use a keyboard and the various logging in and programming procedures).
- Students learn to spell the commands.
- Students develop direction-giving and direction-following skills.
- As they gain skill and experience in the use of LOGO, students can move from concrete to more abstract levels of thinking.

(d) CAL: Modeling

Modeling CAL is courseware enabling a student to learn how models can be made. In addition to simulation, modeling is one of the eight forms of CAI/CAL. Modeling is distinguished from simulation in that the student develops a model on his own which represents a situation in reality. The model itself in this form of CAL is continually subject to discussion and is not regarded as a fact as occurs in simulation. Modeling aims to develop the ability to systemize complex relations within a system. Modeling involves executing certain purpose tasks in order to record the inter-relationships within a certain system. This happens in two steps:

- definition of a system from reality,
- representation of this system in a model

Modeling involves learning to make a model of something, such as making a mathematical model, drawing a flower in LOGO or making a programme for a 'programmable logical controller' (PLC) that resembles a robot. Simulation in contrast, involves learning to experiment with a simulated reality. Although models are used while doing this, the simulation programmes are 'discovery environments' aiming to transport reality into the classroom. The student trains or does exercises while learning to see connections between quantities and components of a system.

(e) CAL: Discovery

Discovery is a general term to describe activities using an inductive approach to learning; that is, presenting problems that the student solves through trial and error or systematic approaches. It approximates laboratory learning outside the classroom. Using the discovery method in CAL the learner employs an information retrieval strategy to get information from a database.

(III) Intelligent Computer Assisted Instruction (ICAI)

Intelligent computer assisted instructions are computer programmes that instruct the student in an intelligent way. They are designed to incorporate techniques from the artificial intelligence community to provide tutors, which know what they teach, who they teach and how to teach. The philosophy behind the intelligent CAI is that it should function much like an instructor with whom the student visits and requests help solving the problems. ICAI is intended to draw best from both traditional CAI and reactive learning environments and then to construct systems that emulate a real teacher working with an individual learner. The necessity of human dimension in instruction cannot be overlooked and thus the realistic view if ICAI would be, to look at it as an assistant to the teacher, which can encourage the learner to learn and practice, arouse learner's curiosity. These type of computers programmes can be of three type:

(a) ICAI: Expert Systems

An expert system is a computer programme dedicated to solving problems and giving advice within a specialized area of knowledge. A good system can match the performance of a human specialist. The field of expert systems is the most advanced part of AI and expert systems are in wide commercial use. The basic components of an expert system are a "knowledge base" (KB) and an "inference engine" (IE). The information in the KB is obtained by interviewing people who are expert in the area in question. The interviewer or "knowledge engineer" organizes the information elicited from the experts into a collection of rules, typically of "if-then" structure. Rules of this type are called "production rules". The inference engine enables the expert system to draw deductions from the rules in the KB. For example, if the KB contains production rules "if X then Y" and "if Y then Z", the inference engine is able to deduce "if X then Z". The expert system might then query its user "is X true in the situation that we are considering?"

Characteristic Features of Expert Systems

Expert systems differ from conventional computer systems in several important ways:

- Expert systems use knowledge rather than data to control the solution process.
- The knowledge is encoded and maintained as an entity separate from the control programme. As such, it is not compiled together with the control programme itself. This permits the incremental addition and modification of the knowledge base without recompilation of the control programmes. Furthermore, it is possible in some cases to use different knowledge bases with the same control programmes to produce different types of expert systems. Such systems are known as expert system shells since they may be loaded with different knowledge base.

- Expert systems are capable of explaining how a particular conclusion was reached and why requested information is needed during a consultation.
- Expert systems use symbolic representations for knowledge and perform their inference through symbolic computations that closely resemble manipulations of natural language.
- Expert system often reason with Meta knowledge: that is, they reason with knowledge about themselves and their own knowledge limits and capabilities.

(b) ICAI: Intelligent Tutoring System (ITS)

Intelligent tutoring systems (ITS) represent the merging of three technologies: (1) the principles of programmed instruction, (2) the computer and (3) artificial intelligence (AI). Referred to as an ITS, it is software with an artificial intelligence component designed to teach a skill or convey information by means of a one-on-one, interactive relationship between teacher and student, just as with a highly skilled tutor. During this teaching-learning process, the computer assesses the learner's style of learning, past learning experiences knowledge and his/her response repertoire and then generates an interactive, coherent sequence of instruction. Like a good teacher, it also "remembers" the learner's errors and helps the learner to analyze and correct them. In its most advanced form, a computer programmed as an intelligent tutoring system can mimic the behaviour of an expert teacher.

Main Components of ITS

The traditional ITS have five main components, namely:

Student Model

The student model stores information that is specific to each individual learner. Such a model tracks how well a student is performing on the material being taught. A possible addition to this is to also record misconceptions. Since purpose of the student model is to provide data for the pedagogical model the system, all of the information gathered should be able to be used by the tutor.

Pedagogical Module

This component provides a model of the teaching process. For example, information about when to review, when to present a new topic and which topic to present controlled by the pedagogical module. As mentioned earlier, the student model used as input to this component, so the pedagogical decisions reflect the needs of each student.

Domain Knowledge

This component contains information the tutor is teaching and is the most important since without it, there would be nothing to teach the student.

Generally, it required significant knowledge engineering to represent a domain so that other parts tutor can access it. One related research issue is how to represent knowledge so easily scales up to larger domains. Another open question is how to represent domain knowledge other than facts and procedures, such as concepts and mental model.

Communication Module

Interactions with the learner, including the dialogue and the screen layouts, are controlled by this component. How should the material be presented to the student most effective way? This component has not been researched as much as the others but there has been some promising work in this area.

Expert Mode

The expert model is similar to the domain knowledge in that it must contain the information being taught to the learner. However, it is more than just a represent of the data, it is a model of how someone skilled in a particular domain represent knowledge. Most commonly, this takes the form of a runnable expert model, i.e. that is capable of solving problems in the domain. By using an expert model, the tutor can compare the learner's solution to the expert's solution, pinpointing the places where the learner had difficulties.

(IV) Intelligent Computer Simulation (ICS)

Computer simulation with artificial intelligence is known as intelligent computer simulation. These types of computer simulations used intelligent models and have the capabilities to control the unexpected circumstances.

(2) Computer as Help Tool

The computer can also serve as a tool during instruction. As a tool, it can be used in a class in different ways like:

(I) Instructional/Learning Tool

Tool applications, comprising the most frequent use of computers in classrooms, include: (1) Word Processing, (2) Spreadsheet and (3) Database Software. While originally designed for purposes other than teaching and learning, tool software packages are being used effectively in enhancing the instructional process. Common examples include the use of word processing software to assist in teaching writing and the use of electronic spreadsheet programmes to assist in teaching scientific formulas.

The popularity of tool software is primarily due to the fact that it is the easiest of all the various instructional software types to integrate into a curriculum. Teachers can use tool software without making major changes to the established curriculum.

(a) Word Processing

e.g. *Microsoft Word, ClarisWorks*

With appropriate software, the learner of can use the computer as an instructional tool for carrying out many daily learning tasks, such as word processing and spelling correction are the most useful tools. Word processing is frequently used to assist in teaching writing, especially in a curriculum where writing is taught as a process in which one writes, revises, rewrites and revises. Word processing software makes revisions very easy and avoids the drudgery of handwriting or retyping extensive amounts of text. A word processing programme is an electronic word handler: words are typed through the keyboard and displayed on the monitor as they are typed. When the text is complete, the computer can save it permanently on a disk and/or give the same typed output on a paper, using a printer. As Hagen (1983) noted, written language skills for the students with special needs are among the most difficult to acquire. A word-processing programme can eliminate many of the writing barriers. A word processor allows changes in the written text with simple editing commands. Words can be inserted and deleted, sentences and paragraphs can be rearranged, and punctuation and spelling can be checked. A word processor may simplify helps a student's tasks who is differently able or is disabled in completing a written assignment and make it considerably more fun. Students to do writing assignments are commonly using commercial word processing packages such as Word Perfect and Microsoft Word at various grade levels.

Most teachers are familiar with word processing programmes in that the teacher likely uses such a programme to create lesson plans, student/parent communications and personal correspondence. Students make use of word processors in similar ways. Certainly, research papers, projects, and other written communications can be accomplished with the use of a word processor.

Aside from simply making student work appear "neater", word processors have pedagogical importance in that they have been found to encourage students to write more and to more easily edit and revise their work. In this way, they are powerful tools in developing writing, critical thinking, and research skills. Further, word processors as a technology-based tool encourage and motivate certain students who have difficulty with the manual task of handwriting. Finally, many students take greater pride in work that has been produced with a word processor. This motivates these students to continue writing and performing the other learning tasks associated with their writing.

Word processors are not just used within Language Arts curricula. Students may word process work related to any subject area. Also, word processed work often becomes the basis for importing data into databases, spreadsheets, and presentation programmes. In this way, the word processor is often the cornerstone application within integrated application suites such as *Microsoft Office*, *Microsoft Works*, or *ClarisWorks*.

Key Benefits of Word Processing

- Word processors encourage students to edit and revise their work to a much greater extent that is often the case with pencil-and-paper writing. Thus, word processors are key tools when teaching the writing process.
- Word processors produce "neater" end products thereby increasing student pride in their work.
- Word processing and the use of a computer keyboard is a key—virtually mandatory—basic skill for most post-school jobs and careers. Virtually all jobs require some familiarity with a keyboard.
- Some students who have difficulty with the manual task of writing (e.g., motor deficiencies, dyslexia, etc.) find it easier to use a word processor to write than to use pencil and paper.
- Word processors are about putting words on paper (or increasingly, into some sort of electronic format). Thus, they can be used *anywhere* where writing is required.

Figure 9.2 shows the features of word processing software.

Desktop Publishing

A variation of word processing software that has grown significantly in popularity is desktop publishing software, which combines standard word processing features with graphics capabilities to produce visually stimulating print material. Desktop publishing can be used to create professional quality newsletters, school newspapers and flyers. It can also be easily integrated into course work and extra curricular activities.

(b) Spreadsheets

e.g., Microsoft Excel, AppleWorks

A spreadsheet is a programme, which organizes "cells" of numerical data into tables of rows and columns much as one would find in an accounting ledger. Through the use of equations (written in a simple programming language unique to the particular spreadsheet programme in use) the spreadsheet programme is able to perform basic mathematical functions across the rows and columns. For example, it is possible to total a column of numbers, divide that total by cells within the column and report the resulting average elsewhere on the spreadsheet. Most spreadsheet programmes provide a capacity for graphing data. Graphs can range from simple X-Y line graphs to more complex three-dimensional representations.

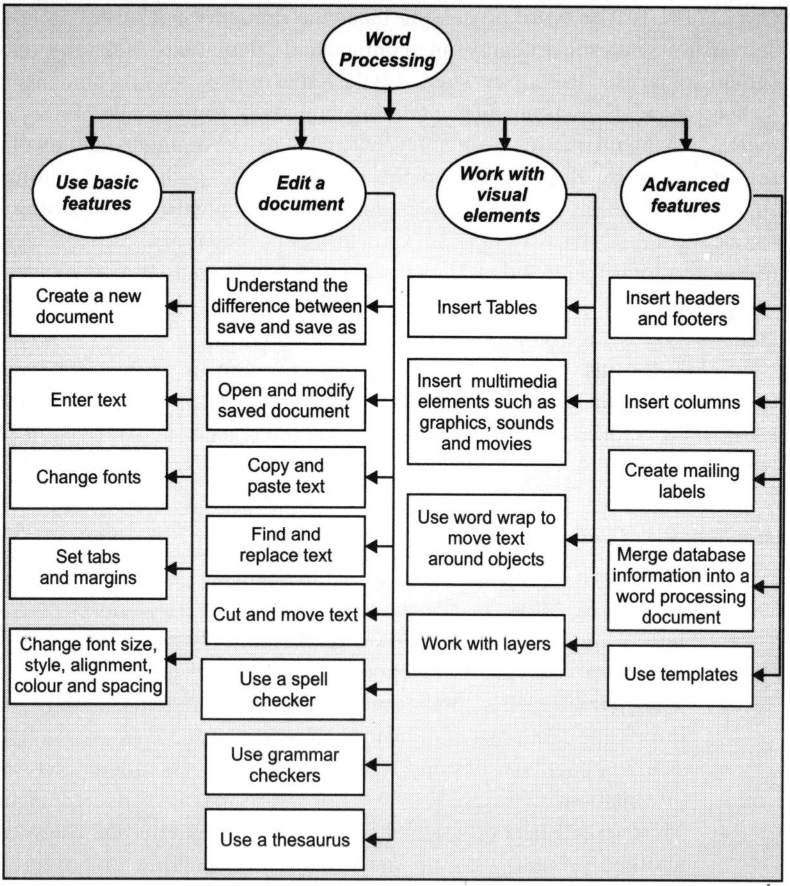

Figure 9.2: Educational Features of Word Processing Programmes

Spreadsheets are excellent tools for students to collect and analyze data and thus work well in curriculum units that call for students to deal with both interdisciplinary content and process/information analysis tasks. Students can design spreadsheet layouts, collect the data to fill in the various rows and columns and then write equations to analyze the data they have collected. In this way, a spreadsheet becomes a vehicle for learning about and representing both simple and more complex relationships between numbers and pieces of information.

Standard electronic spreadsheet programmes are being used for a variety of subjects. Mathematics, science and business education make extensive use of spreadsheet software for all sorts of instructional applications involving the manipulation of numbers. Almost any subject in which, mathematical formulas or statistical analyses are utilized can integrate spreadsheets into the curriculum. Just as word processing takes the drudgery out of typing text, spreadsheets take the drudgery out of doing hand calculations. Naturally, they should not be used in courses where it is desirable or necessary for students to do hand calculations as practice in refining their mathematics skills. However, there are many instructional situations where the nature or understanding of a formula is more important than the mathematical practice of adding, subtracting, multiplying or dividing numbers. In these situations, spreadsheets can be most effective. Commercial spreadsheet packages also provide easy-to-use graphing features that allow students not only to do a mathematical formula but also to visualize it. Lotus 1-2-3 and Excel are some of the commercial packages commonly used in many schools.

While the use of spreadsheets is very common in mathematics and science curricula, they can be used any place where data collection and analysis is required. Many teachers use spreadsheets in social studies curricula where students might collect numerical information and organize it chronologically.

Key Benefits of Spreadsheets

- Provides a highly integrated use of mathematics in a wide range of subjects. Anything that can be counted and categorized can be placed into a spreadsheet whereupon mathematical operations can be performed amongst the categories.
- The structure of a spreadsheet encourages students to think of information in terms of domains and sets.
- Allow students to see the relationships between ordered sets of information.
- Most spreadsheet programmes easily produce graphs and charts as another (visual) way of analyzing and reporting quantitative information.

Example Uses

- A school mathematics teacher can use spreadsheets, graphing software and *Hypercard* as tools for students to investigate the relationship between observations and data. Students can measure and record the volume of water stored in different bottles when those bottles are filled to different heights. Clearly, bottles of different shapes will hold different amounts of water at different filling heights. When this data is graphed, students then compare the curves of different graphs with the bottles they represent. The goal here is for students to develop a sense of the relationship between physical shapes and their one-dimensional data representations. Further understanding of these relationships is demonstrated by having students predict the appearance of a graph based solely upon

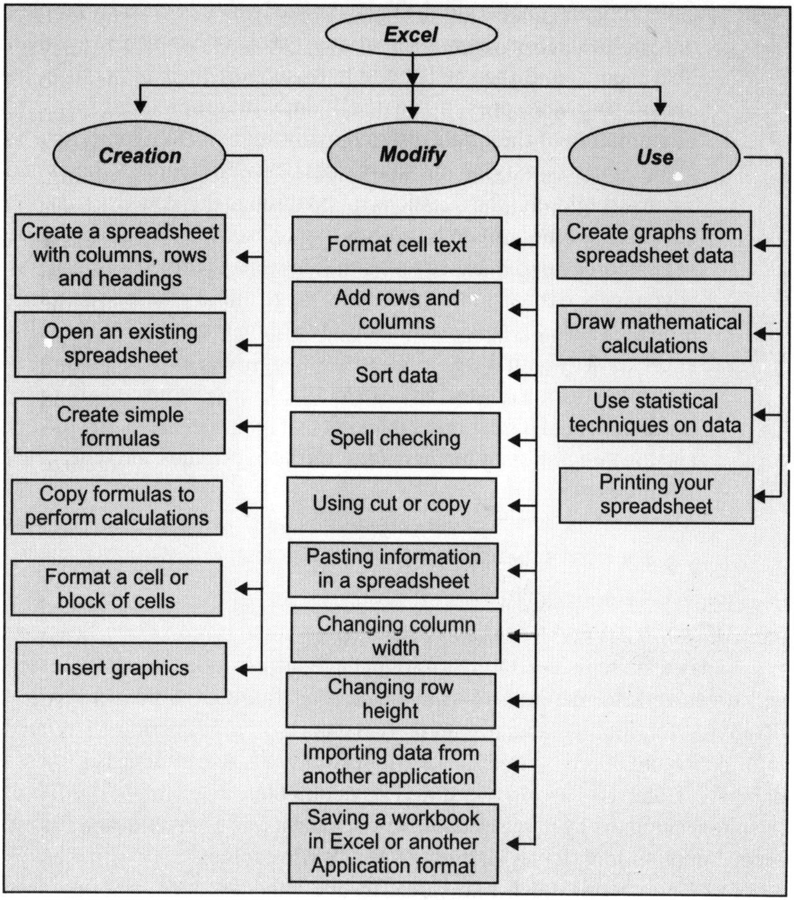

Figure 9.3: Instructional Features of Excel

examination of the physical bottle. Students also write descriptions of their predictions. In these written passages, students must set out hypothesis and develop written proofs. Finally, students use a *Hypercard* stack, which takes them through a series of other data/observation/prediction/proof exercises. For example, students can predict relationships between a person's height and shoe size and that between study time and test grades. In all of these cases, the technology is a tool that aids in the development of process skills related to mathematics and scientific reasoning.

- Students can use databases and spreadsheets as research tools in an interdisciplinary history, science and mathematics project. The project can be collecting birth and death data from local communities. After collecting and analyzing the data, the students can create a number of hypothesis from their observations—such as "women live longer than men"—and then will be able to support their hypothesis by organizing and presenting their data in graphs, tables, etc. Examination of their data also led many students to hypothesize as to the causes of varying mortality rates between centuries, sexes and amongst children. The questions raised through this data examination gave rise to other research projects, not all of which made direct use of technology or databased research. This type of project offers many advantages over a more traditional (e.g., library based) research project. These advantages include development of technology skills such as keyboarding, computer graphing and spreadsheet manipulation; student exposure to primary sources of data; development of higher order thinking that linked statistics and history and the integration of mathematics into social studies and other "real world" explorations.

- Microsoft has an excellent curriculum guide, which explains how its popular *Excel* programme can be used for simple classroom projects.

(c) Databases Management Programmes

e.g., *Microsoft Access, FileMaker Pro*

Today's students need to learn to manage information, to retrieve, sort, and organize information and to evaluate their findings. Students can use databases for inquiry and research. A database is a collection of related information organized for quick access to specific data. A telephone is a printed database. Database can also be stored in a computer; an example is a list of telephone numbers by name or company. A database is a versatile and easy to learn computer tool. It can be thought of as a file cabinet.

Databases work much like spreadsheets, although they are often used where textual information is more important than numerical data. A *database management programme* is used to create, organize, and manipulate information in databases. Databases are primarily used for creating "records" of collected information. Most database management programmes allow for some degree of numerical analysis of the collected information (e.g., counting, grouping, sorting by rank order, etc.).

Databases are often used in interdisciplinary curriculum units. They become a vehicle for information collection and organization. The manipulation of information within a database calls for mathematics and critical thinking skills. These skills are further enhanced when a student *designs* a database using a database management programme.

There are two types of databases. Students create classroom databases. Students can design information sheets and questionnaires; collect the data input relevant facts and then retrieve them in a variety of ways. The facts selected might include student information, book reports or sample math problems. Another type of database is the commercial database. Commercial databases are either purchased on diskettes or accessed via telephone hookup to a computer in another location. Standard database packages such as dBase are easy to use and can be learned readily by older students (Figure 9.4).

Key Benefits Databases Management Programmes

- The act of creating databases—using a database management programme—encourages students to understand categories of information, and the relationship between categories.
- A database gives structure to otherwise disparate information. When a student adds records to a database, s/he must understand enough about any given piece of information (e.g., a book or a movie) so that s/he can complete a number of descriptors about that piece of information (e.g., the title, date of creation, author/director, etc.).
- Creating a database requires that a student sufficiently investigates a subject such that s/he can create an adequate number of descriptive fields of information relating to that information.
- Creating a database is a productive exercise in terms of learning how to search or use a pre-created database.

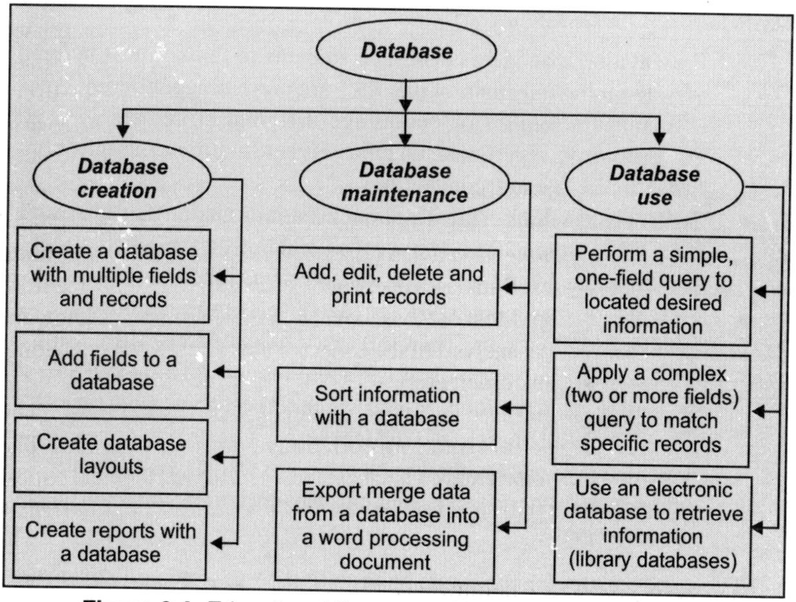

Figure 9.4: Educational Features of Database Programmes

- Databases can be created to catalog virtually any type of information, in particular, qualitative (versus quantitative) information.

(d) Presentation Tools

e.g., *Microsoft Powerpoint, Hyperstudio*

Presentation tools allow students and teachers to take text, numerical data, graphs, sounds and visual images and organize this information into "multimedia" presentations. While it is possible to use multiple media (e.g., sounds and images) within a presentation, it is also possible to create a text-only presentation. It is important to remember that although most presentation tools allow for the creation of very sophisticated products, the degree of sophistication and complexity is very much under the control of the author.

Virtually any student project can result in a presentation. Presentations can be made before an entire class or be designed for individual viewing. Multimedia presentation tools can be integrated into any lesson or unit that would otherwise result in a "paper and paste" project product.

While a presentation tool such as Powerpoint is simply software, this software usually requires the use of particular hardware to acquire digital images/sound and to display the resulting multimedia presentations. Nevertheless, much of the material that makes its way into most presentations results from other software applications such as word processors and spreadsheets (which create tables and graphs).

Key Benefits of Presentation Tools

- Presentation managers encourage students to think in a structured way about the information that they are presenting. Different types of managers require or encourage different structures — e.g., PowerPoint is very linear whereas HyperStudio encourages non-linear, multi-layered, connections.
- Students must think critically about *what* information they choose to place into a presentation. The act of assembling the presentation using the software encourages reflection and critical thought.
- Presentation managers are designed to display information to a large number of individuals. Therefore, the student successfully using a presentation manager must think about the information that s/he is presenting as something, which much appeal to an *audience* that extends beyond oneself and the teacher.
- Presentation managers allow students to mix textual, visual, and audio information in the same presentation. This encourages multiple modes of expression.

The act of creating a multimedia presentation is extraordinarily engaging for many students. Thus, the use of presentation managers very much encourages engaged learning.

(e) Internet

The Internet is one of the most exciting new technology "tools" available to teachers and much is written about the instructional benefits of using this resource. In its broadest sense, the Internet is telecommunications. A vast network of networks, the Internet allows students and teachers to reach out to a world of information that can be accessed, analyzed and brought into research and other projects. Further, the Internet provides students with the capability of *becoming* information providers. Whether through sending electronic mail or by publishing World Wide Web pages, students can place their knowledge and work before the interconnected users of the Internet.

Some describe the Internet as a vast "library." This analogy is only partially correct. Like a library, the Internet contains many pieces of information. This information is held on World Wide Web servers (i.e., web pages) and by individuals with, which anyone with electronic mail can communicate. But unlike a library, the Internet has no particular order to the information it contains. Anything and everything, published by anyone who has computer access to the 'net', can be found on the Internet. Thus, the Internet is really more of an electronic "town square" than an organized library. This presents challenges and problems for the students using the Internet. In this wide-open information universe, critical thinking and research skills must become much more refined than when using a closed information universe such as a traditional library or even a CD-ROM encyclopedia. Many teachers believe that the critical thinking skills that grow out of successful Internet use are the major educational benefit of the Internet.

The networked world of the Internet provides a wonderful ground for student collaboration. Students can electronically "meet" with individuals connected anywhere else on the Internet. This means that students researching a particular subject can communicate with adult researchers, access primary information sources and gain in-depth content area learning experiences. Students can share cultural experiences with peers located around the globe. Students can share their work with anyone by publishing it on the World Wide Web. Indeed, the availability of the Internet means that four walls and a particular geographically bounded community no longer define "school". The Internet brings the world to teachers and students.

Key Benefits of Internet

- Students have access to a truly astronomical amount of information including original research and primary sources. This challenges the student's research, critical thinking and problem-solving skills.
- Students can publish their work before a global audience of peers thereby adding perceptions of importance to their work and increasing pride in ones work.

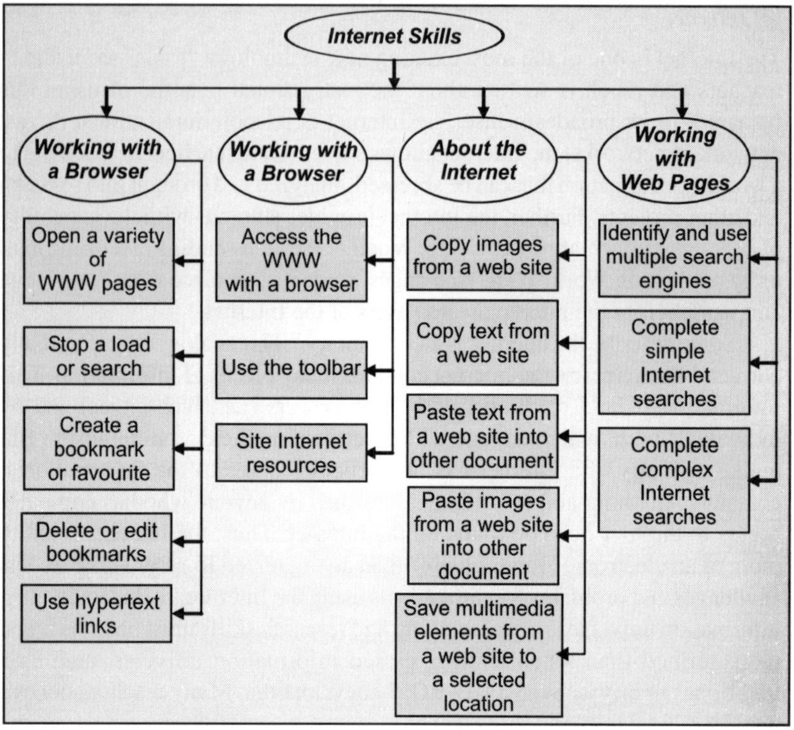

Figure 9.5: Educational Features of Internet

- Students can communicate with peers and individuals around the planet thereby increasing cultural understanding.
- On the Internet, students can electronically collaborate with other students around the globe to solve problems and create information and knowledge. The Internet is a huge arena for collaborative learning.

II. Computer Supported Instruction

In addition to using the computer as a tool during instruction, teachers are increasingly using it as a tool for preparing instruction. The computer can be used to generate teaching materials that incorporate written materials and visuals. Word processing software and desktop publishing systems can be used to generate worksheets, handouts, manuals and announcements. Computers can also be used to produce large banners, visuals, flowcharts, diagrams, posters and drawings for viewing on the computer screen, for projecting or for use in printed form. Computers can produce overhead transparencies and slides. All of these computer generated materials provide learners with opportunities to better understand the material being studied.

Graphics can display mathematical relationships and properties of mathematical functions in ways not previously possible.

Students can learn from producing graphics on the computer. The graphics tablet is a device that facilitates the input of non-textual materials. The tablet is connected to the computer and a special pen is used to draw whatever visual needed. Graphics can be animated and some programmes will handle movement automatically within the parameters specified. Others require each frame of the animation to be drawn as in film animation. Another source of visuals is commercially available files of computer "clip art" on disks. These disks include drawings of people, objects and shapes. The computer to change their size or to combine components of different drawings can manipulate these visuals.

The computer can be used not only for preparing materials but also as a presentation tool. The output from the computer can be projected onto a screen for group viewing using an LCD panel and overhead projector or using a video projector. For the above discussion it is clear that you can see the computer is a valuable tool for the teacher as well as for students.

III. Computer Assisted Testing (CAT)

Computers can be used to store and file banks of test items. The test items can be filed by subject content, objective measured or level of difficulty. Items in the bank can be readily updated and modified, new items added and old items deleted with minimal effort. From the pool of test items the instructor can choose the items to include on an examination or the computer can be programmed to select the items, either randomly or according to specified parameters. The computer can be programmed to select items based on variables in each category used to classify test items.

The computer also can be used to print out a copy of the test in as many different forms as desired or to administer a test to a student who is sitting at a computer. In the latter case, the computer can provide immediate feedback regarding right and wrong responses and keep a permanent record of the learner's achievement on the test. Test scoring and analysis can be computerized by typing the student responses into the computer by using mark-sense sheets during the test that can be read by the computer or by having the student take the test at the computer. The computer can display the number of students selecting each alternative, as well as the raw scores and standard scores of each student. In addition, group data such as means and standard deviations can be calculated.

IV. Computer Managed Instruction (CMI)

Computer managed instruction (CMI) refers to the use of computer system to manage information about learner performance and learning resource options in order to prescribe and control individualized lessons. There is considerable impetus for using CMI because of the increasing emphasis being placed on individualized instruction. Individualized instruction means that students will be moving through the checkpoints in the educational process at different times via different paths. You can imagine the management problem this entails if you think of one teacher responsible for teaching five subjects or major topics, with twenty objectives in each subject, to thirty students. This adds up to a minimum of 3000 checkpoints. The computer can help solve management problems like this by performing a number of specific functions such as administering, scoring and analyzing tests; prescribing media, methods and activities and keeping students records.

(3) Computer as an Object

The computer cans itself be the object of instruction. For example, in computer literacy courses students learn about computers and in vocational training trainees learn to use computers on the job for data processing and analysis purposes. In this role, the computer is treated like any other machine one is learning to use. When a learner is studying computer programming, the computer and the associated software are the objects of instruction.

This role of the computer is like the "Tutee" application of the computer. The computer is of paramount interest to the computer science teacher. The teaching of programming and computer science is based on the premise that a student can benefit from direct interaction with the computer because it is through this interaction that the student learns real problem solving paradigms and skills. The computer provides an unprecedented opportunity for a student to have access to a controlled, responsive environment, which challenges his intellectual and creative potential. Seymour Papert, one of the most well known advocates of using the computer as tutee or object has said *"The child programmes the computer and in doing so, both acquire a sense of mastery over a piece of the most modern and powerful technology and establish an intimate contact with some of the deepest ideas from science, from mathematics and from the art of intellectual building.*

To develop object or tutee applications, both teacher and student need to learn to programme a computer. In object mode, the student programmes or teaches the computer to perform some task. Learning computer programming is the best way to develop an understanding of how a computer works. In the tutor (computer as a "learning environment") and tool (computer as a "help tool") applications described earlier, understanding how a computer functions is not the instructional objective. In object applications, the computer itself becomes a focus of learning. In present time, educators might consider one of the three most popular object (tutee) programmes being used in schools today: Logo, BASIC and Pascal

(4) Computer as an Instrument

I. As a Source of Information

In education, computer can be use as a source of information. A computer network allows individual computers to share courseware, data and peripheral devices such as printers. Information from multiple sources in multiple locations can be accessed through the local area network (LAN). A LAN is a software and hardware system that connects computers, printers and other devices. The heart of the LAN is the file server. This computer serves the file needs of the user computers. The file server contains one or more hard drives. These hard drives contain the programmes that can be served to the user as well as maintain the files the user creates and accesses. File servers can be accessed from the computers attached to the network, which are called workstations.

Adding a modem to the network allows students with their own modem at home to dial into the school network. Networks extend schools beyond their physical walls and beyond their normal operating hours. Networks allow each workstation on the network both to receive data from and to send data to any other workstation on the system.

II. For Administration

Administrative applications of computer system consist of three broad categories:

(a) Database to manage data and information
(b) Electronics spreadsheets to manage numbers, and
(c) Office automation, especially word processing, to manage words and communications

(a) Databases

Database applications are by far the most important of the three categories mentioned. They involve the management of information about the various activities of a school in the form of data elements, records and files. Unlike spreadsheets and word processing applications that become popular with the introduction of microcomputers, database management systems began evolving on large mainframe computers in the 1950's. dBase is an example of database management system. One of the most important features of database software is the ability to generate reports. Generally, a query language is provided that enables users to access data in many different ways. These languages are very powerful for creating customized reports and temporary data files.

Figure 9.6 illustrates some of the major administrative database applications. Each application area has a unique role in contributing to the overall data management resources of a school. The student applications tend

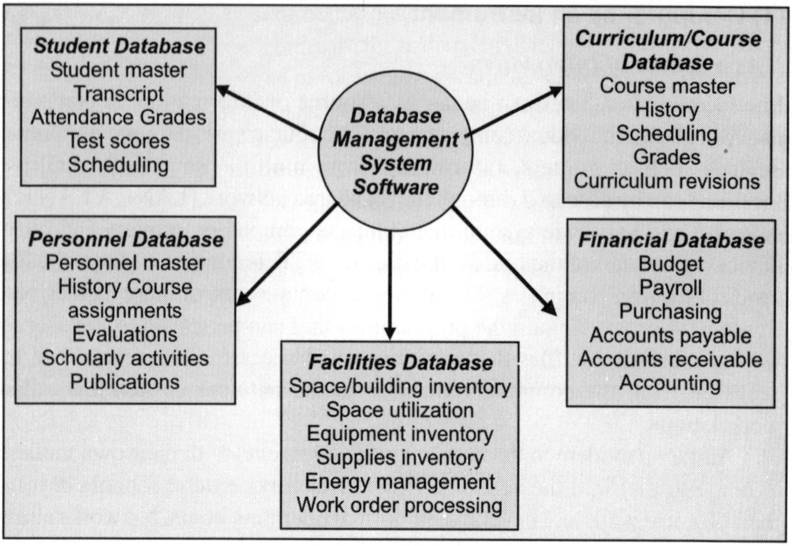

Figure 9.6: Common Database Applications

to be the most complex because of the amount of data that needs to be collected. In addition, student data are volatile and subject to frequent change. Applications such as attendance reporting and scheduling require extensive data collection efforts and careful coordination. Student applications are important since certain areas such as achievement and performance come under a good deal of scrutiny, especially from outside the school. Administrators need to have good access to data such as retention, attrition, graduation rates and test scores. Student enrollment data are also usually critical for various purposes and accurate data on students in attendance become a necessity for various reporting purposes.

Curriculum and course applications are vital for the internal academic operations of a school. Curriculum meetings and discussions are, in many schools, the centerpieces of academic planning. Administrators and teachers collect extensive amounts of data in order to develop new courses and modify existing ones. Data on student performance tied to curriculum and course enrollment become critical for such planning. A good curriculum and colure database also is necessary for developing a student scheduling application, one of the most time-consuming activities undertaken in many schools when done manually. Personnel and financial applications are frequently the first database systems to be implemented. For any administrator, the management of a budget is a critical responsibility. Access to up-to-date and accurate information on budgets and finances is a necessity and affects all of a school's operations. Personnel files are important complements to the financial data files for purposes of managing a budget, since the major costs in school operations are for personnel items such as salaries and fringe benefits. Facilities are generally the last of the database applications to be implemented. Facilities data are not as critical or volatile and do not need to be as tightly integrated. However, applications such as space utilization, equipment inventory and supplies inventory should not be ignored because they contribute to overall effectiveness and efficiency. In developing an overall plan for database management systems, administrators should assess their ability to collect and maintain data in the five major application areas identified in Figure 8.6.

(b) Electronic Spreadsheets

Electronic spreadsheets have grown significantly in popularity for applications that require frequent manipulation of numbers (e.g., budget, accounting, enrollment projections). Lotus 1-2-3 is an example of electronic spreadsheet programme. The major benefit of spreadsheet software is that the arithmetic operations can be performed automatically so that a change in any one cell will almost instantaneously change all other cells that may be affected. This provides "what if" facility. Figure 9.7 provides a chart of some of the major administrative applications appropriate for electronic spreadsheet software.

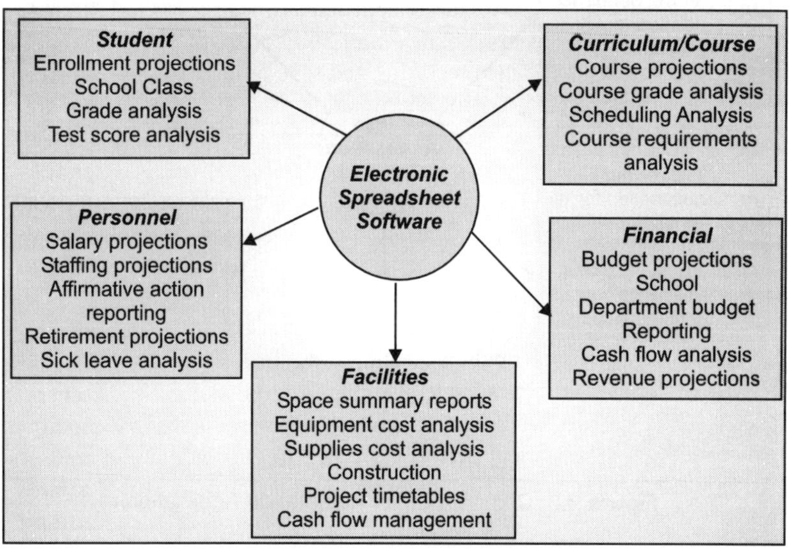

Figure 9.7: Common Spreadsheet Applications

Electronic spreadsheet software is effective in manipulating any aggregate data that is typically presented in tabular form. The number of reports using student data in this fashion is endless. Enrollment projections at various levels test score analyses and grade analyses are common applications. For academic planning and scheduling, electronic spreadsheets can be very effective in doing course enrollment projections. Personnel files are also important sources of data for spreadsheet applications. Staffing projections related to enrollment and course offerings can be routinely done.

Spreadsheets were designed initially for financial applications and have become commonplace in most accounting and budgeting offices. Entire budget planning processes are conducted with school board members, managers and others using the printed output from spreadsheets as the basis for discussion. These documents can easily be changed and recalculated many times over the course of the budget negotiation cycle. The graphics capabilities of spreadsheet programs can produce pie charts and bar graphs on budget information.

(c) Office Automation

In office automation, word processing is increasingly being used in conjunction with other software such as desktop publishing, electronic mail and databases. The first use of word processing with other software came with the need to merge data from database management systems with text. The best example

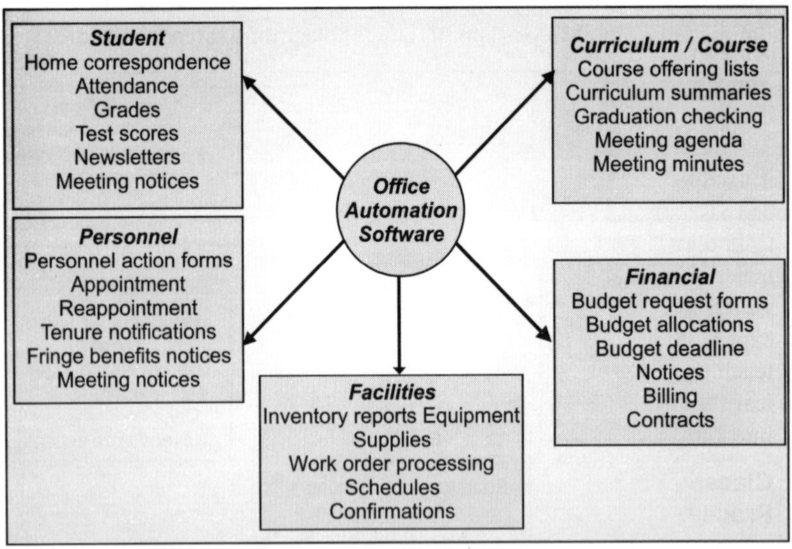

Figure 9.8: Common Office Automation Applications

is the merging of addresses from a database file with the text of a letter. This not only saved the time that would have been needed to key the addresses but also made good use of the information resources available from the database management system. Figure 9.8 provides a chart of some of the common uses of text with database information that are typically performed in school systems.

10

Models of Computer Use in Education

After studying this chapter, the reader will be able to: Classify the different models of computer use in teaching-learning process

The first uses of computers in education can be traced back 30 years ago, and especially in the last decade experts have been emphasizing large potentials of computer based learning in schools. It is a fact that these potentials are not being fully exploited. The problem is that it is not sufficient just to introduce computers as a tool for organizing information into the educational process, but the ways of learning need to be changed as well (Reinhardt, 1995).

Computer technology can enhance educational process in schools only if used correctly- in itself. It is a fact that technology is neither good nor bad. To achieve improvement in education through the use of computer technology, it is necessary to educate teachers, develop appropriate learning materials, and introduce new learning models. In today's information society, which has replaced industrial society, traditional learning is slow and expensive. The new technologies need to be complemented with modern teaching practices where a teacher is a coach to students and helps them learn using their own methods, and to successfully transform information into knowledge.

Classification of Models of Computer use in Teaching-Learning Process

Curriculum mapping is a good way of ensuring that computers are used in a balanced way across all the areas. However, if students use new technology in just a single mode at school or college, they would leave with a restricted idea of its effects and capabilities. There are many classifications of models in which computer technology can be used in teaching and learning. The important classifications of models of computer use in education are discussed below:

(1) Classification by Software Type: Tutor, Tool, Tutee

The most well-known classification system is provided by Taylor (1980). Here CAL is described by reference to three modes of computer use:

Model I: Computer as Tutor: The use of the computer as a tutor is to deliver instructional or learning material to enhance the student's learning. It is used to process information. It is considered an attractive approach for a student who has difficulty in learning. According to Taylor (1980), if the tutor is used properly, it is far more flexible than any book. To function as a tutor in a specific subject area, the computer must be programmed by an expert. In the context of use, the computer presents the student with some subject-matter content together with a set of questions or directions; the student responds and the computer completes the learning cycle by evaluating the response, before presenting further content.

Model II: Computer as Tool: The use of the computer as a tool is to aid or to facilitate academic work or the learning situation. It is not to take the place of the educator or tutor. It is an instructional tool rather than a teaching tool (Cunningham, 1990). Mastery of the computer as a tool is not needed alone. It is mastery of using the computer with the computer programme that is needed. As a tool, the computer records results, analyzes individual and group work and compares answers with those of peers, and evaluates the strengths and weaknesses of each student. The student's records can be compiled for immediate use or can be kept for later use by the student or the teacher or both (Holmes and Kidd, 1982).

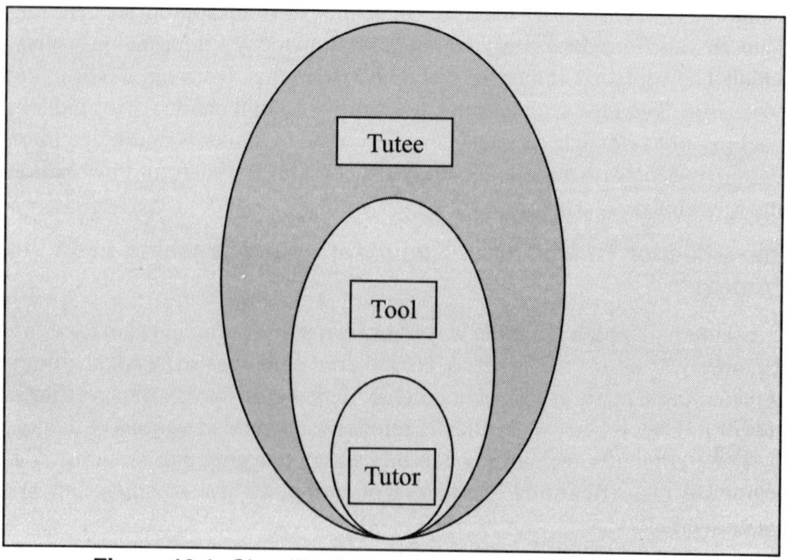

Figure 10.1: Classification of computers by software type

To function as a tool, the computer needs to operate generic software applications, such as a word processor, a spreadsheet, statistical package, etc. Students can then use these applications to assist them in a task in one or more subject areas, such as a word processor to help with writing in English; or a spreadsheet to help with analysis of data in a Maths problem; or perhaps a data-handling tool to support the classification of geographical information.

Model III: Computer as Tutee: The computer as a tutee means that as the student inputs information into the computer for the delivery of knowledge at a later time, the student learns as well. This type of classification will not be considered. 'To use the computer as a tutee, is to tutor the computer; for that the student or teacher doing the tutoring must learn to programme, to talk to the computer in language it understands. The computer makes a good tutee because of its dumbness, its patience, its rigidity and its capacity for being initialized and started over from scratch (Taylor, 1980, p. 4). Common uses of the computer as a tutee include the use of Prolog to create logical and expert systems, the use of LOGO for describing mathematical environments or the use of authoring systems, such as Authorware Professional or Hypercard, to write multimedia software.

(2) Classification by Educational Paradigm

Another useful way to classify computer applications in education is to look at the role the computer plays in stimulating instructional activity. In 1997 a team of researchers at the university of East Anglia headed by Stephen Kemmis produced a report called "How Do Students Learn?". Kemmis's classification scheme divides the role of computer technology in education into four classes that he called paradigms: instructional, revelatory, conjectural and emancipatory. Specifically, the computer can

- deliver instruction, when used in the **instructional mode**
- clarify information, when used in the **revelatory mode**
- answer what-if questions, when used in the **conjectural mode**, or
- free the student from burden some tasks and release effective learning time for more important activities, when used in the **emancipatory mode**.

The above roles of the computer, which often overlap, are discussed below:

Model I: Instructional Use of Computers: When used in the instructional mode, the computer delivers instruction to the learner by fulfilling the roles traditionally played by teachers, tutors and textbooks. Software of this paradigm embodies programmed learning techniques: the material to be learned is broken down into smaller parts, so that the learner can concentrate on each separately and in turn; each part of the material is accompanied by a learning task; and, regular rewards and reinforcements are provided for the

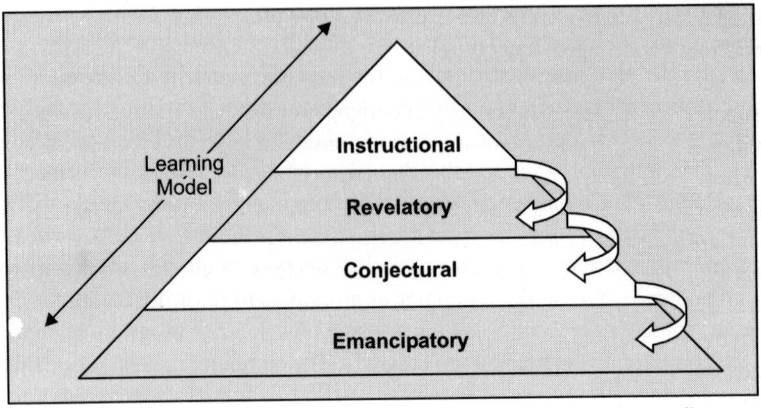

Figure 10.2: Classification of computers by educational paradigm

successful completion of learning tasks. If problems are encountered with any of the sequenced tasks, the learner is routed around a *remedial loop* in the programme and is thereby provided with extra support and tuition. This procedure continues until the learner successfully completes the task and moves onto the next task.

This paradigm covers software of a tutorial type, as well as drill and practice software. In both these software types, the learner is presented with structured content material together with exercise questions, intended to give practice in a particular intellectual skill, until mastery is achieved. When the computer is used in this mode, it should exploit the full advantages of computerized instructional programmes, such as tutorial and drill and practice, otherwise, it may be better to have a teacher, tutor, or textbook deliver the instruction.

Model II: Revelatory Use of Computers: In the revelatory model, the computer mediates between the student and a model of a real world phenomenon. In other words, the computer helps reveal to the students what something is like? The essence of software within this paradigm is that the student is encouraged to explore a model or simulation of an event, phenomenon or experience, whilst the underlying structure of the model or simulation remains hidden. The model or simulation is progressively revealed to the student as they undertake a process of discovery or experiential learning. The most common forms of software in this paradigm include imaginary simulations (historical or adventures) or models of real-world phenomena (e.g. volcano, nuclear explosions). Such software depends upon underlying structures, which have been determined by the designer of the software and are not made available to the learner to modify or change. This fact illustrates an important difference between exploring a model or simulation, and actually building a model, a much more complex cognitive process which lies outside the confines of this paradigm completely.

In science and social studies classes, for example, revelatory programmes can supplement or replace laboratory experiences or field trips when the actual activities would be too time-consuming, expensive, dangerous and technical.

Model III: Conjectural Use of Computers: In the conjectural model, the learner conjectures by asking "what if" questions and testing the hypotheses or configurations that may answer these questions. Essentially, in this model of learning, the computer programme provides students with high levels of control over the learning experience as well as opportunities to express and test hypotheses and ideas. Computer applications in this category include microworlds, model building programmes and some tool applications (such as spreadsheets).

A. *Microworlds:* A microworld is a computerized setting in which the rules of the "world" are defined by the learner or by the programmer to enable the learner to test hypotheses and develop an intuitive understanding of concepts functioning in that world. An excellent example can be found in Sunburst's *Sir Isaac Newton's Games*. The student must decide what to do to move the object around the track in various environments, such as on earth, near the sun, or far off in space. In the process the student develops a scientific model for motion in a particular microworld and uses that model to predict actions that will achieve the goal of movement around the track. Both science process skills and accurate concepts of real world motion are developed.

B. *Model Building Situations: Laws of Motion* is a good example of a programme in the model-building category. It allows students to build a scientific model for Newtonian motion while they experiment with the movement of a block down an inclined plane. Students can change the mass of the block and of the bucket used to pull the block, as well as the angle of the plane and the friction and net force produced. The students make predictions about what will happen and try to achieve designated results and the computer displays the results of their experiments in slow and real time motion, gives stop-action snapshots at equal time intervals and shows graphs and tables of the data.

Model IV: Emancipatory Use of Computers: This model is concerned with reducing workload, so that teaching and learning can take place free of the time consuming processing of data. Two types of labour in learning are distinguished in this context: authentic labour and inauthentic labour. The former is labour that is integral to the learning process; the later is labour, which is not central, but may be an accessory to the learning process.

In the emancipatory model, computers free (emancipate) students from inauthentic labour or non-productive work - that is, from work that does not contribute to the active, generative support of lesson objectives. Examples of such work include repetitive typing or calculation, technical set up, record keeping, and organization of data into productive patterns. Examples of emancipatory applications include word processing, database management programmes, spreadsheets, microcomputer based laboratories and telecommunications.

A. *General Tool Programmes:* Word processing programmes can facilitate writing of reports of any kind. Database management programmes provide a great tool for organizing information for easy retrieval. Electronic spreadsheets are useful to help students make repeated arithmetic computations in tables of data they have collected from experiments or to make projections of various kinds. Both spreadsheet and database printouts can usually be transported to the word processing programme and patched into the student's written report. Telecommunications programmes enable the learner to go beyond the walls of their own classrooms to seek and share information with a much larger world.

B. *Microcomputer Based Laboratories:* Microcomputer Based Laboratories (MBL's) are combinations of hardware and software that free students by enabling them to use the computer as a data collection, tabulation, and analysis device in the science class. With MBL's the computer collects data in real time and the student watches the experiment in progress. This encourages active concept development and the application of process skills. Learning becomes more concrete and intimately connected to observable phenomena. The use of the microcomputer in the emancipatory mode can help students achieve important goals of the traditional curriculum.

(3) Classification by Learning Situations

There are at least five models in which computer technology resources can be used in learning situations. These five initial models are:

Model I: The Support Model: In the support model, a student uses the computer to enhance the presentation of work. The computer can help by increasing the accuracy that the student might otherwise be able to achieve. There are a great number of tools that are currently used in schools, or which are available. For example:

- Word processors and other office applications

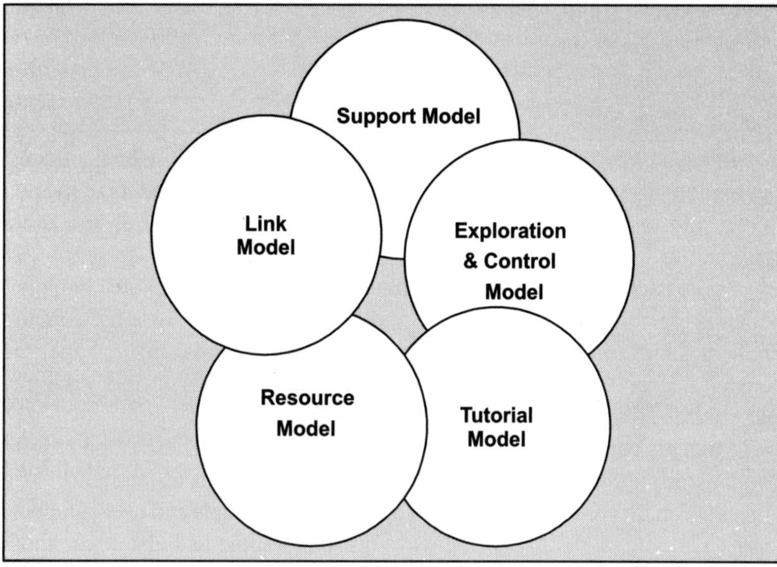

Figure 10.3: Classification of computers by learning situations

- Presentation graphics
- Computer Aided Drafting and Design
- Desk-top publishing
- Spelling and grammar checkers

In essence, the computer in support model enables the student to create or file information, which is usually transferred to paper. Images could quite easily be put on paper using a pen or pencil but the computer increases the accuracy the student can achieve. In so doing, the computer has an important role to play in raising the self-esteem of students and giving them confidence to continue to succeed in their learning.

Model II: The Exploration and Control Model: In the exploration and control mode, the student is able to examine and build situations. This kind of work is often associated with adventure games, where an important historical event is encapsulated in software. Students can explore this crucial moment in time and place, whilst making their own decisions about the events that unfold. Other software enables students to control a real, experimental situation, in a science laboratory for instance or by using robotics. Several environments for exploration or control are available. These include:

- Hypercard,
- Toolbook,
- Stella,
- LOGO,

- Model Builder,
- Expert Builder,
- Intellecta, and
- Sense and Control.

In each case the software provides a framework within which students can explore a situation. Additionally, students to construct models of the real world, and experiment with variations within these models can use these applications.

Some packages enable the student to place information in the computer, which is logically linked and which relates to a specific knowledge domain. Such packages can include databases, expert systems and statistical analysis packages. Expert systems, through the computers' function of rigorous logic, can provide advice about a knowledge domain.

Students can construct Multi-media presentations. These often require good planning skills, and anticipating the effect upon an audience of a presentation. In combining graphics, photographs, sounds and texts, students learn to anticipate the likely pathways through a topic and also learn about the subject himself or herself. Other students to explore the topic can subsequently use Multi-media constructions.

In the Exploration and Control mode, students might create applications, which will subsequently be used in any of the other models. This aspect of computer use is covered to some degree in the Information and Systems strands of the Technology area. However, in the later, the emphasis is upon the use of data as a resource. In considering modes of computer use, the emphasis is upon the subject matter or topic encapsulated within the scenario or simulation. Also, the Technology area gives students the important chance to examine the social effects of technology.

Model III: The Tutorial Model: In the tutorial model, the student will expect to learn new knowledge or skills. This model is characterized by the information system presenting information at an appropriate level and pace for the student. It will also give students opportunities to develop at their own pace and to receive feedback upon their progress. The tutorial model is currently seen as being technically possible in core areas such as Mathematics, Literacy and Science. These areas are seen as ones in which a judgment based upon the testing of objective principles is possible, rather than subjective areas such as Art or English. In our country, certain amount of effort is being put into professional development for teachers using the tutorial mode and multi-media workstations are being put into most teachers' centers.

Model IV: The Resource Model: In the Resource model, the computer is used to access information and other resources. When situated in the school library, this is often the way in which information technology plays a useful role. Several examples can illustrate the resource model:

- using PC-Globe to investigate relative population densities by country and latitude
- using a computer based library catalogue
- accessing the World Wide Web using an interface such as Internet Explorer, Netscape Navigator or Mosaic
- participating in a Newsday, where the computer provides continuously updated information.

When using the computer in resource model, students are developing questioning skills. They are solving problems by stating them and re-shaping them to fit different resource frameworks.

Model V: The Link Model: The link model is typified by the computer being used for communication between individuals. This represents an important role for computers in life for the coming century. In utilizing digital communications, we see a personal involvement and a picture of relationships, missing from the other models. Examples include the use of electronic mail for the low-cost exchange of textual messages, to desktop video conferencing for visual personal communication. This mode comes to the fore in projects such as the "Classroom Without Walls", or the "Global Schoolhouse".

Computer-mediated communication can enhance students' motivation to use the technology and broaden their sense of cultural identity as well as give them a global context for their thinking. In the link model, time-displacement and position independence are possible. Because of the structure of digitized communications, cost is unrelated to distance. This makes class dialogues between India and Canada for example, both relevant and easy.

There are other features of the link model that are worth exploring. Heather Govier in the UK found that the screen formed a 'safe haven for the gaze' in an examination of disturbed children. In the same way, young adolescents can often send important personal messages about themselves and others through this medium. Although the messages can travel instantaneously, they can contain nuances and feelings that individuals might find difficult to vocalize or place in a more public forum.

(4) Classification by Impulses to Learn

This classification focuses on the issue how computers can help students in the learning process. The present classification has three models of computer applications in learning process. The three models are as follows:

Model I: Learning From Computers: A computer is used as a tutor or for drill and practice. In this model we have a one-way information flow from the computer to the student in which the student answers questions, the computer evaluates the answer and depending on the correctness of the answer proceeds to the presentation of the next block of information. This was the

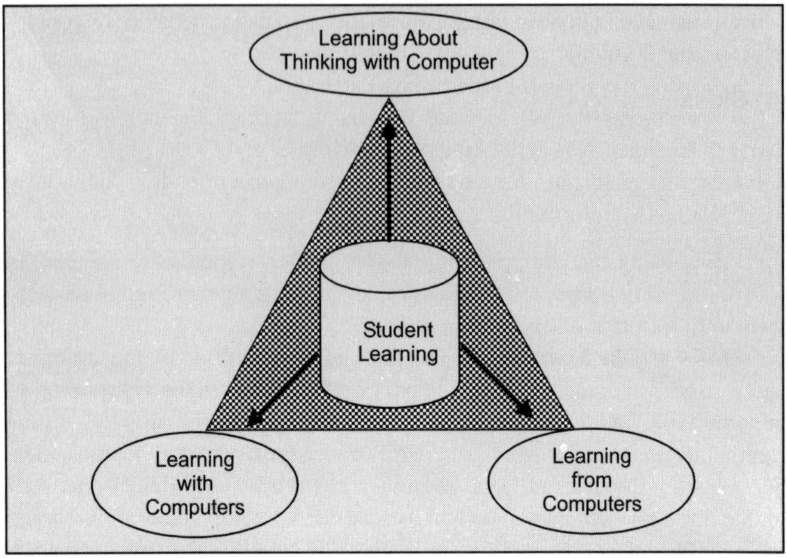

Figure 10.4: Classification of computers by impulses to learn

prevailing method used in the beginnings of computer use in education, but, more recently, it is being avoided since it does not allow for independent thinking in solving problems. The method could only be used in certain phases of the education process for practice or testing of knowledge, but not where new material is being learned.

Model II: Learning With Computers: In this model, a computer is used more like a student's partner which, through simulations and games, helps the student make his or her own discoveries and in that way successfully learn the presented material. The student makes his/her own decisions about how to interact with the computer, since there are no rigid rules that are to be followed. This model of computer usage is especially effective in learning new material, for it replaces lecturing and students are introduced to the new content in an interesting way.

Model III: Learning About Thinking with Computers: A computer is used to aid students develop new patterns of thinking, which can help them in different learning situations. This is achieved by teaching students to programme in a programming language such as LOGO, which is also appropriate for younger students.

(5) Classification by Subject

Essentially this system provides for classification of software by school subjects. For example, all those software programmes that can be applied to, say, Social Studies. Not a useful system when discussing principles of educational computing but helpful when simply wishing to describe resources appropriate to specific content areas taught in schools

(6) Classification by Use

None of the other ways of thinking or classifying CAL appear to accommodate software uses made by teachers in setting the parameters of the learning experience for children—and for young children in particular. Fatouros, Downes and Blackwell (1994) have attempted to redress this by offering a classification of CAL based on software use, with specific attention given to the role of the teacher in determining how a software item might be deployed to engage learning, in young children in particular. They say:

> Whether the software is incorporated within a learning centre for children to explore freely or it is implemented as a planned activity within a unit of work, teacher decisions about implementation have a significant impact on the learning processes that are generated. For example, language and social skills may be developed through the use of a typical drill and practice programme if the activity is implemented in such a way s to promote discussion and negotiation between a pair of children using the software, rather than having an individual child use the software as a means of knowledge testing (p. 186).

Fatouros, Downes and Blackwell (1994) offer a classification system based on the key domains or learning areas that teachers plan for young children to explore:

- images,
- sounds,
- text,
- stories and ideas,
- facts and figures, and
- consequences

These areas broadly define domains that span developmental areas and curriculum areas for early childhood education; and they emphasize the integrated nature of young children's learning. For example, when children are exploring images, they may be developing physical and social skills and general cognitive processes, including understandings in art, mathematics and language. By focusing on images they are able to do this within a meaningful context, which is based on their own view of the world (Fatouros, Downes & Blackmore, 1994, p. 187).

(7) Classification by Role

In 1984 Higgins came up with a two-way classification of roles called magister and pedagogue.

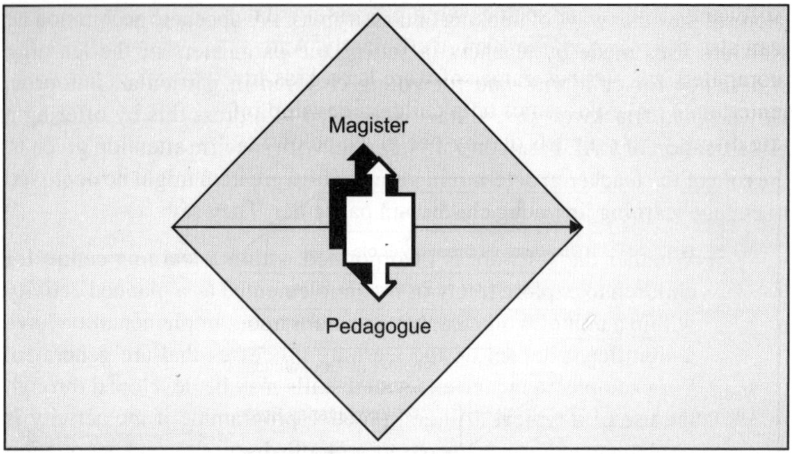

Figure 10.5: Classification of Computers by their Role

Model I: Magister: Magister was any activity in which the computer evaluated student performance and, like the traditional schoolmaster, dictated the order in which learning was expected to occur.

Model II: Pedagogue: Pedagogue was all those activities, such as games, simulations, access to tools and look-up tables of information, in which the computer was providing the services of a slave, like the pedagogue who in ancient Rome escorted rich children to school.

The main force of this argument was that, whereas learners probably need both magister and pedagogue during the course of their learning, the computer performs more effectively as pedagogue and the human more effectively as magister.

(8) Classification by Computer as a Tool

There are six areas in which children or learners can be used computer and software as tools – tools for learning, creativity, productivity, research, communications and entertainment. As a learning tool, computers can help develop memory skills, offer after school study or tutoring sessions, allow children to experiment and investigate abstract science and math concepts through simulations. As a creativity tool, computers provide access to an infinite colour palette and fine tuned keyboard, which keeps children busy creating art and music. As a research tool, computers offer children access to information that wasn't available at their school or local library. As a communication tool, computers and software can enable children to share experiences with their next-door neighbor or with other children as far as Europe or Pakistan, all electronically. As a productivity tool, computers and software programmes such as word processing, databases and spreadsheets can also help children work more efficiently. And, as an entertainment tool, computers and various game software keep kids involved for hours. Many entertainment programmes help children develop important skills. Now we are discuss these models one-by-one given below:

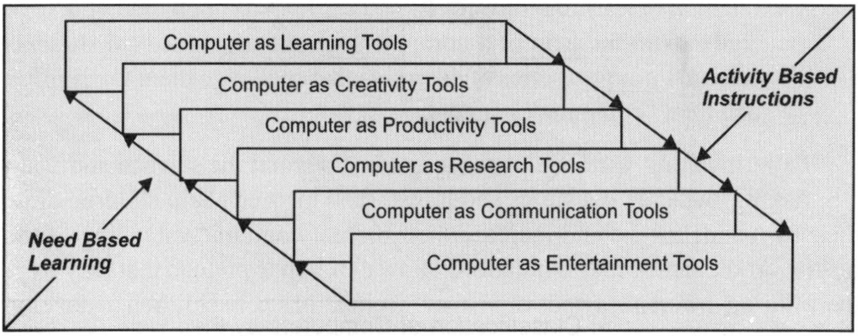

Figure 10.6: Classification of computers by computer as a tool

Model I: Computer as Learning Tools

Memory Practice: Regardless of whether it is multiplication exercises or spelling, there are certain facts that children must learn through memorization in their early educations. And the key to learning these is memorization. Computer software is available to provide children with memory recall exercises, from math facts to science definitions to English vocabulary words. Using a computer to practice facts is fun, which for most children means spending more time with the exercises. Computers are also infinitely patient and (unlike many of us) will work with a child even if it takes 100 tries before they provide the correct response. Children can also receive instant feedback, no more waiting until the next day to see the results, so children do not practice mistakes.

A. ***Tutoring:*** There are times when a student needs extra tutoring help and possibly a different approach from the way that a teacher has presented the material during the class. Computer tutorials offer students a new approach to the subject, as well as one-on-one assistance. Many educational computer software programmes are designed to present information in a step-by-step manner and allow a child to catch up on the steps and concepts they were not able to understand in the formal classroom setting. With computer tutorials, children are free to work at their own pace.

B. ***Experimenting:*** While no teacher or parent can allow children to experiment with dangerous chemicals unsupervised or to cut up cadavers to see just how human body parts fit into place, computer can. Science and math simulation software programmes make these and other words come alive, safely, right on the screen. The programmes encourage children to learn through discovery and experimentation. Even medical students rely on experimental interactive learning tools to help guide them through their course of study. With the help of a computer, for example, medical students can run through a series of exercises that challenge them to diagnose and treat "computer" patients.

Experimenting with computers goes well beyond the science and math lab. Asking "what if" questions about historical facts can help children draw their own conclusions and increase their memory and understanding of the results. At the same time, simulations allow children to pretend that they were there during different periods of history. Simulations help children to develop decision-making skills, which are critical for children's future. In social studies simulations, for example, children learning about Indian history can actually make decisions and from within their computers, change the course of history for a minute and see what would have happened.

Model II: Computer as Creativity Tools: Some students shy away from art and music because they are not immediately proficient using traditional tools. And, even though they have a wealth of creative ideas, they fail to express them because others in the class seem to be better painters or composers. With computers, all students have access to a new array of creativity tools from computer painting and drawing tools to musical composition and desktop publishing programmes, making it easier for them to express and explore their creativity.

Model III: Computer as Productivity Tools: With computers, productivity is always on the rise. Word processing and database management programmes help students, young and old; organize their thoughts and information. For example, if a high school student uses a computer and a word processing programme to prepare a term paper, there is no problem revising the first page. Before computers, the student would have been forced to recopy the entire document but with a computer, they simply key in the changes and reprint. By making written communications easier, computers can't help but boost our children's productivity and Communication skills.

Model IV: Computer as Research Tools: Here's another area that students can explore with the help of a computer and a database programme. Now, pulling together background information on a topic takes on new meaning. Besides the traditional resource materials- encyclopedias, books, etc., there are software and computer tools that provide students with access to online database information and research reports. In addition, there are a number of research analysis and organizational tools available.

Model V: Computer as Communication Tools: Like the telephone, computers have the power to bring people closer together. Through networking technology, computers across the room or across the word can be connected to allow people to communicate, share thoughts and information. Through an electronic mail programme and modems, students in each country can tell each other about their activities. Through these types of electronic communication links, children can strengthen their ability to express themselves in writing and prepare themselves for the increased use of electronic communications in the workplace.

Model VI: Computer as Entertainment Tools: Computer can be a lot of fun. There is a number of entertainment software available that can keep children "working" on the computer for hours. Besides just being fun to play, many games are educational in nature and many others develop eye-hand coordination and strategy skills. Played alone, with a friend or parent, these games can also help to bring people closer together, even if it is in the sprit of computer competition.

11

Computers and Higher Order Thinking Skills

After studying this chapter, the reader will be able to: Understand the complex process of learning through computers; Categorize higher-order thinking skills and lower-order thinking skills; Discuss the Bloom's Taxonomy of educational objectives; Comprehend the instructional elements for fostering higher-order thinking in the classroom; List the questions related to the higher-order thinking skills; Describe the questions for quality thinking at each level of Bloom's Taxonomy; Construct the higher-order thinking skills model; Examine the model for use of computers for higher-order thinking skills; Choose the different computer software in relation to Bloom's Taxonomy

In recent years the computer has become an increasingly desirable tool for the classroom. The growing demand to produce a population skilled in technology has put pressure on educational systems to incorporate technology into the learning environment with a primary goal of producing students who are proficient in computer skills and able to function in society at a competent level. Andrew R. Molnar of the National Science Foundation in Washington D.C., states, *"Research shows that educational technology, when properly applied, can provide an effective means for learning"*. It has been asserted that technology advocates have not been held accountable, however and in the business world computers will help corporate productivity and in education, the benefits accrue to the individual learner (Muller, 1997). But just what are these benefits? Unfortunately, in today's world, the work place is about performing and not about learning new skills. This makes it especially difficult for today's students to understand the relationship between academic exercises and real world benefits.

The desire for computer proficient students has been married to the long-standing objective of educators to enhance academic performance. Technology is being proposed for use as a tool to improve academic performance and enhance test scores, especially at the elementary level (Woodall, 1998). Many classrooms now have computers. Some are used rarely, if at all, if the teachers are not trained. If educators, from primary level through university level education, are going to use the computer as an instructional tool, one must ask, does the computer impact grades? John Anderson of Pittsburgh's Carnegie-Mellon University found that students' grades went up one letter if they used his intelligent, computer-assisted instructional tutorials in geometry, algebra and teaching programming languages (Anderson, 1993).

To increase the contact between young people and computers, volumes of software have been designed to allow academic skills to be practiced and independent learning to be done by individual students. The touted success of this dual objective has become the foundation for educational institutions to promote the enhancement of the learning environment by including computer exercises in the classroom curriculum. Does an individual, computer-based academic skill-building format produce a learning environment of maximum quality? Kulik's analysis of many studies found that one could achieve a 10-20-percentile point increase in scores through computer-based education. What is of special interest is Kulik's finding that peer tutoring was even more effective than the computer in enhancing performance (Kulik, 1991).

As vital as it is to encourage computer proficiency in this information-driven millennium era, it is important to keep in mind that the primary goal of education is to promote learning. Using the computer for instruction presents unique challenges for educators related to student lack of motivation, varying levels of computer literacy and shortages of time for adequate orientation to a new medium of instruction. The amplification of student's thinking and over-all cognitive skills by using tools such as the computer must be constantly analyzed to ensure that actual changes in learning outcomes are being accomplished. A tool is only useful if it increase one's ability to produce quality work. The responsibility of an educator is to teach students how to learn.

There is a strong perception, especially at higher levels of education, that the computer is an excellent tool for the conveying and managing large volumes of information. This is especially useful from the instructor's point of view but may not be highly productive from the learner's perspective. The major problem with learning today is that there is a tendency to confuse information with learning; making information available does not guarantee that students will learn from it. An alternative mode, however, is emerging allowing students to take greater control of the computer, interacting with the machine and concurrently confronting new ways of thinking and new subject material. This type of interaction with the computer is believed to encourage higher order skills.

It is a serious matter that the use of computers in education has traditionally been associated with the use of drill-and-practice programmes in the classroom. In this form of instruction, students receive information stored inside the computer (such as text or pictures), the computer delivers the instruction in a pre-determined fashion (following some sort of programme 'algorithm'). Although a certain amount of interactivity can be found in such instructional software, the general intention is that the computer will control the learning structure with the students being, as such, generally the passive recipients of such information and instruction. But the question must be asked:

- Is this all that the computer can do in an instructional process?
- How can we increase the student's participation in such computer-based instructional situations?
- How can we develop critical and problem solving skills in the learners
- How can we achieve the higher order teaching skills (HOTS) with the help of the computer?

The Complex Process of Learning through Computers

The use of computer technology to enhance learning is not a simple process of loading the computer with the software, turning on the computer and sitting the students in front of the computer. It is a more complex process, which involves many facets of an IT (Information Technology) related learning environment. Many policy makers and also teachers assume that *"introduction of IT into schools and classrooms will lead automatically to improvements in students' learning, so they concentrate their efforts on the provision of hardware and software and on teachers' acquisition of technical competence in using them"* (Somekh, 1998). Many teachers commonly believe that if students are motivated by IT and they are busily engaged in computer related activities they will automatically be learning. Learning depends heavily on the type of learning tasks teachers designed for their students. Now some of the fundamental questions arise here are as follows:

- How can teachers use computer technology more effectively?
- How can teachers promote higher order cognitive skills through the use of technology?
- What kinds of software should a teacher use to help promote students thinking?
- How can teachers effectively design learning tasks that will promote higher order cognitive process?

What are Higher-Order Thinking and Critical/Creative/Constructive Thinking?

Higher-order thinking essentially means thinking that takes place in the higher-levels of the hierarchy of cognitive processing. In 1956, Benjamin Bloom headed a group of educational psychologists who developed a classification of levels of intellectual behaviour important in learning. The contributors to

Bloom's Taxonomy published their proposed classification scheme in three separate volumes, for the three domains of learning: cognitive, affective and psychomotor. Their first volume addresses those outcomes in the cognitive domain (Figure 11.1).

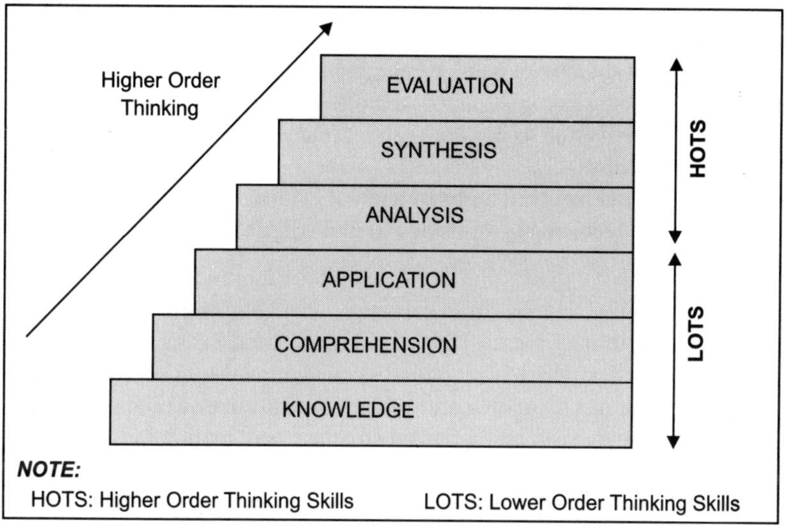

Figure 11.1: Blooms' Taxonomy of Educational Objectives

Table 11.1 shows the categories and sub-categories of learning outcome in this volume:

1. **Knowledge**
   - 1.1 Knowledge of specifics
     - 1.11 Knowledge of terminology
     - 1.12 Knowledge of specific facts
   - 1.2 Knowledge of ways and means of dealing with specifics
     - 1.21 Knowledge of conventions
     - 1.22 Knowledge of trends and sequences
     - 1.23 Knowledge of classifications and categories
     - 1.24 Knowledge of criteria
     - 1.25 Knowledge of methodology
   - 1.3 Knowledge of universals and abstractions in a field
     - 1.31 Knowledge of principles and generalizations
     - 1.32 Knowledge of theories and structures
2. **Comprehension**
   - 2.1 Translation
   - 2.2 Interpretation
   - 2.3 Extrapolation

3. **Application**
4. **Analysis**
   4.1 Analysis of elements
   4.2 Analysis of relationships
   4.3 Analysis of organizational principles
5. **Synthesis**
   5.1 Production of a unique communication
   5.2 Production of a plan or a proposed set of operations
   5.3 Derivation of a set of abstract relations
6. **Evaluation**
   6.1 Judgements in terms of internal evidence
   6.2 Judgements in terms of external criteria

From the above discussion, it is clear that Bloom identified six levels within the cognitive domain, from the simple recall or recognition of facts, as the lowest level, through increasingly more complex and abstract mental levels, to the highest order, which is classified as evaluation. More specifically, the six levels of Bloom's taxonomy allow the student to create a relationship that can be interconnected in an organized structure and applied in a variety of ways.

Though controversy has followed Bloom's theory, studies have shown that the elements of higher cognition fit well with the experience of the student, using technology, to reach beyond traditional rote memorization of the text material. The knowledge objective is viewed as a single frame, whereby students learn to memorize certain pieces of information (Ross, 1993). This cognitive skill allows the student to know specific information on its own without having to use critical thinking. At the comprehension level, the learner moves away from the single frame model and into the linear model. Students are able to understand the information and recognize it in other forms. Relationships between events, facts, problems or solutions are important. Linear layouts are designed to force this process. The linear model is in comparison to a horizontal line, where directions are given and followed, not allowing for critical thinking skills to be mastered (Ross, 1993).

The third level of the cognitive objective pyramid takes the learner to the jump linear model of application, which is the first level of higher order thinking. The level of application allows the learner to apply the knowledge and understanding to new situations that may lie outside the baseline definition of the concept. At the next level, analysis allows individual learners to further work with the same information but in different patterns and with opportunities to compare one set of information with another. By breaking down the information into understandable components, the learner is able to continue branching by comparing and contrasting the information. The students must be able to relate these facts to a problem in an analytical way using both inductive and deductive processes. The students' role at this level is to know how and when to put the parts back together so that the organization of the whole becomes clearer. Computer technology allows the learner to jump from branch to branch in exploring the material necessary to meet his or her own needs. At this level, using the "back and forth" technique is used to access information. Synthesis in Bloom's taxonomy is discovery.

Bloom's Taxonomy is the most widely accepted hierarchical arrangement of this sort in education and it can be viewed as a continuum of thinking skills starting with knowledge-level thinking and moving eventually to evaluation-level of thinking. A common example of the application of the major categories in Bloom's Taxonomy, is shown below, applying the taxonomy to the Pledge of Allegiance:

- ***Knowledge*** statements ask the student to recite the pledge. Example: *"Say the pledge"*.
- ***Comprehension*** statements ask the student to explain the meaning of words contained in the pledge. Example: *"Explain what indivisible, liberty, and justice mean"*.
- ***Application*** statements ask the student to apply understandings. Example: *"Create your own pledge to something you believe in"*.
- ***Analysis*** statements ask the student to interpret word meanings in relation to context. Example: *"Discuss the meaning of 'and to the Republic for which it stands' in terms of its importance to the pledge"*.
- ***Synthesis*** statements ask the student to apply concepts in a new setting. Example: *"Write a contract between yourself and a friend that includes an allegiance to a symbol that stands for something you both believe in"*.
- ***Evaluation*** statements ask the student to judge the relative merits of the content and concepts contained in the subject. Example: *"Describe the purpose of the pledge and assess how well it achieves that purpose. Suggest improvements"*.

[Wiederhold, C. (1997). *The Q-Matrix/Cooperative Learning and Higher-Level Thinking*. San Clemente, CA: Kagan Cooperative Learning.]

When we promote higher-order thinking then, we are simply promoting thinking, along with the teaching methodologies that promote such thinking, that takes place at the higher levels of the hierarchy just provided, notably application, analysis, synthesis, and evaluation.

Critical/creative/constructive thinking is closely related to higher-order thinking; they are actually inseparable. Critical/creative/constructive thinking simply means thinking processes that progress upward in the given direction. First one critically analyzes the knowledge, information, or situation. Then they creatively consider possible next-step options, and then finally, they construct a new product, decision, direction, or value. The evaluation step listed above with the Pledge of Allegiance would require this sort of thinking.

Instructional Elements for Fostering Higher-Order Thinking in the Classroom

Below is given some instructional elements that will foster the higher order thinking in the classroom:

1. Remember to ask for it; that is, for discovery, invention, and artistic/ literary creation.
2. Great curiosity and new ideas with enthusiasm; these can often lead to the most valuable "teachable moments."
3. Expose learners to new twists on old patterns and invite looking at old patterns from new angles.
4. Constructively critique new ideas because they almost always require some fine-tuning.
5. Reset our expectations to the fact that there will be many more "misses" than "hits" when reaching for workable new ideas.
6. Learn to invite contrary, or opposing, positions; new possibilities are often discovered in this way and existing thoughts, patterns, and beliefs can be tested and strengthened.

Questions that Invite Higher-Order Thinking

The questions related to the higher order thinking are given below:

- How is this study like another you/we have read? This question encourages students to make connections and see analogies.
- Does this story/information make you aware of any problems that need attention? This amounts to asking students to see themselves as active participants in problem identification as well as problem solving.
- What does this mean to you and how might it affect others? This pair of questions gives students a chance to express their own interests but also to empathetically consider and understand the views of, and possible consequences to, others.
- Is there anything wrong with this solution, and how else might this problem be solved? These questions are the heart of successful critical analysis.
- What more needs to be known or done to understand or do this better? This is a pointed request for creative problem solving that invites thinking "beyond the lines."

- What is a contrary way of seeing this? Being able to examine issues from multiple points of view helps the students to clarify their thoughts.

Questioning for Quality Thinking at Each Level of Bloom's Taxonomy

The different questions related to the quality of thinking at different level of Bloom's Taxonomy are given below:

***Knowledge*:** Identification and recall of information
Who, what, when, where, how?
Describe ____________________.

***Comprehension*:** Organization and selection of facts and ideas
Retell ___________ in your own words.
What is the main idea of ______________?

***Application*:** Use of facts, rules, principles
How is ______ and example of _______?
How is _______ related to ____________?
Why is __________________ significant?

***Analysis*:** Separation of the whole into component parts
What are the parts or features of ____________?
Classify __________ according to ___________.
Outline/diagram/web ____________________.
How does ______ compare/contrast with ______?
What evidence can you list for ______________?

***Synthesis*:** Combination of ideas to form a new whole
What would you predict/infer from ___________?
What ideas can you add to _______________?
How would you create/design a new __________?
What might happen if you combine ___________ with ____________?
What solutions would you suggest for _________?

***Evaluation*:** Development of opinions, judgments, or decisions
Do you agree with _________________?
What do you think about ________________?
What is the most important ______________?
Prioritize _________________.
How would you decide about _________________?
What criteria would you use to assess __________?

Higher Order Thinking Skills Model (HOTSM)

Certainly before we claim we can achieve the higher order cognitive objectives with the help of the computer, we should be fairly clear about what we mean by "higher order thinking or cognitive objectives or skills". For this purpose, we will see the difference between knowledge, comprehension, application, analysis, synthesis and evaluation.

Knowledge: Knowledge is defined as the remembering of previously learned material. This may involve the recall of a wide range of material, from specific facts to complete theories but all that is required is the bringing to mind of the appropriate at information. Knowledge represents the lowest level of learning outcomes in the cognitive domain.

Table 11.1: Higher Order Thinking Skills and their Descriptions

Higher Order Thinking Skills (HOTS)	*Description*
Focusing	Brainstorming, Goal setting, Defining the problem
Information Gathering	Prioritizing, Formulating questions, Examining different points of view
Remembering	Associating, categorizing
Integrating	Summarizing, Abstracting
Organizing	Comparing, Classifying
Analyzing	Identifying attributes, Relationships, Patterns, Examine, Subdivide
Imagining	Visualizing, Predicting, Speculating,
Designing	Planning, Drafting, Revising
Generating	Inferring, Inducting, Elaborating
Evaluating	Establishing criteria, Testing ideas, Conclude, Verifying ideas and outcomes, Interpret, Measure

Comprehension: Comprehension is defined as the ability to grasp the meaning of material. This may be shown by translating material from one form to another (words to numbers) by interpreting material (predicting consequences or effects). These learning outcomes go one step beyond the simple remembering of material and represent the lowest level of understanding.

Application: Application refers to the ability to use learned material in a new and concrete situation. This may include the application of such things as rules, methods, concepts, principles, laws and theories. Learning outcomes in this area requires a higher level of understanding.

Analysis: Analysis refers to the ability to break down material into its component parts so that its organizational structure may be understood. This may include the identification of the parts, analysis of the relationships between parts and recognition of the organizational principles involved. Learning outcomes here represent a higher intellectual level than comprehension and application because they require an understanding of both the content and the structural form of the material.

Synthesis: Synthesis refers to the ability to put parts together to form a new whole. This may involve the production of a unique communication (theme or speech) a plan of operations (research proposal) or a set of abstract relations (scheme for classifying information). Learning outcomes in this area stress creative behaviour with major emphasis on the formulation of new patterns of structures.

Evaluation: Evaluation is concerned with the ability to judge the value of material (statement, novel, poem, research report, principle) for a given purpose. The judgments are to be based on definite criteria. These may be internal criteria (organization) or external criteria (relevance to the purpose) and the student may determine the criteria or be given them learning outcomes in this area are highest in the cognitive hierarchy because they contain elements of all of the other categories plus conscious value judgments base on.

As you can see that higher order thinking is actually starts with the comprehension phase and it increases up to evaluation phase. From comprehension to evaluation there are so many thinking skills and sub-skills. For the higher order thinking skills model we have identified the various types of thinking skills involved when using IT for learning.

Model for Use of Computers for Higher Order Thinking Skills (HOTS)

For developing HOTS (Higher Order Thinking Skills) among the students, it is not sufficient to give the traditional computer environment (e.g., Drill-and-practice, Tutorial etc.) The learning environment should be dynamic and helpful for the learner to stimulate his/her thinking pattern. The Computer environment has the power to make this and from this we can achieve the higher cognitive skills described earlier. Now the question is what kind of computer environments is helpful for achieving HOTS. It is obvious that there are various types of computer environments for various types of thinking skills. We can categorize them into four categories of IT use (Chen & Hsu, 1998; Wong & Williams, 1998). We classified the categories based on the pedagogy when students use the computer material for learning. For example, we found lots of software programmes, which can be used for individualized teaching and they are suitable for the acquisition of skills and knowledge. Thus, the first category of the computer environment is for "direct instruction", the second category involves using computer for resource-based learning, the third as an instructional tool and the fourth category involves the use of computer in creating various multimedia projects. Now we are explaining each of the computer environments one-by-one given below:

(1) Use of IT for Direct Instruction/Explicit Teaching

Models of Learning Associated with Direct Teaching Mode

Relevant models of learning associated with the direct teaching mode are drawn from behaviourism and cognitivism. Drawing from the works of Skinner and Thorndike, behaviourism is based upon a stimulus-response-reinforcement concept. The behaviourist perspective suggests that "knowing is an organized accumulation of associations and components of skills". It is in focusing on learning as a series of accumulated associations that behaviourism establishes its approach to teaching and learning. One of the implications is that individual students must have the opportunity to respond to instructions and receive feedback based upon the individual student's response. This form of learning theory is most appropriately applied to drill-and-practice mode. In this mode, the computer provides a stimulus (question), the student answers (response) and if correct, the computer provides reinforcement. Meta analysis research studies on the effectiveness of drill-and-practices have shown that this mode is effective in increasing student learning (Kulik, Kulik & Bangert-Drowns, 1985). Another popular mode commonly found in computer-based instruction is the tutorial mode. In this mode, the computer plays the teaching role and teaches students certain contents. To test their understanding of the concepts taught, students will be tested and it is usually done through multiple choice question formats. However, this approach is appropriate for the acquisition of basic skills but does not greatly help to promote higher-order cognitive processes.

IT for Direct Instruction/Explicit Teaching

Direct Instruction, also known as Explicit Teaching "is a systematic method for presenting material in small steps, pausing to check for student understanding and eliciting active and successful participation from all students. This model of instruction is well grounded in Behaviorist Theory. It has also been classified as a 'transmission' model (as opposed to an 'information-processing' model). Rosenshine, (1986, p. 60) details six teaching functions as an important sequence in the method of explicit teaching. They are: daily review, presenting new material, guided practice, corrections and feedback, independent practice and weekly and monthly reviews. This method has been shown to be particularly effective in the "teaching of mathematical procedures and computations, reading decoding, explicit reading procedures such as distinguishing fact from opinion, science facts and concepts, social science facts and concepts, map skills, foreign language vocabulary. They are less relevant for teaching in areas that are less well-structured, for example, teaching composition, reading comprehension, analyzing literature or historical trends." (Rosenshine, 1986, p. 60)

Higher Order thinking Skills Framework in Direct Instruction/Explicit Teaching

This is the most commonly used instructional mode when students work with computer-based instructional materials. Traditional computer-based instructional materials are based on the direct teaching approach to teaching.

In this type of instructional mode, the computer delivers instructions and the student responds to the instruction. At the end of the instructional process, students are tested for their understanding of the materials learnt.

There are two major categories of educational technology that support this method of teaching. One of the first applications of computer software in the classroom was in the form of drill and practice programmes. There are many that take the task of providing guided and independent practice to students. Some computer-based instructional software will employ a drill-and-practice approach to teach basic skills, e.g., the acquisition of numerical operating skills like addition, subtraction, multiplication and division. This mode serves a purpose, as they are good for the acquisition of basic skills.

Another type of software that supports this model is the tutorial type of programme. In a tutorial programme instruction is usually expected to stand-alone; the student should be able to learn the topic without any help or other materials from outside the courseware. Tutorials should address all instructional events i.e. all six teaching functions that Rosenshine defines. Tutorials can be categorized as linear or branching tutorials. A linear tutorial gives the same instructional sequence and feedback to all learners. A branching tutorial directs learners along alternate paths depending on how they respond to questions and whether or not they show mastery of certain parts of the material. Emulating a good teacher is difficult for a person, let alone a computer, but there are some very good tutorials available.

Other examples of direct teaching mode include simulation and instructional games. While the direct teaching mode of the courseware does not really promote thinking in general, this form of instructional approach is still important as they help to teach students skills and help them to acquire concepts that are necessary for higher- order cognitive processes.

Behaviourism is based on the premise that it is meaningless to theorize about the working of the brain, since we can only study the behaviour of people in responding to stimuli (Leahey and Harris, 1993; Schultz and Schultz, 1992). The consequence of this premise is that there is an emphasis on strategies such as repetition that encourage 'parrot' fashion learning rather than higher order cognitive processes. The cognitive psychology movement rejects this premise, instead surmising that a person's responses to stimuli is individual and depends on the person's cognitive state and on the mental processes occurring. The important consequence of the cognitive position is that rather than being concerned with the best way to elicit the desired response, teachers are concerned with the learner's cognitive activity and the mental models that they form. With cognitivism, the authors of the courseware who intend to use direct teaching method as a form of delivery should keep in mind the various information processing principles:

- reduce the content into small chunks of information (Miller, 1956)
- use advance organizers by presenting new concepts and ideas to students before they are taught (Ausubel, 1977)
- provide linkages for new information to existing information (Bransford, 1979)
- employ various memory strategies to help students to transfer from short-term memory to long-term memory.

(2) Use of IT in Cooperative/Collaborative Learning

Models of Learning Associated with Cooperative Learning

Cooperative (sometime known as Collaborative) Learning is a model of teaching with a set of common attributes and features. It is cognitive in nature. It also has several variations. The following are its essential features: students work in teams to master academic materials, teams are made up of high, average and low achievers and are racially and sexually mixed, reward systems are group-oriented rather than individually oriented. (Arends, 1994, p. 344) Some of the variations are:

- ***Student Teams Achievement Divisions (STAD)*** where team members use work sheets or other study devices to master the academic materials and then help each other learn the material. Individually students take weekly quizzes and are given an "improvement score". This score is based on the degree to which the score exceeds a student's past average. Teams strive to get a good team improvement score.
- ***Jigsaw*** where each student on the team would be responsible to become 'an expert' in one aspect of the academic task and are responsible for teaching that aspect to the others. Members from different teams who are to be experts on the same topic meet to help each other learn their aspect of the task. They then return to their group to share what they learned and plan their presentation to the class.
- Group Investigation where students are involved in planning both the topics for study and the ways to proceed with their investigation. Students will choose a topic for study, proceed with an in-depth investigation of that topic and prepare and present a report to the whole class.

IT for Cooperative Learning

There are two types of technology that support Cooperative Learning. The first category includes those types of programmes that will provide the environment for collaboration. Included here are the types of software that we usually think of as tools:

Table 11.2: IT Tools and Examples

Tools	*Examples*
Word Processors	Word, WordPerfect
Spread Sheets	Excel, Lotus 1-2-3
Databases	Access, FoxPro
Drawing Programmes	Corel Draw, Paintbrush
Desktop Publishing Programmes	Microsoft Publisher, Print Shop
Script Writing Tools	Hollywood High, 3D Movie Maker
Multimedia Presentations	Power Point, Hyper Studio, Podium

Each of these tools provides the environment for students to produce a product that they can share with the class or publish in a newsletter to parents or publish on the World Wide Web (WWW) to the world. Learning content material, learning to work together and valuing each other for their multiple intelligence are all goals of cooperative learning that teachers can focus on in this environment.

There are many programmes that will provide the resources that students need to complete the research that is needed for class presentations. There are several very good multimedia encyclopedias (*World Book*, *Grolier's Interactive*, *Compton's Interactive*, *Encarta 97*, and *Britannica CD 97*). There are many informative CD's on a wide variety of subject areas, Medio's *JFK Investigation*, DK Multimedia's *The Way Things Work*, Mindscapes's *How Your Body Works.* These programmes can collect an enormous amount of information that is easily searched and copied into word processors for use as notes to share with fellow teammates.

The Internet is a resource of hundreds of thousands of documents on any subject imaginable. By using the search engines, Alta Vista or Yahoo, for example, a student can find much information on virtually any topic. Some instruction and class discussion on techniques for searching and evaluation of sources is needed to get the most of working in this environment. When we view our task of encouraging students to be lifelong learners, these become indispensable tools. The WWW is also a great resource for the pictures and sounds that go into making a great classroom presentation. The Lycos search engine has the capability to search the web for these resources.

(3) Use of IT in Resource Based Learning

Models of Learning Associated with Resource-Based Learning

Many educational psychologists found the behavioural and cognitive approaches unsatisfying. After rejection of these theories, a new theory "constructivism" came into existence. This approach is based on the work of educational philosopher John Dewey and educational psychologists Lev Vygotsky, Jean Piaget and Jerome Bruner. They propose that children actively construct knowledge and this construction of knowledge happens in a social context. Vygotsky proposed that all learning takes place in the 'zone of proximal development'. This 'zone' is the difference between what a child can do alone and what he can do with assistance. By building on the child's experience and providing moderately challenging tasks teachers can provide the 'intellectual scaffolding' to help children learn and progress through the different stages of development.

IT in Resource Based Learning

The methods of constructivism emphasize student's ability to solve real-life, practical problems. Students typically work in cooperative groups rather than individually; they tend to focus on focus on independent learning rather than on instructional sequences that require learning of certain content skills. The job of the teacher in constructivist models is to arrange for required resource and act as a guide to students while they set their own goals and 'teach themselves'. In this mode of use of computers, the role of the teachers has shifted away from the traditional role of content provider to one who provides scaffolds to enable students to learn from non-traditional sources such as from Internet and Electronic multimedia encyclopedia. The students themselves and not the teacher bear the responsibility for gathering and synthesizing the information. In this approach, the teacher steps out of the traditional role of 'content expert' or 'information giver' and instead lets the students find their own facts and information. The teacher in this approach acts as a 'facilitator', to help students get started to when they have problems. The general flow of events is as follows:

- The class examines a topic
- The teacher create questions about the topic
- Students find information about the questions
- Students organize their information and respond to the questions

Teachers and students both need to realize that both traditional as well as new (e.g., Internet) sources are valid places to look for information.

Higher Order thinking Skills Framework in Resource Based Learning

In this approach, there is an emphasis on inquiry learning. Traditional approaches bring us packaged information in neat parcels designed for easy student consumption. An inquiry based (or discovery) approach, however, requires that students enter the often messy and confusing "real world" to search for their answers. It is more challenging for students but it is also can lead to higher level thinking much more effectively than the "spoon-feeding" techniques. The Table 11.3 summarizes the contrasts between the traditional model and the resource-based learning model

Table 11.3: Differences between traditional model and resource based learning model (Rakes, 1996)

Traditional Model	*Resource Based Learning Model*
Teacher as "expert"	Teacher as facilitator
Textbook as source	Variety of sources
Focus on facts	Focus on questions
Information is packaged	Information is discovered
Emphasis on product	Emphasis on Process
Assessment is quantitative	Assessment is quantitative and qualitative

(4) Use of IT as Mind Tools

Jonassen and associates (Jonassen, Carr & Yueh, 1998; Jonassen, 1996) have been advocating the further use of computers for instruction. They argued that technologies should not be used only as instructing tools but as knowledge construction tools that students learn with. In other words, students should not just learn from the computer, which is used as a vehicle for delivering pre-packaged learning materials but to function like designers in manipulating data and information and the computers as tools for this process. Based on constructivist approaches to learning, students themselves are constructing knowledge as they go about exploring and using the IT tools. This is a move away from the traditional teaching and learning where the teachers "teach" the content and students will passively "receive" information. In using the computer and its software as a constructivist tool, the computer does not teach but provides the environment where students can "manipulate" data and information and thus enable the students to observe changes.

Jonassen (1996) identified many different kinds of software programmes that can be used by students and each different kind of tool will be suitable for different goals. He used the term "Mind tools" to describe various computer software such as spreadsheet and database applications, expert system shells, concept-mapping programmes, multimedia and hypermedia development software.

Mind tools imply a higher level of interaction between the students and their computers. Mind tools are also related to critical thinking or higher order thinking, because they can help people look more closely at issues and not make quick decisions. Instead, students can search the web, gather data, use spreadsheets to analyze and demonstrate that their conclusions are valid. Moreover, mind tools also fit well with another concept: Bloom's taxonomy.

Benjamin Bloom's taxonomy, comprised of six levels, or types, of learning, has been a model to help teachers construct test questions and learning activities. However, it has also become a touchstone for teachers examining the impact of learning on critical thinking (Teaching Using Bloom's Taxonomy, 2002). The first three items—knowledge, comprehension and application are sometimes referred to LOTS, or lower order thinking skills and the next three items—analysis, synthesis, and evaluation are called HOTS, or higher order thinking skills. While the lower order skills are important for building a foundation, it is the higher ones that need to be developed for overall problem solving skills, as well as to help prepare students for the work place. In addition, the concepts of designing real world tasks for students and constructing knowledge are hallmarks of the third concept influencing computer classrooms: constructivism.

Constructivism is an approach to teaching/learning that comes from the work of psychologists and educators like Bruner, Piaget, and Vygotsky: it stresses the need for learners to construct knowledge for themselves, and encourages reflection, authentic tasks and collaboration.

Constructivism reshapes classroom dynamics, focusing on students becoming active learners and teachers serving as facilitators. Along with the other changes, constructivist classrooms promote collaboration, communication, and cooperative learning (Connecting student learning, 1999). All of these contribute to creating a student-centered classroom where active learning occurs, as students work alone or with classmates to find information on a research question, ask questions about it, look for connections to previously discovered data, and determine whether or not their sources are valid. Communicating with each other and the teacher—using an online discussion board, for examples—leads to reflection, which helps students analyze their own learning.

Another feature of the constructivist classroom is the creation of opportunities for real world problem solving. An excellent example is provided by Hoffman and Scheidenhelm (2000), who present four reasons for using computers in education. Two of them address mind tools: first, that computers help students reflect on and solve problems, and second, that computers allow students to tackle more complex problems (p. 12).

Using Bloom's Taxonomy to Make Software Choices

Table 11.4 shows the computer tasks and tools to that are fit into the Bloom's taxonomy.

(5) Use of IT in Creative Projects

Self-made multimedia projects could be used from within two different approaches:

Multimedia as an Instructive Tool

One is as an instructive tool where students learn some content through a multimedia presentation created by the teacher (e.g., using some multimedia creation software such as Power Point by Microsoft or Director by Macromedia). This kind of approach has become increasingly common in classroom settings.

Table 11.4: Bloom's Taxonomy and Software Choices

Bloom's Category	*Key Words and Example of a Computer Task*	*Level in the Hierarchy*	*Software tool/ product*
Knowledge (Finding out)	Recall, Name Define spreadsheet in a word-processed sentence.	Lowest (LOTS)	Internet search, Table, Word document
Comprehension (Understanding)	Summarize, Discuss Give an example of a way to use a spreadsheet.	Middle (LOTS)	Internet search, Word document
Application (Making use of the knowledge)	Demonstrate, Solve Open Excel and create a simple budget in a spreadsheet.	Top (LOTS)	Excel Spreadsheet
Analysis (Taking apart the known)	Compare data, See patterns Manipulate the spreadsheet to see how quickly car loan can be paid off if payments are doubled.	Lowest (HOTS)	Excel spreadsheet, Word table, Access database
Synthesis (Putting things together in another way)	Combine elements, Create Go back to the spreadsheet and reduce amount for miscellaneous expenses and increase loan payment, plus set aside savings.	Middle (HOTS)	Excel spreadsheet, Word table, Access database query
Evaluation (Judging outcomes)	Judge, Criticize, Defend Based on your evaluation of the two budgets, write a couple of paragraphs defending the revised budget.	Highest (HOTS)	Database query, Word table, Word document

Multimedia as a Constructive Tool

It requires that the students themselves create their own multimedia programme or presentation. In this approach, the students are expected to build sophisticated presentations to communicate some rich content. These projects can take many forms, with the teacher assuming whatever degree of technical management necessary (for software and hardware): from very high teacher software control (such as is necessary for lower primary students) to very high student independence (when students are very comfortable with software). In both cases, however, the teacher still adopts a facilitative role during the learning process. That is, the teacher may need to directly help the students with the multimedia development software but it is the students who make most of the decisions for the content and design.

The constructivist approach to teaching is gaining momentum. Educators have realized that for students to be successful in the twenty first century they need to be lifelong learners. Helping them to develop the skills necessary to become lifelong learners requires a different approach to teaching and learning. The direct instruction method that was used almost exclusively in the earlier part of this century, though still effective for some skills, is giving way to a more cooperative approach. The use of direct instruction is useful for the acquisition of basic skills and key concepts but does not promote higher order cognitive processing. The use of IT in resource-based learning is a good and easy start to constructivist approach to learning. One that involves students working together toward common goals, teachers serving as 'experts', and coaches, and facilitators, and sometimes just plain getting out of the way and letting students discover things for themselves. What is technology's role in this movement? It is supporting the choices that teachers make every step of the way by providing the environment, the content, the experiment, and the place for students to 'put it all together' to share with other students, parents, and the world.

12
Computer Aided Laboratory Experimentation

After studying this chapter, the reader will be able to: Comprehend the different goals for laboratory experimentation; Analyze the current laboratory practices; Understand the role of computers in the laboratory; Describe the application of computers in laboratory organization and management activities; Describe the application of computers in pre-laboratory activities; Describe the application of computers in laboratory activities; Describe the application of computers in post-laboratory activities; Understand the main functions of coordination for computer aided instruction laboratory; List the main duties of the computer aided instruction laboratory coordinator; Identify the minimum qualifications of the CAI laboratory coordinator; Discuss the computer lab related activities; Discuss the person related activities

Every field of knowledge can be divided into its two parts: theoretical knowledge and practical knowledge. Therefore, *Theoretical Knowledge + Practical Knowledge = Complete Knowledge.* Here, one question is arises in our mind that, what is knowledge? The answer of this question is that- "knowledge is the structure of theories, laws, facts, principles, etc". Theoretical knowledge of every subject contains all these facts, theories, laws, principles, etc. For a clear understanding with the subject, theoretical knowledge is compulsory but we can't fully understand the subject without practical knowledge because practical knowledge is helpful to test the theoretical knowledge and for generating the new knowledge of that subject. So, laboratory or experimentation practice for each subject is very important and it is helpful to make the knowledge and experiences life long and permanent.

Goals of Laboratory Experimentation

The main goal of the laboratory experimentation or practice is to provide students with good practical hand and analytical mind. The conventional laboratory working is routine and boring and is a mere formality in the eyes of students. It leaves no choice and provides practically no degrees of freedom to them for the creativity and to test their innovative ideas. They feel that the existing system allows them to follow the mechanical ways of performing the experiments only. The subject does not emerge from their within.

The main goals of the science laboratory are as follows:

***Goal I*:** The Art of Experimentation: The introductory laboratory should engage each student in significant experiences with experimental processes, including some experience designing investigation.

For many students an early experience with a stimulating scientific process in which they control the steps of an investigation can be a critical "turn-on" to science. Students completing the introductory laboratory should understand that science is an experimental in nature and that observation and experimentation are as important as concepts and theories. To achieve this goal, the following considerations are important:

- A conscious distinction should be made between laboratory exercises and lecture demonstrations on the one hand and laboratory experiments on the other hand. The former provide critical experience with phenomena under the control of the instructor, whereas in the later case, student decisions on how to design and conduct the experiment influence its outcome.
- Laboratory investigations should encourage students to add some of their own ideas to experiments and their interpretation. Even in conventional investigations, instructors can "programme in" unexpected surprises and applaud those special moments when students achieve intellectual discoveries or develop experimental techniques on their own.
- Laboratory investigations should engage students in the process of formulating and asking an interesting question of nature. Students then select the methods and apparatus needed to make progress toward finding an answer. A portion of each laboratory course can be reserved for student-designed projects. With guidance and monitoring by faculty and teaching assistants, these projects can provide a creative climax to a laboratory course. Careful planning can make this a viable option even in large laboratory sections and programmes.

***Goal II*:** Experimental and Analytical Skills: The laboratory practice should help the student to develop a broad array of basic skills and tools of experimental physics and data analysis.

While it is imperative that students have a broad experience with techniques using laboratory equipment, it is impossible to prescribe precisely which equipment should be used in all introductory laboratory courses. The learning objectives of each laboratory experiment should determine the equipment to be used. At the same time, it is advisable to have students use many different types of basic laboratory apparatus to make observations.

Computers, when used as flexible tools in the hands of students for the collection, analysis and graphical display of data, can accelerate the rate at which student can acquire data, abstract and generalize from real experience with natural phenomena. The digital computer is an important tool for an inquiry-based course in science because it has become the most universal tool of inquiry in scientific research. However, computer simulations should not be used as substitutes for direct experience with science apparatus. Students should have experience in analyzing experimental results at various levels of sophistication, ranging from purely qualitative to highly quantitative. Students should be able to graph data and describe the relationships between quantities both in their own words and in terms of the mathematical relationship between the variables. Students should understand the uncertainty associated with measurement and the distinction between experimental uncertainties and mistakes in reading or recording information. Students should learn enough about uncertainties to understand the inherent limitations of measurement processes.

***Goal III*:** Conceptual Learning: The laboratory work should help student's master basic science concepts.

A growing body of research in science education indicates that a majority of students have difficulty learning basic science concepts in a course built around traditional lectures, textbook problems and verification experiments [Arons, A.B. (1990) & McDermott, L.C. (1993)]. These studies indicate that for improved leaning, students must actively confront difficult concepts. Effective learning may also be assisted by close interaction of students with their peers in this process. The laboratory can be an excellent environment for active learning [Laws, P.W. (1991)].

The laboratory has long been considered useful to develop conceptual understanding, but some recent courses have been developed that rely heavily on laboratory experience, in contrast to lecture, for the primary development of conceptual understanding of science. In such programmes conceptually oriented laboratory experiences may constitute a portion of the laboratory programme, the entire laboratory programme, or the entire course. The use of computers with laboratory interfaces allows real-time recording and graphing of physical quantities. The qualitative use of real-time graphing in microcomputer-based laboratories (MBL) has increased interest in using the laboratory to enhance conceptual understanding. The combination of two factors—laboratory course design based on an understanding of the preconceptions students bring to the study of science from their past experience and the continuing development of MBL and other laboratory technology-has the potential to significantly improve the effectiveness of laboratory instruction.

***Goal IV*:** Understanding the Basis of Knowledge in science: The laboratory should help students understand the role of direct observation in physics and to distinguish between inferences based on theory and the outcomes of experiments.

Science is a complex structure of concepts, hypotheses, theories and observations that are interrelated in such a way that it is often difficult to separate inferences based on theory from direct observations based primarily on laboratory experiments [Rothman, M. (1972)]. Students should understand that experimental evidence is the basis of our knowledge of the laws of science and that science is not merely a collection of equations and textbook problems.

The majority of students enrolled in both the high school and college level do not have sufficient concrete experience with everyday phenomena to understand the subtle interplay between observation and the construction of science theories. The processes of observing phenomena, analyzing data, and developing qualitative verbal models and mathematical models to explain observations afford students a unique opportunity to relate concrete experience to scientific tneories [Feynman, R.P. (1964)].

***Goal V*:** Developing Collaborative Learning Skills: The laboratory should help students develop collaborative learning skills that are vital to success in many lifelong endeavors.

Specific attention should be given to the quality of the small-group collaborations in introductory science laboratory programmes.

Current Laboratory Practices

In order to understand how computers can contribute to improving the laboratory practice, an examination of the current laboratory practice to identify its drawbacks and causes are essential. Today, we have old fashion, outdated and routine laboratory functioning. The students are more interested in the result as the teacher also stress on this, irrespective of the fact that the working instruments and the materials are of low quality. If a student fails to complete the experiment on to the scheduled date, is forced to go on the next experiment. The teacher usually does not pay any attention on his problems. Possibly, because of tight laboratory schedule. In this way, he proceeds without any understanding. Lack of understanding makes him disinterested in the lab-work. Further, there is no scope for the students to use their creative instinct. If some students observe something new, the teachers discourage them, as they usually want their students to finish their course first.

There are many drawbacks of traditional or current laboratory practices as follows:

- Impracticable teacher-student ratio.

- Teacher's concentration is on completing the syllabus in a required time period and less on the skills development.
- Students' lack of knowledge in design of the experiments.
- Results are rarely analyzed.
- No discussion occurs on the results of the experiment.
- No discussion occurs on the applications or improvements in the experimental design.
- Problem of copying and manipulation of the results.
- Results are merely checked for its correctness.
- At the end of the experimentation the student does not know what skills he should have mastered during the performance of the experiment.
- Mechanical process.
- Emphasis is on the product not on the process.

Computers in the Laboratory

Computers may be utilized to overcome some of the above-mentioned problems/situations and make the laboratory practice effective to the student and the whole educational system. The entry of the computers in the laboratory can change the picture of the traditional laboratory practices. It can shift the old fashion, outdated and routine laboratory functioning into active, demanding, skillful and meaningful laboratory functioning. The application of the computer for laboratory work can be classified into four distinct stages:

Application of Computer in Laboratory Organization and Management Activities

For successful laboratory experimentation, a teacher's first job is to organize and manage the laboratory classes. For completing this job, a teacher performs different kinds of activities. Computers help considerably in the process by automating the following activities of the teacher or in other words we can say that with the help of the computer, a teacher can make the above activities interesting and automating.

- Teacher can prepare in detail a list of working, non-working apparatus and equipments.
- The teacher for allotting different types of experiments to the students can prepare a computerized list.
- Student's work and progress can be checked by the teacher with the help of the computerized data and previous records stored on in the computer.
- The teacher can obtain a soft copy or hard copy showing records of the individual learner at any time.
- Student's record can be stored in the computer for future purposes.

- Computerized records of the students on the different experimentation can be helpful for the teacher in decision-making about the learner.

Application of Computes in Pre-Laboratory Activities

In conventional laboratory practices, students go to the laboratory without serious preparation. It is real fact that if you do not know, where are you going? Why are you going? Then you cannot reach your destination successfully. Similarly, if the student does not know what experiment is he going to do?, what are the aims and objectives of the experimentation?, what types of previous knowledge, experiences and skills are required for that practical?, what are the experimental designs to extend the lab work?, what is the experimental process and what apparatus amd equipments should be used to conduct the experiment, then the student cannot successful in the process of experimentation. In other words, the whole educational system will be fail. The computer may use in the pre-laboratory activities discussed above, which are to be carried out by the student before the actual laboratory work in the following manner

Computer can be used to familiarizing the student with:

- Objectives of the experiment (in behavioural term)
- Skills to be acquired during the experiment
- Previous knowledge, experiences and skills required for conducting the experiment
- Necessary precautions during the experimentation
- Experimental design for the experiment
- Experimental setup and equipments to be used
- Experimental procedure and steps involved during the experiment
- Possible errors involved in measurement
- Background theory of the experiment
- Necessary equipments and apparatus
- Recording of observation
- Necessary calculations
- Interpretation of the results
- Reporting of the experimentation
- Pictorial representation of the results

One important question arises here that the textbook or laboratory manuals can perform the above functions of the computer, then why there is a need to add computer for this purpose. The answer of this question is that the important functions such as: design of experiment, the procedure of conduction the experiment, familiarization with the experimental setup and equipments can be done more effectively with the help of the computer through its fast operating speed, animation graphics, and data retrieval. Figure 12.1 illustrates the role of the computer in pre-laboratory work.

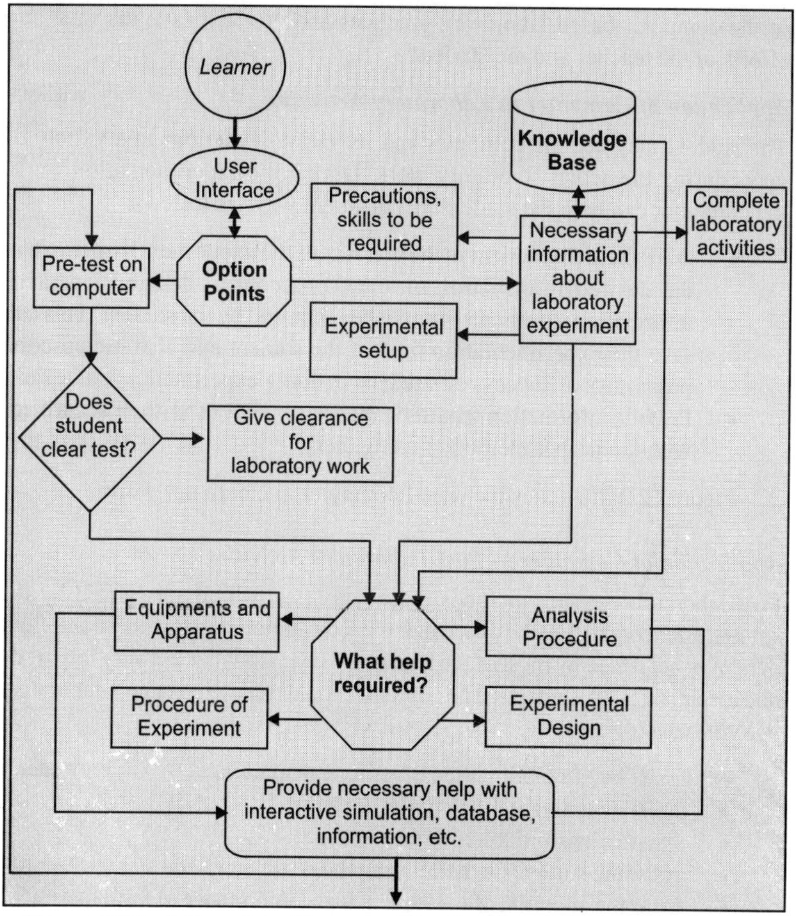

Figure 12.1: A Complete Diagram of Applications of Computers in Pre-Laboratory Activities

Are You Prepare for the Laboratory Work?

An important thing is to remember here is that with the help of the computer we can only prepare students for the laboratory work. After this preparation, the students will experiment in the actual (real) laboratory. But the question is how a teacher identify that these students less with necessary knowledge and skills. For this purpose, the computer may administer a pre-test on the student to examine the student preparedness to conduct the required laboratory work. If the student fails to clear the test, the computer assists the student to learn the required aspect. The student may be permitted to proceed with the actual laboratory work only after clearing the pre-test. This is an important function of the computer-based laboratory practices and this will save the time and efforts of the teacher and the student.

Application of Computer in Laboratory Activities

The student may use the computer and its various functions in a variety of ways during the actual laboratory work. During the experimentation work, the computer can help the student in a different ways as follows:

- guide/help the student in the conduct of the experiment by providing the desired information on data, procedures, design, necessary information, formulae as and when required by the student. This can save the experimentation time of the student and also increase the possibility of success of students in doing experiment.
- Provide information regarding the instruments used, their accuracies with the proper method of using them.

Figure 12.2 illustrates the use of computer in laboratory work.

Application of Computer in Post-Laboratory Activities

Post laboratory session includes those activities, which are carried by the student after conduction the experiment. In conventional setting these activities generally neglected by most of the teachers. These activities are very important and essential for the students. The computer could be utilized in post-laboratory activities as follows:

- assist in completing the necessary calculations
- assist in analyzing the obtained results
- assist in interpretation of the results
- assist the students in comparing the results with the standard results
- focus the attention of the student to the importance of the experiment, applications and the implications of the investigation

Figure 12.3: illustrates the use of computers in post-laboratory activities.

Coordinator for Computer Aided Instruction Laboratory

For smoothly functioning of the computer-aided laboratory experimentation in the schools, there is a need to appoint a person as a coordinator of the laboratory, who is capable to doing this job. The lab coordinator is much more responsible for the effective functioning of the computer-aided laboratory, because the main functions of the coordinator are:

- to supervise a computer-aided instruction laboratory
- to organize, schedule and assist in evaluating a variety of laboratory activities

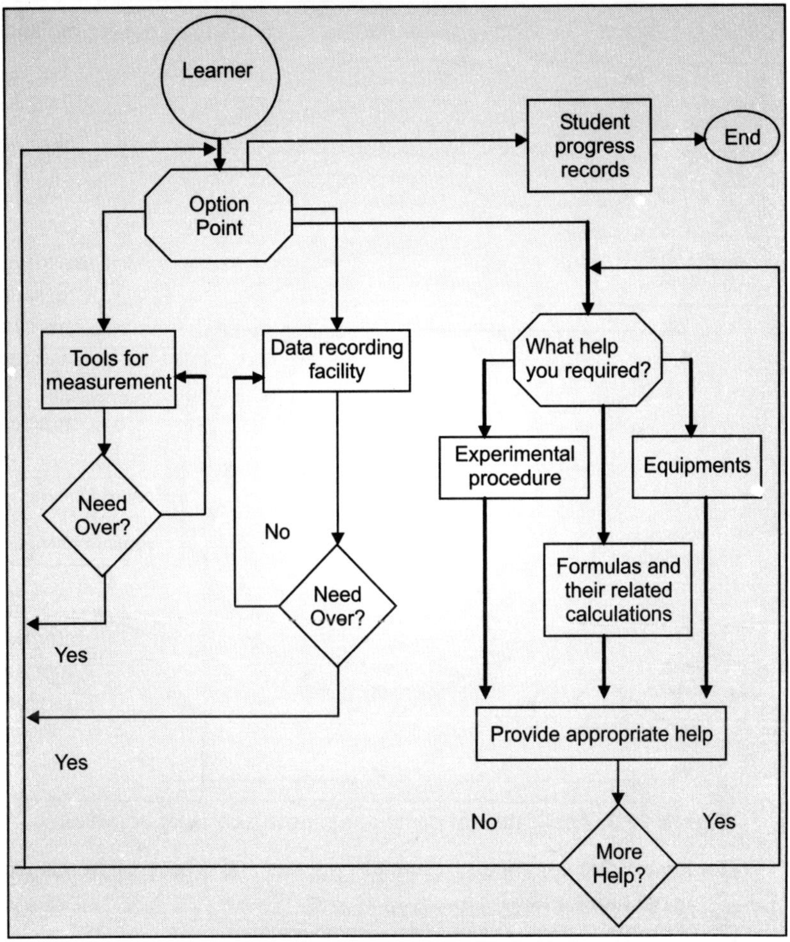

Figure 12.2: Application of Computers in Laboratory Activities

- to provide tutoring services to students in the discipline assigned
- to assist instructors with laboratory teaching exercises
- to provide a wide range of technical, supervisory and paraprofessional assistant to students, faculty and tutors.

Main Duties of the Computer Aided Instruction Laboratory Coordinator

The main duties of the CAI laboratory coordinator are given below:

(1) Coordinate and supervise the laboratory activities, including monitoring computer network software and hardware operating status.

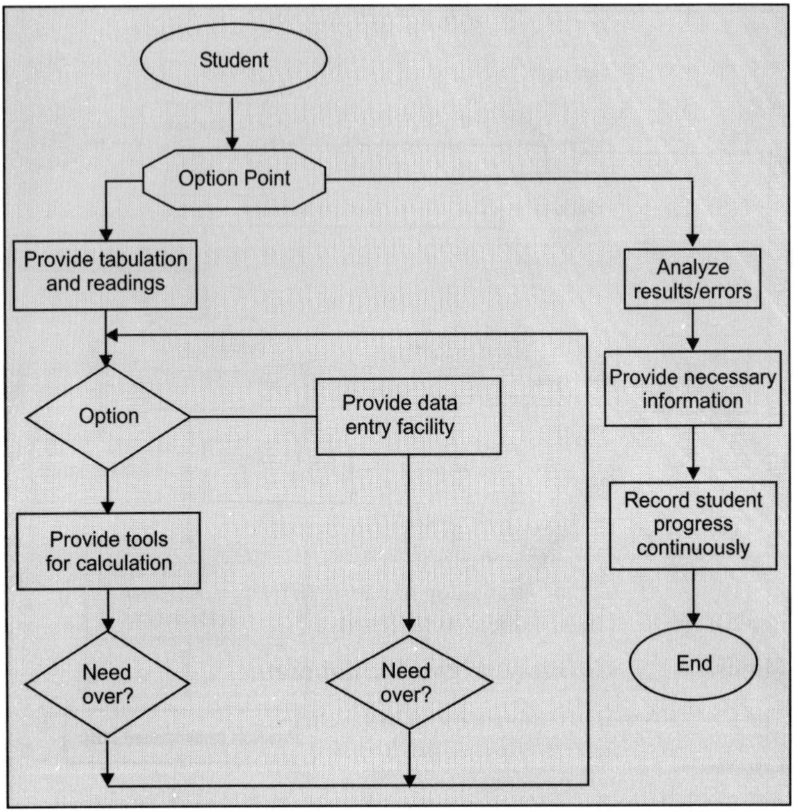

Figure 12.3: Application of computer in post-laboratory activities

(2) Ensure that computers, terminals, printers and other peripherals are in operating order.
(3) Perform minor maintenance when necessary.
(4) Report and document equipment problems or failures.
(5) Supervise and tutor students in the use of the laboratory facilities and in the areas in which the students need assistance.
(6) Identify student needs and determine remediation plans for students with weaknesses in the assigned subject are.
(7) Advise students on study methods and learning strategies.
(8) Assist in developing and monitoring the budget for the laboratory and develop record keeping systems and statistical reports as assigned.
(9) Select, train, supervise and evaluate student assistants and/or tutors; check student time cards for accuracy and turn into payroll.
(10) Assist in the administration of laboratory assignments, exercises and

tests under the direction of an instructor or other certificated staff member.

(11) Meet with faculty in order to be familiar with their lesson plans and expectations for student competencies.

(12) Create and maintain student and faculty computer files; ensure that only authorized persons are using the computer equipment.

(13) Supervise student computer operations and provide students with assistance and training in the operation of the computers and other laboratory equipment.

(14) Assist in the training of faculty and tutors in the use of the laboratory equipment and facilities.

(15) Refer telephone inquiries to appropriate resources.

(16) Maintain a reference library and files of resource material for faculty and student use.

(17) Assist in the design, development and implementation of software to monitor and improve the effectiveness of the laboratory.

(18) Assist in the preparation of instructional aids to be used by students or faculty in the laboratory.

(19) Assist with the orientation of part-time faculty.

(20) Perform related duties as assigned.

Minimum Qualifications of the CAI Laboratory Coordinator

The CAI laboratory coordinator should have the

Knowledge of

- Laboratory equipment, materials, supplies and procedures as used in the subject area laboratory.
- Principles, practices and applications of the assigned subject material at the level of the course taught in the school.
- Principles and operations of the computer equipment and software utilized in the laboratory.

Skills to

- Perform a variety of instructional assistance, tutoring and related support functions within the academic subject area assigned.
- Select, train, supervise and evaluate student assistants, hourly clerical support and tutors.
- Assists students in understanding the basic fundamentals of the subject area assigned.
- Operate, configure, troubleshoot and demonstrate the use of computers and other equipment in the laboratory.
- Analyze the laboratory procedures and make constructive suggestions

for improvement.
- Develop and maintain record keeping systems for the laboratory.
- Communicate effectively and tactfully, both orally and in writing.
- Understand and carry out both oral and written instructions.
- Organize, coordinate and schedule a variety of laboratory activities.
- Establish and maintain effective work relationships with those contacted in the performance of required duties.

Experience and Training

Any combination of experience and training that would likely provide the required knowledge and skills is qualifying. A typical way to obtain the knowledge and skills would be:

Experience

- Work experience in the operation and maintenance of a computer-assisted teaching laboratory.
- Work experience as a tutor in the assigned subject at the level taught at the school.
- Minimum two year of work experience in operating computers to those used in the laboratory assigned.
- Experience in the field of CAI/CAL.

Education

- Equivalent to an associate degree in the subject assigned, supplemented by course work and/or training in computers comparable to those in the assigned laboratory.

Work Models for CAI Laboratory

The CAI laboratory coordinator (or teacher) should have the knowledge that what kinds of activities he will do in the laboratory from beginning to the end of the school session. These activities are the guidelines for the coordinator, which can help a coordinator for effective functioning in the lab. Below we are given three work models for CAI laboratory activities under two categories: computer lab related activities and person related activities.

Computer Lab Related Activities

Model I: Programme Planning and Preparation

Computer Lab Duties

1. Prepare computer lab for use at the beginning of the school year.
2. Organize computer lab materials to be used: computer disks, documentation and manuals, computer software catalogs, computer magazines and supplies (stationary, etc.).

Administrative Duties

1. Develop or assist in developing a yearly plan for making computer lab programme improvements (new hardware upgrading, etc.)
2. Handle computer lab finances and improvements.

- Manage computer lab budget.
- Select or assist in selecting new computer software.
- Order or assist in ordering computer software.
- Select or assist in selecting new computer hardware.
- Order or assist in ordering computer hardware.
- Obtain or order supplies.
- Establish content and schedule of computer lab related reports (on status of lab, computer software, inventory, budget, etc.).

Model II: Training and Learning

Computer System Management

1. Engage in continuing education in the areas of: (a) computer hardware, including upgrades and new technologies and (b) computer software, including new versions and products.
2. Attend technology, in-service meetings, workshops, seminars, etc.

Model III: Computer Lab Administration and Operation

Computer System Management

1. Manage user accounts on file server (networked computers).
    - Add new accounts (register new students on network system).
    - Delete unused accounts.
2. Open the computer lab at the beginning of the school day.
    - Unlock the computer lab room.
    - Start the system (networked computers).
    - Have students turn on computers in appropriate manner (stand-alone computers).
3. Manage computer files.
    - Be able to locate files.
    - Add data or records to files.
    - Edit files.
    - Delete data or records from files.
    - Make file backups.
4. Communicate with others using telecommunication tools (e-mail, etc.).
5. Maintain security.
    - Protect confidentiality of student records.
    - Provide safe storage for computer software master disks.

- Prevent the introduction of viruses to the system or disks.
- Introduce measures to avoid system break-ins (Provide effective passwords, restrict physical access, etc.).

6. Close the computer lab at the end of the day.
   - Shut down the system (networked computers).
   - Have students turn off their computers in appropriate manner (stand-alone computers).
   - Lock up the computer lab room.
7. Install new computer software and updates on stand-alone computer or network hard drives.
8. Change directory setup if necessary.
9. Duplicate computer disks as needed (backups, computer software where licensing agreement permits copying).
10. Handle computer hardware maintenance.
    - Maintain hard drive(s) for stand-alone computers or network system.
    - Organize files on hard drive.
    - Delete unnecessary or corrupted files.
    - Compress or defragment files (Use a computer programme designed to group files together on hard drive. File access time is improved).
    - Rebuild desktop periodically on individual computer if appropriate.
    - Conduct computer hardware maintenance (other than hard drive maintenance) (Change printer ribbon or cartridge, etc.).
    - Clean computer hardware (monitor, keyboard, disk drive, headphones, mouse, printer, etc.) in proper manner.
11. Handle computer software and hardware failure.
    - Identify computer software and hardware problems.
    - Apply solutions to common computer software and hardware problems.
    - Make computer software support calls for assistance with software problems.
    - Arrange for computer hardware repairs.

Computer Lab Duties

1. Provide computer lab displays: bulletin boards, posters and charts.
2. Maintain a neat and orderly computer lab room.

Deal with special situations: power outage, fire, earthquake, bomb threat, drills, etc.

Administrative Duties

1. *Keep lab records*: warranties, computer hardware serial numbers, documentation of network organization, description of standard network functioning and log of network problems.
2. Provide computer lab related reports (on status of lab, computer software, inventory, budget, etc.).
   - Create reports.
   - Deliver reports.

Person Related Activities

Model I: Programme Planning and Preparation

[Person: Teacher]

Communications and Interactions

1. Discuss schedule for groups and individuals.
2. Discuss long-range instructional plan.
3. Establish teacher's role in computer class (participation or non-participation).
4. Establish content and schedule of reports on student achievement and activity.

[Person: Students]

Instruction

1. Handle introductory business.
   - Assign user passwords.
   - Assign student seating.

Behaviour Management

1. Introduce lab rules and procedures.

Evaluation

1. Establish student records (attendance, instructional progress, test scores, etc.).
2. Determine current level of student knowledge and skills at the beginning of the year.

[Person: Assistants]

Lab Assistance

1. Obtain assistants for the new school year: students, parents and volunteers.

[Person: Visitors]

Lab Visits

1. Establish policy for dealing with unscheduled visitors: students too early for scheduled classes, friends of students in class, etc.

Model II: Training and Learning

[Person: Teacher]

Communications and Interactions

1. Provide teachers with information regarding available software.
2. Provide in-service for faculty on computer-related issues.
3. Assist teachers with computer-related questions.

[Person: Students]

Instruction

1. Develop lesson plans.
   - Identify instructional objectives.
   - Determine instructional strategies.
   - Decide upon computer software to be used.
   - Plan individualized or group lesson assignments.
   - Determine instructional aids or material needed.
2. Obtain or prepare instructional aids: charts, transparencies, student work examples, etc.
3. Obtain or prepare student materials (worksheets, information pages, etc.) to be used in lessons.
4. Introduce instructional units or programmes (overview, instructional objectives).
5. Instruct students, using instructional software, applications programmes, etc.
6. Adjust instruction where possible to meet individual learning requirements.
7. Answer student questions and assist as needed.

[Person: Assistants]

Lab Assistance

1. Train assistants

Model III: Computer Lab Administration and Operation

[Person: Teacher]

Communication and Interactions

1. Handle re-scheduling and cancellations.
2. Discuss short-range instructional plan.

3. Coordinate computer lab instruction with classroom instruction (so that classroom instruction is reinforced).
4. Facilitate implementation of teacher's role in the computer lab.
5. Report on student achievement and activity.
   - Provide reports on students (software system with report generating capability).
   - Generate reports.
   - Deliver reports.
   - Discuss reports with teachers.
   - Advise teachers regarding students (software system with no report generating capability).

[Person: Students]

Behaviour Management

1. Monitor student activity.
   - Make certain that the right student is at the right station.
   - Make certain that students on the right lesson.
   - Monitor for cheating and other irregular activities.
   - Monitor for proper use of computer software and hardware.
2. Recognize and encourage positive student behaviour.
3. Deal with student misbehaviour.

Evaluation

1. Assess student progress (tests, quizzes).
2. Maintain student records (attendance, instructional progress, test scores, etc.).
3. Assign report card grades for computer lab class.

[Person: Assistants]

Lab Assistance

1. Work with assistants.
   - Schedule assistant time.
   - Supervise assistants.

[Person: Visitors]

Lab Visits

1. Conduct tours and demonstrations of the computer lab.
2. Deal with unscheduled visitors.
3. Meet with parents of students at: parent-teacher meetings, computer lab open houses, etc.

13
Computer Assisted Assessment

After studying this chapter, the reader will be able to: Understand the assessment in relation to the pedagogical perspectives (Behaviourism, Cognitivism and Constructivism); Define computer-assisted assessment (CAA); Discuss types of computer-assisted assessment; List the advantages of computer-assisted assessment; List the limitations of computer-assisted assessment; Define objective tests; Comprehend different types of questions used in objective tests; Acquaint the parts of an objective test question; Discuss the pedagogical issues related to objective type tests; Know that what types of learning can be tested using objective tests; Define question banks; Define optical mark readers; List the advantages and disadvantages of optical mark readers; Tell how to implement tests; Know the security in testing students; Define feedback and guessing in assessment process; Describe the technique of assessment of students' abilities in cooperative and collaborative learning environment; Discuss the methods of assessment of students' abilities and traits in cooperative and collaborative learning environment

Assessment is an important element of the curriculum design and therefore, its inclusion is critical. It measures learner's depth of understanding of concepts and their ability to apply them in real world situations. One of the main focuses of instruction today is to instill in learners the skill of learning how to learn; for this, assessment has to be largely diagnostic and formative in order to assess learners while the learning is actually taking place rather than after it has taken place as it is normally done in traditional settings.

Further, assessment instruments and activities should be congruent with learning objectives, enable learners to assess their progress, to identify areas for immediate review and even fine tune learning objectives to accommodate the special needs, characteristics and situation of individual learners. Laurillard (2002) argues that innovative learning and teaching must be matched by innovations in assessment.

The three pedagogical perspectives (Behaviourism, Cognitivism and Constructivism) emphasize different aspects on what should be measured and how:

Behaviourism and Assessment: The behaviourist approach focuses on the assessment of accurate reproduction of knowledge and skills.

Cognitivism/Constructivism and Assessment: The cognitive/constructivist view emphasizes the assessment of broad conceptual understanding, participation, extended performance, and excellent performance through recognition. It also promotes the assessment of process as well as outcome through varied methods such as self and peer assessments.

Situativism and Assessment: The situative perspective emphasizes assessing participation and authenticity of practice. Both cognitive and situative perspectives advocate varied assessment methods, including teacher assessment, peer assessment, self-assessment, online portfolios of student work and reflection

Using new technology, students can obtain just-in-time rich feedback, make corrections to their work and structure learning experiences around their individual needs; assessment can focus more on building feedback loops directly into the learning process. In a web-based blended approach, assessment can be easily administered more frequently, and it can be ongoing and cumulative.

Computer-Assisted Assessment (CAA)

It is late in the evening and Pallavi has just finished studying a chapter on the elasticity of demand in a free-market economy. She has worked through a couple of example calculations at the end of the chapter and has re-read the relevant lecture notes but is still unsure whether she has really grasped the topic. She uses the PC in her study bedroom to log in to the course's Website and selects the self-test on 'elasticity of demand'.

The computer presents her with ten questions, which she must answer within 30 minutes. Some are simple and just require him to select the right answer from a list, but others are much more complex and need careful thought and some calculation. She finishes with 5 minutes to spare and clicks the Submit Test button. Within a few seconds he sees his score (58% - OK, but not that good) and a page of feedback on his answers. She prints this out and decides that another hour or so of study tomorrow should sort out any problems so that when she takes the test again his score will meet his personal goal of 70 per cent

This story highlights many of the features that make computer-assisted assessment (CAA) a powerful educational tool in the right circumstances:

- on-demand formative testing;
- access from anyplace at anytime;
- instant marking and automated feedback

What is CAA?

Computer-assisted assessment (CAA) is a common term for the use of computers in the assessment of student learning. Various other terms are used, such as computer-aided assessment, computerised assessment, computer-based assessment (CBA) and computer-based testing. These terms are largely interchangeable.

CAA encompasses the use of computers to:

- deliver, mark and analyse assignments or examinations
- collate and analyse data gathered from paper forms, using an optical mark reader (OMR) with hard copy question paper and an OMR-readable answer form
- record, analyse and report on achievement
- collate, analyse and transfer assessment information through networks

CAA is generally used for objective testing. An objective test is one in which each question is designed to have an unequivocally correct answer or set of answers. In contrast a subjective test, for which there is no uniquely correct answer, examines the ability of the student to respond clearly and develop an argument. The multiple-choice question (MCQ) is the most commonly used type of objective question. While objective tests are used largely to test knowledge and comprehension, with careful design they can also asses higher learning outcomes such as the application of knowledge and analytical skills.

Because they can be marked quickly and easily and can cover a wide range of course content, objective tests are particularly appropriate for informal self-assessment to give students ongoing feedback about their progress. They can be used in this way throughout an undergraduate course or prior to a course or section of course for students to test their own ability and suitability. For formal assessment, however, their contribution to final marks is likely to decline as student progress through their degree programmes and the range of abilities being examined becomes more comprehensive and demanding.

CAA software can provide immediate supportive feedback for each question, tailored to the answer given, making this particularly suitable for informal self-assessment. Superior graphical and visualization exercises can also be included with the use of multimedia files such as graphics, sound and video clips. Most software offers a facility for reporting results and analyzing student responses.

Types of CAA

There are three main methods of delivering tests that make use of CAA – paper based, computer based and web-based tests.

Paper-based Tests

Paper based tests usually involve a traditional exam setting, with students sitting at desks in a classroom or hall. Students receive a question paper, an answer sheet and instructions on how to complete the answer sheet.

A typical question paper would contain around sixty questions to be answered in an hour, depending upon the degree of difficulty of the questions. In a multiple choice test the body text of each question, or stem, is followed by a number of possible response options of which only one, the key, is correct. The incorrect options are known as distracters.

It is essential that the distracters have some degree of plausibility or else they are not worth including as part of the question. One of the most important features of a good multiple-choice question (MCQ) is that it has good distracters.

It is not possible to suggest an optimum number of options for a MCQ, but it is worth noting that too few options makes guessing easier and that too many makes the construction of good distracters difficult.

Answer papers usually contain a series of options, often labelled A to E, for each question. Examination candidates are required to make horizontal marks through the options of their choice in much the same way that a National Lottery ticket is completed. Completed papers are collected and fed into a scanner to be marked by Optical Mark Recognition (OMR). OMR software reads and marks each question for each paper. Detailed reports are automatically produced and this allows analysis of student understanding of items of knowledge. It is perhaps this analysis, which is one of the major benefits of CAA.

It is extremely important that the instructions to students are clear, precise and unambiguous. OMR will recognize and reject papers that have not been completed correctly. These papers may then have to be hand marked, and would not figure in reports produced by the system. OMR will also identify individual questions that appear to have been marked incorrectly – for example by registering more than one mark or no mark at all. The member of staff operating the OMR can then make a visual check of the question and when the intended response is absolutely clear manually input this into the system.

Good instructions to students, both written and verbal, considerably reduce the need for manual intervention. When OMR is to be used for summative assessment it is preferable that students are first given the opportunity to complete an answer sheet under trial conditions.

Computer-based Tests

Computer based tests can be delivered via floppy disk, CD ROM, hard disk or local network. Students are required to sit at a PC, questions appear on the monitor and responses are input using the mouse or keyboard.

Students may receive immediate feedback either after each question, which is particularly useful for formative assessment, or on completion of the assessment. Tests are marked instantaneously and results are added to a report file.

A group of students can sit a test in a computer laboratory, and, for a networked system, a lecturer in another part of the institution can access these results as soon as the test is completed. This form of assessment, which receives little or no manual input once the tests have been input into the system, is more commonly referred to as Computer Based Assessment (CBA).

One advantage of CBA is that the technology allows the use of multimedia. Graphics, sound, animation and video can all be used to good effect. As well as enhancing the presentation of questions this can also help in constructing questions to test higher order skills.

Web-based Tests

Web-based tests can offer all of the advantages of computer based tests with the additional facility of allowing the user to access the test from any PC connected to the World Wide Web. This is particularly useful for distance learning. For formative assessment students with an Internet connection can access the tests from their own homes at their own convenience.

For summative assessment this can allow students from different parts of the world to take the same test at the same time.

Additionally, web-based tests allow links and access to all of the resources available via the World Wide Web, and this can be used to good effect for formative assessment.

One slight disadvantage is that feedback is not as immediate as with computer-based tests.

For this reason feedback is generally given at the end of the test rather than at the end of a question. As technology advances it is unlikely that this will be a consideration in the not too distant future.

With a little training it is possible to write multiple-choice tests for delivery over the World Wide Web using Javascript. There are however, a number of systems, both commercial and non-commercial, which make the authoring of web-based tests much simpler.

Use of CAA

The following are the three main types of assessments for which CAA is used:

Diagnostic – tests, which are taken to determine a student's prior knowledge of a subject.

Formative – assessments which assist learning by giving feedback, which indicates how the student is progressing in terms of knowledge, skills and understanding of a subject. In CAA, this often takes the form of objective questions with feedback given to the student either during or immediately after the assessment. Formative assessment may be monitored by the tutor, used purely for self-assessment or used to contribute marks to a module grade.

Summative – assessments which give a quantitative grading and which aim to make a judgement about the student's achievement in a particular area. Summative assessment can include marked coursework as well as an end of unit examinations and can incorporate feedback to the student. It must be formal, structured and invigilated.

Advantages of CAA

- A wider variety of assessment methods may be possible than with other forms of assessment.
- Lecturers can monitor the progress of students through more frequent assessments.
- Students can monitor their own progress; self-assessment can be promoted and at times convenient to students.
- Detailed, specific feedback is available to students during and immediately after test.
- A wide range of topics within a body of knowledge can be tested very quickly.
- Computerized marking of tests can result in a great saving of staff time in the longer term.
- More frequent assessment of students is made possible by the automatic marking of scripts.
- Large groups are more easily assessed.
- The potential to introduce graphics and multimedia allows for inclusion of questions not possible with paper assessments.
- Can reduce cheating through the randomization of questions.
- Eliminates the need for double marking.
- Students report reduced stress levels sitting CAA exams as compared to traditional exam taking situations.
- Marking is not prone to human error, marker fatigue or subjectivity.
- Formative assessments can be repeated as frequently as desired to aid student learning.
- Adaptive testing can be used to match test to the student's ability.
- Students can be provided with clues and marked accordingly.
- Students acquire information (IT) skills.
- Diagnostic reports and analyses can be generated – for example, to see which areas of the curriculum are not understood.
- The quality of questions can be monitored by looking at facility and discrimination.

- Can aid with the transmission and administration of marks which can be automatically entered into information management systems and student records databases.

Limitations of CAA

- Construction of good objective tests requires skill and practice and so is initially time consuming.
- Because of the above, testing of higher order skills—analysis, synthesis, evaluation—is difficult, but not impossible. (See TRIADS).
- Questions tend to address factual content and may therefore encourage learning of surface detail rather than an appreciation of underlying concepts, though this disadvantage is not proven.
- Can penalise lateral thinking and those who see alternative 'correct' answers.
- Students may obtain the correct answer for the wrong reason or may be encouraged to reinforce misconceptions about the subject while answering questions incorrectly.
- Marks distribution may differ from those produced by conventional essay based papers.
- Implementation of a CAA system can be costly and time consuming.
- Assessors and invigilators need training in assessment design, IT skills and examinations management.
- Hardware and software must be carefully monitored to avoid failure during examinations.
- Students require adequate IT skills and experience of the assessment type.
- High level of organization is required across all parties involved in assessment (academics, support staff, computer services, administrators).
- The nature of the process makes it difficult to retrieve mistakes in compiling questions before the test is taken, placing a heavy duty of responsibility on the question setter.
- Formal assessment by computer is subject to concerns over security.

Objective Tests

Most CAA tests use objective test questions, with answers being selected from or compared to a limited set of pre-defined unequivocally correct responses to a question. While objective tests are used largely to test knowledge and comprehension, with careful design they can also assess higher learning outcomes such as the application of knowledge and analytical skills. The electronic marking of the responses is completely non-subjective because no judgment has to be made on the correctness or otherwise of an answer at the time of marking. (It's worth remembering that an objective test is only as objective as the test's author makes it.) Objective tests are particularly appropriate for informal self-assessment to give students ongoing feedback about their progress.

Types of Questions Used in Objective Tests

Generally the following types of questions are used in objective type tests:

- Multiple choice questions (MCQs) are the traditional 'choose one from a list' of possible answers. Special types of multiple choice questions include assertion-reason questions; multiple combination questions and true/false
- Multiple response questions (MRQs) are similar to MCQs, but involve the selection of more than one answer from a list. These are not usually presented in OMR tests.
- Graphical hotspot questions involve selecting an area(s) of the screen, by moving a marker to the required position, or, in the case of OMR questions, by filling in a block in a particular position linked to a graphic illustration on a specially designed paper answer sheet. For advanced types of hotspot questions (e.g. labeling and building questions) see the TRIADS project.
- Text/Numerical questions involve the input of text or numbers at the keyboard (CBA only).
- Matching questions (selection/association) involve linking items in one list to items in a second list (CBA only).
- Sore finger questions have been used in language teaching and computer programming, where one word, code or phrase is out of keeping with the rest of a passage. It could be presented as a 'hot spot' or text input type of question.
- Ranking questions require the student to relate items in a column to one another and can be used to test the knowledge of sequences, order of events, level of gradation.
- Sequencing questions require the student to position text or graphic objects in a given sequence. These are particularly good for testing methodology.
- Field simulation questions offer simulations of real problems or exercises. See TRIADS for examples of such questions (CBA only).
- Other question types require students to identify and/or manipulate images. Students may be asked to plot a graph, complete a matrix, draw a line or build up an image using parts provided.

Parts of an Objective Test Question

The general parts of an objective type test question are listed below:

- *Stem:* the phrasing of the question. Ensure that it is concise and unambiguous, avoiding negatives ('Which of the following is NOT...?') and grammatical clues to the key.
- *Options:* the alternative answers provided after the stem, one or more of which may be correct.
- *Key:* the correct answer(s) in the list of options. This should be the same length as the distracters and its position in any list should be randomized using the software (unless it is a numeric answer in which case answers should be in ascending order, avoiding any systematic placement of the key).
- *Distracters:* the incorrect answer(s) in the list of options. These should be apparently realistic alternatives that, as far as practicable, cover the full range of options and easily identify misconceptions.
- *Feedback:* a mark and/or comment reflecting the student's performance. This may be presented immediately after the question, at the end of the test or not at all. Feedback may also be provided on the basis of overall test performance. It should be appropriate, helpful, encouraging, varied and un-patronizing.

It is clear that the questions should reflect the aims and objectives of the course and be appropriate to the abilities of the students for whom they are intended. A pre-test during which questions can be tried out, edited and reformulated is considered essential.

Pedagogical Issues Related to Objective Type Tests

Objective tests are especially well-suited to certain types of tasks. Because questions can be designed to be answered quickly, they allow lecturers to test students on wide range of material. The use of CAA in the delivery of objective tests enables the provision of automatic feedback (in terms of scores, hints, praise, and guidance) to the student. Additionally, statistical analysis on the performance of individual students, cohorts and questions is possible.

The capacity of objective tests to assess a wide range of learning is often underestimated. Objective tests are very good at examining recall of facts, knowledge and application of terms, and questions that require short text or numerical responses. But a common worry is that objective tests cannot assess learning beyond basic comprehension. However, questions which are constructed imaginatively can challenge students and test higher learning levels. For example, students can be presented with case studies or a collection of data (such as a set of medical symptoms) and be asked to provide an analysis by answering a series questions. If using a computer, students can be given electronic tools to manipulate or construct objects on a screen. Problem-solving can also be assessed with the right type of questions. Assessing higher learning levels with objective test questions will be considered more closely below.

A further worry is that objective tests result in inflated scores due to guessing. However, the effects of guessing can be eliminated through a combination of question design and scoring techniques. With the right number of questions and distracters, distortion through guessing becomes largely irrelevant. Alternatively, guessing can be encouraged and measured if this is thought to be a desirable skill.

There are, however, limits to what objective tests can assess. They cannot, for example, test a student's abilities to communicate, to construct arguments or to offer original responses. Tests must be carefully constructed in order to avoid the decontextualisation of knowledge (Paxton 1998) and it is wise to use objective testing as only one of a variety of assessment methods within a module. However, in times of growing student numbers and decreasing resources, objective testing can offer a viable addition to the range of assessment types available to a lecturer.

Advantages of Objective Type Tests

The advantages to objective testing can include:

- Significantly reduced marking time
- Speed of assessment (A large number of questions can be asked quickly.)
- Wider coverage of topic content than essay questions; scope of test is broadened.
- Analysis of individual questions is possible
- Provision of automatic feedback to student (when used in computer-based assessment)
- Potential for more frequent assessment
- Questions can be pre-tested in order to evaluate their effectiveness and level of difficulty.

Disadvantages of Objective Type Tests

Disadvantages to objective testing can include:

- Significant amount of time required to construct good questions
- Writing questions that test higher order skills requires much effort.
- Cannot assess written expression or creativity

What Types of Learning can be Tested Using Objective Tests?

Bloom's taxonomy of educational objectives is a useful starting point for categorizing types of questions (Table 13.1).

It is commonly assumed that objective tests are only useful for examining the first three or four levels of learning. However, some educationalists suggest that all six levels can be tested using objective test questions.

Question Banks

Writing good objective questions can be a lengthy and laborious exercise. It is usually faster to edit existing questions from a question bank - a collection of questions normally on one subject. In some software packages, items can be chosen at random from question banks, thus allowing a unique subset of questions to be chosen for each assessment or student.

Questions can also be grouped into banks according to difficulty, area of the curriculum or type of skill being tested, such as recall, comprehension, analysis, and application. Assessments can then be designed which draw a certain number of questions from each bank, thereby ensuring that, while the test is randomized, specific skills and levels of competence will be examined.

Table 13.1: Bloom's Taxonomy and Question Categories

Competence	*Skills demonstrated*
Knowledge	• Recall of information • Knowledge of facts, dates, events, places • Question words: list, define, label, describe, name
Comprehension	• Interpretation of information in one's own words • Grasping meaning • Question words: interpret, discuss, predict, summarize, classify
Application	• Application of methods, theories, concepts to new situations • Question words: apply, demonstrate, show, relate
Analysis	• Identification of patterns • Recognition of components and their relationships • Question words: analyse, arrange, order, explain, connect, infer, compare, categorize
Synthesis	• Generalize from given knowledge • Use old ideas to create new ones • Organise and relate knowledge from several areas • Draw conclusions, predict • Question words: integrate, modify, invent, design, compose, plan, formulate, arrange
Evaluation	• Make judgements • Assess value of ideas, theories • Compare and discriminate between ideas • Evaluate data • Question words: appraise, judge, evaluate, defend, rank, conclude, discriminate, recommend

Some question banks are available commercially, generally associated with textbooks. It is also possible to adapt questions found in textbooks for objective testing.

Subjective Testing

Objective testing is not the only type of assessment delivered using CAA. A subjective test, for which there is no uniquely correct answer, examines the ability of the student to respond clearly and develop an argument. An example is:

- CEILIDH (Computer Environment for Interactive Learning in Diverse Habitats) to aid the teaching of programming languages and includes a facility which "marks" students' programmes, assessing them for style, layout, design and format.

Optical Mark Readers

An Optical Mark Reader (OMR) is a machine which process paper forms by scanning the page for marks such as crosses or ticks. (For example, UNN route questionnaires are processed in this way.)

For assessment purposes, pre-printed paper tests are taken by students using pen or pencil and fed into an OMR at rates of up to 2200 forms per hour. Exam questions must be objective (such as multiple choice or true false) and the answer sheets must be printed on special machine-readable paper.

Advantages of OMR Assessment

The advantages of OMR assessment include:

- Swift, objective marking–input is 10-20 times faster than by keying.
- Large groups can be assessed quickly.
- Automatic creation of reports on exam results.
- No need for special time tabling–run the test in any teaching room, no need to book a PC lab.
- Elimination of data entry errors when recording scores.
- User friendly for students–simply scoring out a box with pencil.
- No technical support is necessary.
- Marking is not prone to human error.
- Allows you to increase the frequency of testing to enhance motivation, develop skills, recognize effort spent learning, or to diagnostically test for weaknesses.
- Feedback is faster than manual marking.
- A wide range of topics within a body of knowledge can be tested very quickly.
- Quality can be monitored by looking at the facility and discrimination of questions and tests.

Disadvantages of OMR Assessment

Disadvantages of OMR assessment include:

- Limitations of question type–only MCQ.
- Construction of good MCQ tests requires skill and practice and so is initially time-consuming.

- Expense of machines.
- Staffing needs.
- Care must be taken to retrieve the question scripts if they are to be reused.
- OMR stationery is delicate and can be spoiled, requiring hand marking.

Implementing Tests

Students find that objective tests require considerable concentration and it is probably wise to limit the test content to no more than one hour's duration, although imposition of a time limit for self-assessment purposes is usually counterproductive. The use of open tests to assess coursework is subject to abuse through collaboration unless supervised, but this is true of conventional activities executed out of class as well. Encouraging this sort of student collaboration may even be considered desirable. The provision of feedback under such conditions is also a significant issue: withholding information can compromise other educational objectives. Using CAA in examination conditions requires careful preparation including back-up plans in case of hardware or software problems. Step-by-step tutorials and checklists are available for summative assessment planning. Sample questions for practice and introductory sessions on summative CAA may be needed to familiarize students with the process so as to reduce anxiety in the exam itself.

Security in Testing Students

The following strategies can help security during CAA:

- Assessments can be randomized to prevent cheating.
- Exam questions can be loaded onto server just prior to the test being taken to prevent unauthorized access.
- Exams can be password protected.
- Customized screens can be attached computers to prevent students from at other terminals during exams.
- Access to other electronic materials (such as those stored on the Internet or the university system) can be restricted during the exam
- Encryption facilities are available some assessment systems. These can prevent unauthorized access to question and answer files.

If assessments are being used summatively, it is likely that invigilation will be required.

Feedback

One of the strengths of CAA is that students can receive feedback quickly as they progress through the assessment. This feedback can take several forms. It can simply mean that the exam scores are available to the student after finishing the exam. More helpfully, particularly in formative assessments, students can be given feedback at the end of every question to tell them whether their response is correct or not.

Most CAA packages allow tutors to enter own feedback, so that a message appears explaining to students why the response is wrong and perhaps directing them to relevant or course materials. Additionally, some packages allow for the inclusion of hints to be made available during exam to help a student the correct answer. (Marks can be adjusted accordingly.) In some cases, students take the summative assessment for an exam mark with no feedback and they have the option at a later stage to go through the exam and receive feedback at the end of each question.

With OMR assessments, a range of reports analyzing students' scores can be generated once the answer forms have been scanned.

Guessing

A common anxiety about objective tests is that students will gain an inflated score simply through guessing. The effects of guessing can be largely eliminated through the use of corrective scoring in which marks are subtracted for incorrect answers. However, corrective (or negative) scoring is a contentious issue, and corrective scoring is unnecessary if the assessment has been well-constructed with good coverage of course content and questions varying difficulty. Alternatively, intelligent guessing be viewed as a useful skill that lecturers may wish to encourage.

Disadvantaged Students

Research to date suggests that if students given adequate training in the use of assessment software prior to the actual test, CAA disadvantage no groups. In fact, some software developers (CLASS and Test IT) claim to include facilities, which aid student's difficulties such as dyslexia or sight impairment. However, as yet, little research has been carried out in this area.

Assessment of Students' Abilities in Co-operative and Collaborative Learning Environment

Assessment is a part of the instructional process, and it plays a central role in supporting learning. Current debates on theories of learning have indicated the need to consider both cognitive and situated perspectives—knowledge and social interaction in computer supported collaborative learning.

Traditionally the purpose of assessment has been testing and ranking of the students. Currently the focus has changed so that *assessment is been viewed as a part of the instructional process and it plays a central role in supporting and enhancing students learning*. There is a link between assessment methods and what learning strategies students use. For example if the test consists mainly of factual and recall questions, students may use memorisation tactics to study to meet the task demands. On the other hand, if assessment tasks involve higher-order thinking, deep knowledge and conceptual understanding, the students are required to use deeper level learning strategies. So one way to influence students learning is to change how learning will be assessed.

Since the contemporary view of learning defines learning as a complex process of interpreting, seeking meaning and constructing new knowledge, also the assessment methods should capture the complex structure and quality of student learning and understanding. Therefore it is necessary to design challenging tasks that assess knowledge, conceptual change and higher-order thinking. It is also important to consider how assessment is conducted and how it can support learning.

Collaborative learning is about collaborating to learn, but also about learning to collaborate and therefore it is useful to assess participants' progress in terms of the quality of the learning process, not just the outcome. It is important to realise, that learning is also a social achievement, and its traces can be seen in increased capacities of groups to collectively create knowledge and deal with problems (Table 13.2).

Table 13.2: Comparing traditional and social-constructivist view from the assessment point of view

	Traditional view	*Social-constructivist view*
Purpose	Summative: to rank and to select	Formative: to support and transform learning, to provide positive effects
Time sequence	Assessment usually follows instruction	A dynamic and ongoing process embedded in instruction
Task	Objective tests, achievement tests, standardised tests	Challenging and collaborative tasks assessing and eliciting thinking and understanding
Inquiry	Learning products	Both learning processes and products
Standard	Criteria not transparent	Expectations made clear to students with explicit criteria and rubrics to scaffold student learning and collaboration
Assessor.	Teacher is the solo assessor	Students play active roles in assessing their own and peers' work
Unit of analysis	Individual learning and achievements	Both individual and collaborative learning; collective knowledge advances
Focus	Assessment is separated from learning	Alignment of learning, assessment and collaboration

Methods for Assessment

The following are the methods of assessment of students' abilities and traits in Co-operative and Collaborative Learning Environment:

Concept Map: Concept mapping has been used as an instructional and assessment tool for assessing student learning and conceptual change. As students draw concept maps, they need to elicit their knowledge, organise the relations among concepts, and construct their understanding of the topic in question. Assessment of concept maps by examing the number of concepts, linkages and hierarchies can show the quality of knowledge.

Self-Generated Questions: Students' self-generated questions can support and characterise reflection and metacognition. Assessment of problem posing and metacognition skills can identify gaps and inconsistencies in understanding.

Project: Project approach has been used as an instructional and assessment tool for assessing student ability to do a systematic and focused inquiry of a problem; focus on research and inquiry skills.

Presentation: Presentation and/or poster tasks have been used for assessing for example student ability to construct relevant presentation and present and discus about it.

Learning Diary: Learning diary has been used for assessing student reflection and metacognition; how student reflect and construct questions based on lectures, seminars and readings.

Case Studies: Case study approach has been used for assessing student problem solving skills. Important aspect is authentic problems and real-life situations.

14
Computer Classroom

After studying this chapter, the reader will be able to: Describe the various types of activity programs in computer-assisted learning; Know the methods for use of computers in the classroom; Discuss the role of computers in classroom; Understand the laboratory-based computer set-up; Describe the advantages and disadvantages of computer assistance; Analyze the teacher's role in relation to the integration of the computer into the system; Comprehend the classroom dynamics

The computer is to be used as a delivery system, a motivator and a power tool for the student (Phillips, 1985) As a delivery system, it is the teaching medium which links the student to the learning task designed by the educator. In turn, learning will take place through the computer. As a motivator, the computer increases the student's interest in the task. As a consequence, he will be motivated to perform and carry out the learning activity. As a power tool, the computer strengthens the demands made on the learner's cognitive level, allowing for individualization and active participation to take place within the learning process.

Types of Activity Programmes

Various activity type programmes exist in computer-assisted learning. Simulation, Problem Solving, Games, Text Construction, Tests, Drill and Practice—with or without remediation and Tutorial are some such activity types (Duffield, 1991). The educator chooses the activity type to use depending on the needs of the student, the education system, the teaching objective, and the education level (Higgins and Boone 1993; Underwood, 1993). Whichever activity type the educator chooses for use will allow the student to employ an active role in his learning process.

Simulation, Problem Solving, and Game Type Activity programmes use higher order learning conditions, and more conceptual and abstract thinking.

They are designed to model real or idealized complex situations a student may come across. The student's learning is exploratory in nature. As such the categories maintain active learning, privacy, freedom and skill application as do the Drill and Practice and Tutorial categories.

In a Simulation type of activity, the student works within a particular framework, similar to an authentic situation, to reach the end result. Another positive aspect about the programme is that it costs less in personal and economic matters.

In the Problem Solving type of activity, a student is exposed to a problem within a certain subject area that involves communication and exploration. In a Game type of activity, the student is engaged in a purposeful activity to accomplish an end result. The end result may be a goal, a prize or a winning score. Thus, communicative needs are indirectly being implemented.

Methods for Use

The individual can use the computer independently or cooperatively in a group; it can be individual or group paced; it can be used for practice or for problem-solving situations. It can also be used for remedial or for mastery purposes. The computer can be used within the classroom session or in a laboratory setting.

The way the educator is to use computer assistance will play a role in promoting an effective learning environment to enhance the students' mastery. Deciding on which method to use enables the educator to create alternative means. However, to do so, it is assumed that the objectives, goals and curriculum have been revised to find the most effective way to incorporate the computer in learning. Malone (1993) stated that the "chief culprit blocking widespread use of technology in schools today is the manner in which computers are integrated into the curriculum. In effect," he noted, "that the models of instructional computing that have emerged are not necessarily meeting the students' instructional needs" (p. 305).

The computer programme may be used in the whole class group cooperative setting, a small group setting or individually. If the computer is to be introduced into the class, it is not to go unused. The educator has to plan how to use it during the class session. For example, if the method of instruction is lecture followed by a whole class assignment, this does not mean the educator has no reason to use it. The computer may be used during the lecture session or may be used by the students to aid them in their whole class assignment. The same belief is true for computers in a laboratory. An institution that installs all its computers in a laboratory must ensure that the educators make effective use of the computers there to enhance the students' learning.

The Classroom-Based Computer

The literature suggests that classroom instruction combined with computer-assisted learning for tasks is not detrimental to enhancing learning (Chin Liou, 1992).

However, using a computer as a word processor or as one of many teaching aids is not what the researcher considers the best use for the computer.

In class use, the computer is considered an aid if it is seen to contribute to productivity or teaching effectiveness (Griffiths, 1991). So, a classroom that is set up around the concept of 'learning center' uses the computer as an additional workstation at which the students may work independently. With such a set-up, there is only a little time of computer use per learner; it may be only up to six to eight minutes per week for an average size class. So, there has to exist enough stability and flexibility within a course curriculum to work within the learning center set-up.

Furthermore, an educator may use the computer as a teaching aid to advance the material of study to the whole class. He can also demonstrate varied application of material on it to the learners. As a teaching tool, it is exciting to use; however, the educator has to make sure that the computer does not become exclusive to his use. To control this, some education institutions may opt to keep the computers in a laboratory.

The Laboratory-Based Computer Set-Up

Similarly, as in the classroom, using the computer for a word processor or resource value power is not what the researcher expects to use the computers for. Nor does the researcher want the lab-based instruction focus to be an independent learning process as opposed to being a tool to enhance the overall learning process.

Computer labs provide the student with opportunities to focus on skills learning or activities during a scheduled time period. In the lab, the student works individually or in a group setting. Barba (1993) noted that two students on a computer is an efficient number and can promote an optimum-learning atmosphere.

Computer-Need Awareness

Computer availability should not be what determines how the computer is to be used. Determining factors should be dependent on the student's needs, the purpose of the computer use, and the programmes available.

In a Drill and Practice or a Tutorial instructional setting, the students should not be given the same time period to use the computer. The students do not learn tasks at the same rate. This is why a student in using a computer is able to pace his own learning to meet his needs. The learning of a subject or the acquisition of a skill is what determines how the computer is to be utilized as opposed to the time spent on the computer.

Thus, how the computer is used is defined by set end points, time and task orientation. An end point within a programme determines how long a programme session is to be. A student works to accomplish mastery of the material within this set end point. Timing the session for a student enables planning within the lab or class session. However, students do not learn at the same pace. Thus, quick learners or high achievers will learn or accomplish more than slow learners or low achievers. Giving a student open time at the computer may seem ideal for a learner-oriented session, but the aggressive and interested student will be the one in such a situation to monopolize the computer time; he would not allow the other students to use the computer effectively. Task-defined learning is based on accomplishing a task. It is not based on just having the learner reach the end of his unit.

Student-Computer Ratio

Educators also need to decide on the number of students using each computer. Again, this decision has to be programme and purpose related. To have one student per computer allows the student to completely attend to the material. Ideally, this condition is conducive to effective learning; however, realistically, this is very expensive.

Research studies note that two or three learner per computer promotes effective group bonding which affects the learning process. However, if the computer programmes are designed to address specific needs of an independent user, the sharing of a computer will probably lead to ineffective group cooperation and learning. One student in this situation will dominate the activity (Geisert and Futrell, 1995).

Deciding on effective group size on the computer depends on the activity. For Simulation or Problem Solving activity type programmes, four to five students per computer still results in effective learning. For Project work within a class setting, it is best to have the project carried out by a large group. To facilitate project work in the whole class, the use of the computer as a tool is recommended for the whole class to see at once.

In short, no matter what the group size at the computer is and no matter what method or what activity type the students are using, the important thing is whether or not a student's performance and mastery are acquired.

Advantages and Disadvantages of Computer Assistance

Advantages and disadvantages exist in exploiting the use of computer-assisted learning. The main advantage for its use is that it enables a student to enhance his learning and improve his performance. The basic disadvantage is that it alone cannot guarantee that useful learning takes place. It creates a medium for learning to take place, but there is no security that actual learning will take place (Phillip, 1985). Kulik and Kulik (1991) noted that computer assistance alone couldn't account for the student's processed learning outcome. Accordingly, to reach such a conclusion, they questioned the feasibility of evaluating all textbooks, all lectures, across time, conditions and places. There exist limitations in all tools. Moreover, there is enough evidence to allow Kulik and Kulik to advance that the use of the computer in education can be as effective as 'live teaching'. Moreover, the fact that the student is able to improve his learning effectively makes computer assistance valuable in the education acquisition process (Sabieh, 1998).

Computer assisted learning provides the educator with a partner to share in the responsibility of the student's learning process. Computer assistance implicitly imitates the educator and integrates the theories and conditions (Sabieh 1998). It does nothing more or nothing less. This may be true, but a change in the education system, as a whole, has to take place. The attitude, the system, the methodology, the curriculum, the objective, the teaching, and the roles have to be modified to integrate the computer into the education process. With the changes made, the responsibility for ensuring learning becomes distributed: the Ministry of Education, the educators, the students and the parents all became active participants within the medium to promote success in the new system. Exchange of ideas, day-to-day policy making and planning could place worldwide, conferences, training programmes and satellite links could be planned to aid the process.

Educators need to have hands-on training to ensure that the computer assistance does not threaten them. They need to learn leadership skills to guide the students, and at the same time they too need guidance from professionals in the field.

Computer assisted learning makes the student an active learner. His learning is learner-oriented, active, and less dependent on the educator. It gives the student the responsibility for his own learning, whether independently or in a group setting. It gives him time to practice sufficiently to secure mastery of concept. It provides immediate feedback to allow him to evaluate his level of mastery and to improve his performance. It gives the student personal feedback. The incentive and pressure to perform is solely his decision. It gives the student a personal feeling of success and accomplishment. It provides intrinsic rewards. It caters to the need of the student; he may be a slow learner, disadvantaged learner, bright student, high achiever, learning disabled student, deficient student or average student.

Holmes and Kidd (1982) noted that immediate feedback is indeed very exciting, but the educator needs to be aware that the feedback given is based on man-made designs and predetermined feedback options. The complexities and variety of language creativity are not accounted for and, thus, an item may be answered correctly, but is registered by the computer as wrong. Computer language exploiting is too limited to deal with the complexities and/or creativity of learning and problem solving angles. That is the reason the researcher advocates the use of Drill and Practice and Tutorial activity programmes.

Feedback does improve performance; however, Kluger and Adler (1993) warned that it is informational feedback and not outcome feedback that aids the learning process. Also, answer-until-correct-feedback was not found to be effective as an enhancement for learning to take places (Morrison, Ross, Gopalakrishnan and Casey, 1995).

Computer programmes are not as advanced or as efficient as educators assume them to be. Even though many programmes have limited use, the educator expects that by introducing the "new" way into the system, the problems he faces will disappear immediately. Computer programmes are man made, and, as such, man has to deal with the complexities of human learning and all the characteristics involved. The designer has to break it all down into simplicities for computer programmeming. This is not easy, and it is very time consuming. Also due to convenience, the computer programmes are bought and used, but they do not really suit the needs of all education systems.

Moreover, educators as well as students may not be able to use the computer or the programmes. It takes time, money and expertise to master effective use of the computer both on the individual and the institutional level. Moreover, the computer world changes rapidly, leaving them unable to keep up with the development. Aware of this dilemma, many computer companies are attempting to develop hardware and software that has improved quality, is more learner oriented and is available at a lower price.

The Teacher's Role in Relation to the Integration of the Computer into the System

The computer gives the educator a tool to enhance the teaching and learning of the student. It gives him the tool to work with students of different achievement levels in one setting. The educator becomes the organizer, the mediator between the computer and the student, the facilitator of instruction, the resource consultant, the stimulator, and the motivator. With computer assistance, the educator has more time to spend with other students who need his aid. The educator encourages (Levesque, 1989), and supports (Hyland, 1993) the learner as well as selecting, presenting, creating, manipulating, organizing, applying, introducing, and discussing learning tasks. He helps the student explore knowledge in an integrated real-life manner.

The educator chooses how to use the computer in the learning environment. He may use it to develop a particular skill and/or for remedial and enriching purposes (Gage and Berliner, 1992). However, he is not to use the computer as a major part of instruction in any situation. He must keep in mind that it is a means to serve an end-purpose. It is his partner in promoting effective learning amongst his students (Geisert and Futrell, 1995).

The teacher may use the computer to develop independent learning. He may choose to group-work the students, making cooperative learning a norm, where each student actively participates with the rest of the group to reach a common end point.

He may use the computer to carry out distant learning and self-directed learning outside an educational setting. It depends on how he classifies computer-assisted learning.

Classroom Dynamics

Given the new roles for teachers and learners outlined above, it is clear that the role relationships between them must change if both are to benefit from the new learning/teaching paradigms.

The Role of the Teacher Changes to Being a Facilitator

The teacher is no longer the sole source of knowledge and information about the subject, nor is s/he the sole provider of texts and exposure to target materials. S/he will need to apply (new found) skills to guiding learners through the labyrinths and excesses of the information society to a principled approach to learning which can be appropriated by learners to help them on the path to self-determined acquisition of skills and knowledge. The most successful teacher in an ICT rich environment is a good learner.

The Role of the Student Changes to Being an Active Participant

The learner is no longer viewed as a receptacle into which the teacher pours wisdom and knowledge but as an agent of change, reacting and interacting with the mass of materials that s/he encounters.

There is Closer Interaction between Teacher and Students

The classroom situation begins to reflect that encountered in modern companies, which have adopted flat, non-hierarchical structures where maximum benefit for all is to be reaped by pooling knowledge and resources in informal exchanges.

15
Computers and Changing Roles of Teachers and Learners

After studying this chapter, the reader will be able to: Comprehend the new roles of the teachers in age of computers; Recognize the kinds of supports that the learners needs from the teachers; Define the status of the teachers; Describe the role of the teachers; Specify the relationship between teacher and the learning process; Identify the factors which creates an educative situation; Discuss how teacher can support cooperative and collaborative learning; Define the new roles of the learners

With rapid advances in technology, the nature of knowledge and learning for the information age is no more the same as that of the industrial age and this has major implications for the strategies to be used for inspiring and engaging today's learners who have grown up surrounded with digital media and are used to having instant access to information. They look for flexible resources that change with their individual needs and prefer to work in student-centered, networked learning environments. All these have major implications for the design and delivery of instruction and demand new responsibilities from teachers as well as students. Moving from teacher-centered practice to this new approach in the online environment often creates dramatic shifts in the perspectives of instructors and their students (Dringus, 2000) particularly in their roles. Some of the challenges and barriers for online learning that have been identified by researchers are the change of roles and responsibilities for instructors (Zheng and Smaldino, 2003).

New Roles of Teachers

In such a student-centered and teacher-supported learning environment, the role of the teacher is no longer the all-knowing "sage on the stage" who expertly transmits knowledge but a facilitator of student learning, an experienced member of a learning community, researcher, consultant, mentor or resource person. Further, since the online environment is different from the more traditional passive classroom, it is important for the instructor to motivate students to adjust their roles to become a more active online learner.

Besides their role shifting, the role of the virtual instructor is to select and filter information for student consideration, to provide thought-provoking questions and to facilitate well-considered discussion (Kettner-Polley, 1999). Within the context of social networking tools, teachers are on the verge of becoming creators of conducive learning environments and designers learning experiences. They need to be creative and be able to pose thought-provoking questions (rather than to provide answers) that stimulate higher-order thinking skills and metacognition, to challenge learners' curiosity and to encourage them reflect on the learning process. Even the most experienced traditional teacher requires additional skills to teach online; they need to explore new pedagogical options that reflect sound online instructional principles and technological innovations.

In online student-centered online learning environment, learning occurs by building on previous knowledge, through interaction with rich learning environments and results from engaging in authentic activities and social interaction and negotiation supported by the teacher. In online education, the nature of interaction between students and their instructors have changed from synchronous in face-to-face instruction to mainly that of asynchronous in a virtual community. Moore (2001) noted that to effectively deliver online courses, faculty must promote student-to-student interaction with minimal faculty intervention, engage students in regular assignments, cultivate students' self-directed abilities and then provide specialized attention to students who lack self-directedness. Due to several such changes, Zheng and Smaldino (2003) argue that, besides being a facilitator, the instructor should also be an instructional designer.

Collis, Vingerhoets, and Moonen (1997) formed a set of key principles for good teaching and learning in higher education the first of which is to "scaffold the learner's increased self-responsibility for learning" (in a VLE). Other factors are to stimulate active engagement, elicit articulation and reflection, and lecture less while giving more feedback and to encourage more frequent targeted communication. In addition, since learners are perceived as constructors of knowledge in the new paradigm, the learners' unique perspective must be evaluated and attached more importance than external criterion-referenced evaluation. All these mean that teachers have to adopt new instructional approaches and assessment strategies, incorporate collaborative tasks and develop technological skills.

Instructors need to scale up their attitudes to teach online, understand what skills are needed and know what they can do to ensure the quality of online instruction. As Deubel (2003) has argued, an instructor's attitude, motivation and true commitment affect much of the quality of online instruction. In addition, instructors must be ready to engage in a range of teaching innovations and for investigating the impact of these approaches on student learning (i.e., the scholarship of teaching and learning).

From the forgoing discussions, online teachers should also have the skills in the following:

- How to motivate students to learn;
- Pedagogical techniques that differ from traditional face-to-face techniques whereby the student and teacher have to actively co-create the learning environment;
- How to establish effective communication and interaction in the absence of nonverbal visual cues;
- Good facilitatory tutoring skills for self-directed learning and for challenging learners' thinking or reasoning skills (problem solving, metacognition, and critical thinking) by asking the 'right' questions which probe their understanding deeply and spark their intellectual curiosity;
- Effective assessment techniques for measuring student achievement and learning including higher order learning outcomes.

Nunes and McPherson (2006) propose the following skills essential for online tutors:

(a) To plan and organise delivery by clearly specifying learning objectives and outcomes;
(b) To set learning agendas and providing leadership and scaffolding in learning activities;
(c) To welcome and embrace diversity of learning outcomes, attitudes and styles;
(d) To adapt supporting styles to the needs of individual participants;
(e) To provide advice on different levels of access to learning materials according to the needs of individual participants;
(f) To create an atmosphere of collaborative learning of which the tutor him/herself is often an integral part;
(g) To be able to cope with and resolve online conferencing conflicts and difficult behaviours;
(h) To encourage active construction of knowledge by being actively involved in discussions, activities and debates;
(i) To develop and implement methods for learner feedback and reinforcement;
(j) To present advance organisers into the content materials and advise on learning pace so as to avoid cognitive overload and information anxiety.

Mason (1998) advocates the organizational, social and intellectual roles of the online lecturer. Bonk and Wisher (2000), Wlodkowski (1999), and Besser and Bonn (1996) identify the following as the most critical skills of an online instructor: Expertise, Empathy, Enthusiasm, Clarity, Cultural responsiveness, Mentor, Provocateur (prompting critical thinking in learners), Observer, Participant, Co-learner, Assistant, Community organizer, Host, Facilitator, Mediator, Patient, Positive, Friendly, Responsive, Caring, Flexible, and Web-smart. Bonk and Wisher (2000) also note that a lecturer who offers web-based courses requires competencies such as: Social, Managerial, Research, Pedagogical and Technical skills. It is important for instructors to be familiar with these essential aspects to enable them build an effective online learning community and integrate it with occasional face-to-face sessions in order to take advantage of both in a complementary manner.

Kinds of Supports that the Learners Needs from the Teachers

When introducing IT-based learning environments the role of the learners changes and in the same manner the role of the teachers is also dramatically changed. The traditional role as mediator of knowledge is outmoded. The new role is more to act as a designer of information systems and as a guide who supports the learners in their learning process. In addition, the learners themselves and computers take over much of the support, control and decisions that the traditional teachers have dealt with. The process of formulating the theoretical basis for a pedagogical model has resulted in an identification of six kinds of support that the learners need, and the learning environment must provide:

Establishing and Maintaining Focus

Establishing focus has much the character of a process of exploration. Often learners come into this process with a rather vague view of what they want. The aim is to make this view more concrete and precise by changing and adjusting the focus. Focus and goals are dynamic entities that change during the process of learning. Changes in focus and goals are made implicitly during the process of learning but also as an active and conscious action of the learner. On the other hand, keeping focus is one of the hardest problems to deal with in information seeking and in learning situations based on information seeking. Some of the problems to keep focus have their roots in information overload. The fact is that keeping track of many parallel goals causes problems for the process of keeping focused.

Active Learning/Reading

In the process of forming or constructing knowledge, an active processing of the topic is important for the result. Therefore, much of the concept of the *learners as knowledge-worker* is captured in the concept of active learning. The learners must have the opportunity to process the material in many ways, both in the domain-space and in the media-space. To actively read a material commonly involves activities such as: editing, extracting meta-information, processing meta-information, making changes in the structure, making notations, searching for information, assessing one's state of knowledge, communicating the way one has processed the topic and much more.

Communicating the Learning Process: One important factor of learning, is to learn from one's own experience but also learning from others' experience is important. In many learning situations most of the people involved, both learners and educators will benefit from a non-competitive mentality.

Confirming the State of Knowledge

To have an idea of what one knows and what one does not know, is a question of confirmation. The possibility for the learners to confirm their state of knowledge plays an important role in every kind of learning situation. Confirmation of the state of knowledge can be done in many ways, from regular examinations, which are used in traditional education, to ways where learners have more control over the process, like self-assessments. It is a great challenge to construct computer-based assessments with the phenomenological approach to knowledge and learning, as the foundation. Individual's ability to interpret and judge information can play an important role. *Knowledge-mirroring* based on visualization of abstract information such as the state of knowledge, goals, focus etc., is an alternative that also provides the learners with the facilities to make self-assessments. In addition, different forums for discussion may serve as way to recognize what one knows and what one does not know.

Managing the Information Overload

In the information society, information overload has become a situation that is well known to most of the knowledge workers and which appears to be inevitable. In a learning environment, the information overload is also a serious problem and the learners must have support to manage it. We can learn from the way scientists and other knowledge workers manage the situation. Commonly, a personal information system is used as a tool for knowledge workers or persons working in an information flow to cope with the situation of information overload. Information about data, information, and knowledge plays an important role in a learning environment, especially in the process to manage information overload; much of the work with organisation and management of information, is based on meta-information.

Finding Internal Factors of Relevance and Motivation

The quality of the outcome from the process of learning is improved if the learners are motivated by internal factors of motivation and relevance. The whole learning environment should encourage the learners to an active and self-designed style of learning but also to arouse the learners' curiosity for the topic.

Teacher's Status

The teacher may have the status of:

Specialist in the Field: Any teacher must have an optimum professional level; through training, examinations and experiment, status as a member of the teaching staff;

Coordinator of the Teaching Process: Teacher's actions will be focused on the selection of the most appropriated means and methods in order to support students knowledge construction to accomplish the requirements of the curriculum; teacher will establish the evaluation criteria for the students and will accept the results as being a feed-back for teachers' own activity; teacher will create the best educational conditions in order to achieve the objectives of the teaching process (E.E. Geissler, 1981);

Formative Trainer: The teacher is a knowledge possessor and a knowledge transmitter; through professional, creative, adapting and readapting capacities, teacher acts upon students' intellectual and professional training.

Educator: By virtue of this status, teacher will be concerned with the providing of a professional, moral and social model for the students: this model will be teachers' own person; at the same time, teacher will be a counsellor for the students, by helping them to solve the different problems they are confronted with and to identify their own resources during their evolution to the adult age;

Partner to Education: This refers to the relationships established by the teacher with the other educational factors: parents, family, local community; in the light of this status, the teacher becomes a partner to mentality and attitude changing, to the interactive action aiming at rendering aware of the adaptation and reforming, of the self-education and improvement.

Member of the Teaching Staff: This status determines teacher's relationships with colleagues, with the leading board members etc. To belong to an educational team means that any teacher has to accomplish some tasks and responsibilities required by the need of efficiency of the educational act.

Having in view these characteristics, it results that the main activities of any member of the teaching staff—projecting, organizing, decision making, coordinating the teaching process, evaluating, solving the specific situations etc.—must be reinterpreted under the managerial perspective, in order to improve the whole activity efficiency.

Teacher's Roles

The specialty literature describes a multitude of roles that the school teacher may exert. According to A.E. Woolfolk (1990), the teacher has the following roles:

A Leader of the Didactic Activity (expert of the teaching - learning act): This role is exerted in order to fulfil the objectives aimed by the educational system; the role is given by the fact that the knowledge volume included in the school programmes and textbooks is assimilated by the students according to the way they have been filtered and transmitted through teacher's personality.

A Motivating Agent: The teacher has to arouse and maintain students' interest, curiosity and desire to learn.

A Leader of the Group of Students: The teacher has to participate in students' different school events.

A Counsellor: After having observed and known students and after having identified their problems, the teacher gives them support, guides and orients them.

A Model: Through his actions and behaviour, the teacher is a positive example for his students; he settles and offers moral requirements, he transmits moral knowledge.

A Reflexive Professional: The teacher permanently tries to understand the psychopedagogical phenomena he is confronted with.

A Manager: The teacher supervises students' activity during the classes, he keeps in touch with students' parents and with the representatives of the local community.

In the specialty literature, there are many debates about the teacher's managerial roles. The roles of the teacher-manager can be defined starting with the manager's general tasks, expressed by the managerial functions, as well as with their turning into specific operational leadership tasks (planning, organizing, decision making, (communication, the information system about the activity, students' participation in their own education process).

According to the specialists in the educational management field, the defining of the teacher-manager's roles has to be realized from an interdisciplinary perspective, including the psychological, sociological and pedagogical domains. This is necessary because the role represents the dynamic and situational aspect of the teacher's (educator's) status in the applying of the formally specified rights and duties related to the educational process leading.

A distinct aspect of the teacher-manager's roles is given by the fact that some roles are imposed, prescribed by the State or by the organization (those of planning, controlling and organizing), while others are acquired through the becoming aware of the necessity of applying the pedagogy actual requirements about students' personality building up and educating (guidance, counselling, communication) (E. Joita, 2000).

The Teacher and the Learning Process

By referring to the teacher's status and role, particularly as coordinator of the learning process, we can identify several ways of approaching the relationship between the teacher and the teaching contents. This relationship defines itself within pedagogical patterns, described through the comparative analysis by Lesne (1997). In the traditional transmitting-normative pattern, the autonomy appears in the field of knowledge as a result of the guided initiation. The teacher is the only possessor of knowledge and the indispensable mediator between information and student. The teacher has a tendency to use the extrinsic motivations. As for the acting predominant factor, there can be noticed the providing of a scientific content within the teaching activity focused on teacher's action. This one is also perceived as the main source of information transmitting. Teacher's first role will consist in information transmitting and in testing their assimilation level.

The alternatives for the previous pattern are the personal-arousing pattern and the acquisition through social insertion pattern. Within the personal-arousing pattern, the student becomes the subject of his own education. Actually, this is about passing from the student who is trained and educated to the student who educates himself. In this case, the function of knowledge transmitting is no longer the central function. The emphasis shifts towards the organizing of the framework and of the activities proper to knowledge accumulating.

Under this approach, teacher's role is that of attitudinal and cognitive mediator between that one who is getting educated and the sources of his information, and this is an aspect requiring the use of some other educational and didactic strategies (Barthelemy, 1997). There is also an alteration of the teacher's position as compared to the teaching contents. He may choose the most appropriate contents, depending on the aimed objectives.

This approach allows the mobilization of all students' personality resources. The formative process is based on student's autonomy, responsibility and learning motivation, consequently the learning process is not destined only to his intellectual development, but to the development of his whole personality. Although the value of this pattern is certain, the specialists emphasize that the teachers are firstly required to construct educative situations. Thus, the teaching act responsibility becomes grater, as well as the exigencies imposed when putting into practice his psycho-pedagogical abilities. At the same time, a special emphasis is placed on the creating of an intrinsic motivation, determined by the pleasure of being in action and by the arousal of the spontaneous interests.

A third pedagogical pattern, the acquisition through social insertion, relies on the formative resources of the real social relations in everyday life. The student is perceived as a social influence agent and, through this, as a self-education agent. As for the acting predominant factor, there can be noticed the teacher's role of supporting the cognitive approach to reality, through a pedagogical activity based on the current actions of those who are getting educated. The knowledge selection relies on scientific and social criteria, which aim at creating some theoretical tools that facilitate the acquisition, through personal efforts, of the real, in its concrete determinism and relationships.

Within this approach, a special emphasis will be placed on the relation between theory and practice, respectively on the connection between the knowledge assimilated by the students and their practical value. At the same time, it is to notice that evaluation is made in the context of the daily activities, the sanctions resulting from the very activity finality and quality.

In the education process, these three models are used to a large extent by the teachers whose option is based on each one's professional knowledge and it continues with students' age and instruction level.

To accept that the teacher constructs educative situations and is an external factor of the instruction doesn't mean to alter teachers' main role, that of initiator and organizer of the education process, but some aspects are however altered, in the sense that between the teacher and the student interferes the educative situation created by the specialist.

Creating an Educative Situation

Creating an educative situation involves the exertion of teacher's coordinator role. This role involves, in its turn:

(1) *Analyzing the available educational resources:* Material resources (teaching aids);
(2) *Didactic projecting:* Formulating the instruction objectives, conceiving the system of educative situations and establishing their temporal sequence, selecting the learning process contents, settling the types of activity the students will participate;
(3) *Students placing in the educative situation:* This is made on the basis of the projected elements, but they could be modified, depending on the momentary variables acting during the instruction process;
(4) *Feed-back providing:* Through which the evaluation is made, if the educative situation or the sequence of created educative situations correspond to the established objectives.

How Teacher Can Support Co-operative and Collaborative Learning?

Learners' adaptation to complex collaborative learning situations, such as sharing knowledge and maintaining coordinated activity, presumes more advanced cognitive, motivational and socio-emotional regulation skills than more conventional and well-structured learning or working situations. Therefore it is not self-evident how to engage in collaborative learning situations.

Teacher play a major role in directing (on-line or face-to-face) discussions, influencing the discussion by entering new topics, sharing new material and redirecting conversational patterns. Learners are needed to feel a sense of security in order to participate to groups' activities. Forming a sense of community, where people feel they will are being treated sympathetically by their fellows, seems to be a necessary first step for collaborative learning.

Teacher can use *pedagogical models*, which have been developed to support and structure collaborative learning. Pedagogical models are based on theoretical framework of learning and offers practical instruction of teaching and learning process.

New Roles of the Learners

The role that learners have in a typical learning situation has not changed much during the last hundred years, especially not in higher education. An involvement of modern information technology in the learning situation will force on a discussion of the learner's role. The role that the learners have in a learning situation is to learn but this role can take different forms. How actively the learners participate in the learning situation is an important parameter for the learning environment. In a learning environment based on a qualitative view on knowledge viewed as understanding, it is necessary for the quality of the learning outcome that learners take a more active role in the learning situation. Consequently, the role of the learners is to actively formulate their own goals for the learning process, be active during the learning process and to keep focus on the learning goals. Another aspect of the active learning is the learners take the role as a teacher. Acting as a teacher serves as much to improve one's own understanding. To learn from other learners and how they have processed the topic or course material, is also an important facility in the learning environment.

Students must move from being a more traditional passive classroom learner to a more active online inquirer who can collaborate with peers in order to develop personal understanding of course content. By these changes in approaches, learners gradually take increasing responsibility for their own learning as they become effective self-directed learners. To become successful self-directed learners, they must accept responsibility for majority of their learning. This involves setting their own time schedules, developing the right study habits and discipline necessary for accomplishing the tasks. Garrison, Cleveland-Innes, and Fung (2004) suggest that online learners must take more responsibility, adjust to a new climate, adjust to new context, synthesize ideas, know how to participate, synthesize ideas, apply ideas or concepts and stimulate their own curiosity. According to Palloff and Pratt (2003) online learners should be willing to take "responsibility" for online community formation and be willing to work "collaboratively". Instructors should clearly explain to students in advance the change in roles they must adapt in order to be successful in online learning environment.

A major advantage of online learning to students is its flexibility; however, this flexibility also poses a challenge to them: they have to adapt the new pedagogical approaches which are a lot different from the teacher-directed approaches; they have to manage their learning time themselves, and develop strategies of creating knowledge and monitoring their own learning process. They must engage in social negotiation activities, often via online discussions, online project work and online collaborative activities. The new approach puts high cognitive demands on some learners, especially on the low ability group. The cognitive load has the potential to cause problems in cognitively ill-equipped learners, making them feel "disorientated," and causing "cognitive overload" in such learning environments (Oren, 1990). Liyoshi, Hannafin, and Wang (2005) suggest that technology as a cognitive tool can help learners in overcoming their disorientation and cognitive burden because cognitive tools are capable of searching, accessing, and organizing and processing a large amount of information. Therefore, if technology can be used appropriately, it can address challenges posed by technology itself.

References

Adams, M. & Bruce, B. (1980). Background Knowledge and Reading Comprehension. Reading Education Report Number 13. Urbana: Center for the Study of Reading, University of Illinois at Urbana-Champaign.

Alessi, L.M., & Trollip, S.R. (1991). *Computer-Based Instruction: Methods and Development*. (2nd Ed.). Englewood Cliffs, NJ: Prentice-Hall. USA.

Alessi, M.S. & Trollip, S. (1992). *Computer-Based Instruction: Methods and Development*. New Jersey: Prentice Hall, Englewood Cliffs.

Ambrose S, *et al*. (2010). *How learning works: seven research-based principles for smart teaching*. San Francisco: Jossey-Bass.

Anderson J.R. (1995). *The architecture of cognition*. Cambridge, MA: Harvard University Press.

Anderson, M. (1993). "Technology Integration for Mainstreamed Students". In T. Cannings and L. Finkel (Eds.), *The Technology Age Classroom (97)*. Wilsonville, Oregon: Franklin. Beedle and Associates, Incorp.

Anderson, P. (2007). What is web 2.0? Ideas, technologies, and implications for education. http://www.jisc.ac.uk/media/documents/techwatch/tsw0701b.pdf

Anderson, R.C. (1977). 'The Notion of Schemata and the Educational Enterprise', in *Schooling and the Acquisition of Knowledge*, eds. R.C. Anderson, R.J. Spiro & W.E. Montague. Hillsdale, NJ: Lawrence Erlbaum Associates.

Anderson, T., Anderson, R., Dalgaard, B., Paden, D., Biddle, B., Durber, J. & Alessi, S. M. (1975). An Experimental Evaluation of a Computer Based Study Management System. *Educational Psychologist*. 11, 184-190.

Anglin GJ. (1995). Instructional technology: past, present and future. Libraries Unlimited, Inc. Englewood, Colorado.

Arons, A.B. (1990). A Guide to Introductory Physics Teaching. Wiley, New York.

Arseneau & Rodenberg. (1998). The developmental perspective. In: Pratt's *Five perspectives on teaching in adult & higher education*. Malabar, FL: Krieger Publishing.

Atkins, M.J. (1993). Theories of learning and multimedia: an overview. *Research Papers in Education,* 8(2), 251-271.

Ausubel D. (1963). The psychology of meaningful verbal learning. New York: Grune & Stratton.

Ayersman, D. J. (1996). Reviewing the research on hypermedia-based learning. *Journal of Research on Computing in Education,* 28, 500-525.

Bandura A., Walters R. (1963). *Social learning and personality development*. New York: Holt, Rinehart & Winston.

Bandura A. (1969). *Principles of behavior modification*. New York: Holt, Rinehart & Winston.

Bandura A. (1973). *Aggression: a social learning analysis*. Englewood Cliffs, NJ: Prentice–Hall.

Bandura A. (1977). *Social learning theory*. New York: General Learning Press.

Bandura A. (1986). *Social foundations of thought and action*. Englewood Cliffs, NJ: Prentice–Hall.

Bandura A. (1997). *Self-efficacy: the exercise of control*. New York: W.H. Freeman.

Bandura A. (1998). Health promotion from the perspective of social cognitive theory. *Psychol Health*. 13:623–649.

Bangert-Drowns, R., Kulik, J., and Kulik, C. (1985). Effective of Computer-Based Education in Secondary Schools. *Journal of Computer-Based Instruction*, 12, 59-68.

Baran B. (2010). Experiences from the process of designing lessons with interactive Whiteboard: ASSURE as a road map. *Contemporary Ed Tech*. 1(4):367–380.

Bastiaens T.J., Marks GH. (2012). Education and information technology 2012: a selection of AACE Award papers. Chesapeake, VA: AACE.

Becker, H.J. (1994). How exemplary computer-using teachers differ from other teachers: Implications for realizing the potential of computers in schools. *Journal of Research on Computing in Education*, 26, 291-321.

Bell, Daniel. (1979). Communications Technology for Better or for Worse. *Harvard Business Review*, May-June, pp. 20-28.

Beothel, Martha and K. Victoria Dimock. (2000). "Constructing Knowledge with Technology." Austin, TX: Southwest Educational Development Laboratory.

Bereiter, C. & Scardmalia, M. (1989) Intentional learning as a goal of instruction. In L.B. Resnick (Eds.), *Knowing, learning and instruction: Essays in honor of Robert Glaser* (pp. 512). Hillsdale (N.J.): Erlbaum

Birl, D.S., & Jon Nichol (1976). *Games and Simulations in History*. Hong Kong Printers Press. Hong Kong.

Black, E. (1995). Behaviorism as a Learning Theory. [On-line]. Available: http://129.7.160.115/inst5931/Behaviorism.html.

Blanchard, K & Cheska, A. (1985). *The Anthropology of Sport: An Introduction*. Massachusetts: Bergin & Garvey Publisher, Inc.

Blankenhorn, J. (1999). "How cost-effective is computer-based training?" *Wood Technology, 126, 29-30.*

Blanton, Betty B. (1998). The Application of the Cognitive Learning Theory to Instructional Design. *International Journal of Instructional Media,* 25, 2, 171-177.

Blease, D. (1986). *Evaluating Educational Software*. Croom Helm, London.

Bloom BS. (1980). *All our children learning*. New York: McGraw-Hill.

Bloom BS. (1984). *Taxonomy of educational objectives*. Published by Allyn and Bacon, Boston, MA. Pearson Education.

Bloom BS. (1985). Developing talent in young people. New York: Ballentine Books.

Bloom, G.S. (1984). The 2-Sigma Problem: The search for methods of group instruction as effective as one-to-one tutoring. *Educational Researcher*, 13(4), 4-16.

Boaler, J. (1999). Mathematics for the moment, or the millennium? What a British study has to say about teaching methods. *Education Week,* 58, 23-29.

Bork, A. (1979). Learning With Computer Simulations. *IEEE Computer*, 12 (10).

Born D.G., Davis ML. (1974). Amount and distribution of study in a personalized instruction course and in a lecture course. *J Appl Behav Anal*. 7(3):365–75.

Bowman, B., F. Grup, *et al*. (1995). "Teaching End-User Applications with Computer-Based Training: Theory and an Empiracal Investigation." *Journal of End User Computing* 7(2): 12-18.

Boyle, T. (1997). *Design for Multimedia Learning*. Hertfordshire: Prentice Hall Europe.

Bransford J.D. *et al*. (1990). Anchored instruction: Why we need it and how technology can help. In: *Cognition, education and multimedia*. Hillsdale, NJ: Erlbaum Associates.

Bransford J.D., Stein B.S. (1993). *The ideal problem solver* (2nd Ed). New York: Freeman.

Bright, G. (1982). Computer Diagnosis of Errors. Unpublished manuscript. Dekalb, IL: Northern Illinois University.

Brooks J., Brooks M. (1993). The case for a constructivist classroom. Alexandria, VA. ASCD.

Brooks L. (2009). Social learning by design: the role of social media. *Knowledge Quest*. 37(5):58–60.

Brown J.S., Collins A., Dugid P. (1989). Situated cognition and the culture of learning. *Educational Researcher*. 18:32-42.

Brown, John Selly. (1977). 'Uses of Artificial Intelligence and Advanced Computer Technology in Education' in (Eds.) Robert J. Seidel and Martin Rubin, *Computers and Communication: Implications for Education*, New York, NY: Academic Press Inc.

Brufee, K. (1993). *Collaborative learning*. Baltimore: Johns Hopkins University Press.

Bruner J. (1966). *Toward a theory of instruction*. Cambridge, MA: Harvard University Press.

Bruner J.S. (1986). A study of thinking. New Brunswick, NJ: Transaction Press.

Bruner, J. (1973). *The Relevance of Education*, W.W. Norton, N.Y. (theoretical background)

Bullough, Sr.V. Robert & Beaty, F. Lamond. (1987). *Classroom Applications of Microcomputers*. Merril Publishing Company, Columbus, pp. 139.

Burke, R.L. (1982). CAI Sourcebook. Englewood Cliffs, NJ: Prentice-Hall.

Burns, H.L. & Capps, C.G. (1998). Foundations of Intelligent Tutoring System: An Introduction. In *Foundations of Intelligent Tutoring System* (Eds. Polson, M.C. & Richardson, J.J.), pp. 1-19, Lawrence Erlbaum Associates, USA.

Burton JK, Moore DM, Magliaro SG. (1996). Behaviorism and instructional technology. In: *Handbook of Research for Educational Communications Technology*. New York: Macmillan.

Butzin, S.M. (1992). "Project CHILD: A New Twist on Integrated Learning System". Technological Horizons in *Education Journal: Curriculum Integration* 20 (2), 90-95.

Byrd, D. (1981). Do educational constituency groups agree on topics for professional development?, *Action in Teacher Education*, no. 3

Caffarella R.S. (2002). *Planning programs for adult learners: a practical guide for educators, trainers and staff developers*. Jossey-Bass: San Francisco, CA.

Caffarella, P.E. (1987). Evaluating the New Generation of Computer-Based Instructional Software. *Educational Technology*, 27(6), pp. 19-24.

Caldwell E.C., *et al.* (1978). Mastery: the essential essential in PSI. *Teach Psych.* 5(2):59-65.

Calhoun JF. (1976). The combination of elements in the personalized system of instruction. *Teach Psych*. 3:73–76.

Callahan C, Smith RM. (1990). Keller's personalized system of instruction in a junior high gifted program. *Roeper Rev*. 13(1):39–44.

Carbonell, J.R. (1970). AI in CAI: An Artificial Intelligence Approach to Computer-Assisted Instruction. IEEE Transcation On Man-Machine Systems, MMS-11 (4).

Carter, D.S.G. (1990). Knowledge Transmitter, Social Scientist or Reflective Thinker: Three images of the practitioner in Western Australian high schools. *Theory and Research in Social Education*. XVIII (3), 274-317.

Case DO. (2012). Looking for information: a survey of research on information seeking, needs and behavior, 3e. San Diego, CA: Academic Press.

Chambers, J.A. & Sprecher, J.W. (1983). Computer-Assisted Instruction: Its Uses in the Classroom. Englewood Cliffs, NJ: Spectrum.

Chase W.G., Simon H.A. (1973). Perception in chess. *Cognitive Psychology*. 4:55-81.

Chi MTH, Feltovich P.J., Glaser R. (1982). Categorization and representation of physics problems by experts and novices. *Cognitive Science*. 5:121-152.

Chi MTH, Lewis M.W., Glaser R. (1989). Self-explanations: How students study and use examples in learning to solve problems. *Cognitive Science*. 13:145-182.

Choy S. (2010). Transformational learning in the workplace. *J Transformative Education*. 7(1):65-84.

Clancy W.C. (1997). *Situated cognition: on human knowledge and computer representations*. Cambridge: Cambridge University Press.

Cobb, P. (1994). Where is the Mind? Constructivist and sociocultural perspectives on mathematic development. *Educational Researcher*, 23(7), pp. 13-20

Coburn, P. *et al.* (1982). Practical Guide to Computers in Education. Addision Wesley, Reading Massachusetts.

Cognition and Technology Group at Vanderbilt CTGV. (1990). Anchored instruction and its relationship to situated cognition. *Educational Researcher*. 19(6):2-10.

Cognition and Technology Group at Vanderbilt CTGV. (1993). Anchored instruction and situated cognition revisited. *Educational Technology*. 33(3):52-70.

Colborn N. (2011). Introduction to instructional design: a brief primer. *Indiana Libraries*. 30(1):15–19.

Collins A., Brown J.S., Holum A. (1991). Cognitive apprenticeship: making thinking visible. *American Educator*. 15(3):6-11.

Collins A., Brown J.S., Newman S.E. (1989). Cognitive apprenticeship: teaching the craft of reading, writing and mathematics. In: *Knowing, Learning & Instruction: Essays in Honor of Robert Glaser*. Hillsdale, NJ: Erlbaum.

Collins A. (2006). Cognitive apprenticeship. Cambridge handbook of the learning sciences. Cambridge, UK: Cambridge University Press47-60.

Collins, A. (1991). The role of computer technology in restructuring schools. *Phi Delta Kappan, 73,* 28-36.

Congram, G. (1995). "Computer-based training simplifies safety compliance". *Pipeline & Gas Journal, 222, 52-54.*

Cosmovici, A., Iacob, L., (coord.) (1998) Psihologie °colarã, Editura Polirom, Ia°i

Coulson R.L., Feltovich P.J., Spiro R.J. (1997). Cognitive flexibility in medicine: an application to the recognition and understanding of hypertension. *Adv Health Sciences Ed.* 2:141-61.

Csikszentmihalyi, M. (1990). Flow: The Psychology of Optimal Experience. New York: Harper & Row.

Cuco°, C. (coord.) (1998). Psihopedagogie pentru examenele de defintivare °i grade didactice, Editura Polirom, Ia°i

Cunia E. Behavioral learning theory. Principles of instruction and learning: a web quest.

Dave, R.H. (coord.) (1976). *Founding of Lifelong Education*. Pergamon, Oxford

De Landsheer, V. (1992). L'Education des adultes, in V. De Landsheer, G. De Landsheer, L'Education et la formation. PUF, Paris

Dembo M.H. (1995). *Applying educational psychology*. White Plains, NY: Longman Publishing Group,.

Deschamps, J.C., Moprales, J.F., Paez, D., Worchel, S. (1999). L'identité sociale. La construction de l'individu dans les relations entre groupes, Grenoble, Presses Universitaires de Grenoble

Dhanjal, R. & Calis, G. (1999). "Computer-based training in the steel industry". *Steel Times,* 227, 13-14.

Dick, W., & Carey, L. (1996). *The Systematic Design of Instruction*. New York, NY: HarperCollins.

Didierjean A., Cauzinille-Marmeche E. (1998). Reasoning by analogy: is it schema-mediated or case-based? *Eur J Psych Ed.* 8(3):385-98.

Dillenbourg, P. (1999) Introduction: What do you mean by "collaborative learning"? In P. Dillenbourg (Ed.), *Collaborative learning: Cognitive and computational approaches* (pp. 1-19): Amsterdam: Pergamon.

Domeshek E., Kolodner J. (1993). Using the point of large cases. *Artificial Intelligence for Engineering Design, Analysis and Manufacturing*. 7(2):87-96.

Dowson, G., Fischer, K.W. (editors) (1994) *Human Behavior and the Developing Brain*. New York, Guilford Press

Driscoll M.P. (2000). *Psychology of learning for instruction*. Needham Heights, MA: Allyn & Bacon.

Driscoll, M.P. (1994). *Psychology of Learning for Instruction: Learning and Instructional Technology*. Needham Heights, MA: Paramount Publishing.

Duchasel, P. (1995). Learning Interfaces. In T. Liao (Ed.), *Advanced Educational Technology: Research Issues and Future Potential* (pp. 207-216). Berlin, Germany: Springer-Verlag.

Duffy T.M., Jonassen D.H. (1992). Constructivism and the technology of instruction: a conversation. Lawrence Erlbaum. New Jersey.

Dumitriu, Gh., Dumitriu, C. (1997) Psihologia procesului de învãþãmânt, Editura Didacticã ºi Pedagogicã, Bucureºti

Durrett, J., & Trezona, J. (1982). How to Use Color Displays Effectively: The Elements of Color Vision and their Implications for Programmers. *Pipeline*, 7, No.2, 13-16.

Dwyer, F.M. (1978). Strategies for Improving Visual Learning. State College, PA: Learning Services.

Edelson D.C. (1993). Learning from stories: indexing and reminding in a Socratic case-based teaching system. Northwestern University.

England, E. & Finney, A. (1996). *Managing Multimedia*. Addison-Wesley, Reading, Massachussetts, U.S.A.

Ertmer P.A., Newby T.J. (1993). Behaviorism, cognitivism, constructivism: comparing critical features from an instructional design perspective. *Perf Improvement Q*. 6:50-70.

Ertmer, P.A., Addison, P., Lane, M., Ross, E., & Woods, D. (1999). Examining teachers' beliefs about the role of technology in the elementary classroom. *Journal of Research on Computing in Education, 32,* 54-72.

Falk, D.R. and H.L. Carlson. (1992). Learning to Teach with Multimedia. Technological Horizons in *Education Journal: Curriculum Integration* 20 (2), 96-101.

Feltovich P.J., Spiro R.J., Coulson R.L. (1989). The nature of conceptual understanding in biomedicine: the deep structure of complex ideas and the development of misconceptions. In: Evans D.A., Patel V.L., editors. *The cognitive sciences in medicine*. Cambridge (MA): MIT Press. pp. 113–72.

Fenwick T.J. (2000). Expanding conceptions of experiential learning: a review of the five contemporary perspectives on cognition. *Adult Education Quarterly*. 50(4):243-272.

Feynman, R.P. (1964). *The Feynman Lectures on Physics*. Addison-Wesley, Reading, MA, Chap.1.

Filipczak, B. (1997). "Training Gets Doomed." *Training* 34(8): 24-31.

Fleming, M., & Levie, W.H. (1978). Instructional Message Design: Principles from the Behavioral Sciences. Englewood Cliffs, NJ: Educational Technology Publications.

Fond-Harmant, L. (1996) Des adultes à l'université, L'Harmattan, Paris

Forster, B. (1998). Computer-based training substitutes for instructors. *Boston Business Journal*, 18 (33), 40-42.

Fosnot C.T. (1989). Enquiring teachers, enquiring learners: a constructivist approach for teaching. New York: Teachers College Press.

Fosnot C.T. (1996). Constructivism: theory, perspectives and practice. New York, NY: Teacher's College Press.

Fox E.J. (2004). The personalized system of instruction: a flexible and effective approach to mastery learning, In: *Evidence-Based Educational Methods*. Academic Press, San Diego.

Franklin, S. & Marasco, J. (1977). Interactive Computer Based Testing. *Journal of College Science Teaching* (September), 15-20.

Gagné R.M., Briggs LJ, Wager WF. (1985). *Principles of instructional design*. Wadsworth.

Gagné R.M., Driscoll M. (1988). *Essentials of learning for instruction*. Englewood Cliffs, NJ: Prentice-Hall.

Gagné R.M. (1962). Military training and principles of learning. *American Psychologist*. 17:263-276.

Gagné R.M. (1965). *The conditions of learning and theory of instruction*. New York, NY: Holt, Rinehart & Winston.

Gagné R.M. (1987). Instructional technology foundations. Hillsdale, NJ: Lawrence Erlbaum Assoc.

Gahan S. (2001). Piaget's theory of cognitive development applied to the classroom. University of Leicester, School Education Social Science Resource.

Gardner, H. (1999). Multiple Approaches to Understanding. In C.M. Reigeluth (Ed.),

Instructional Design Theories and Models: A New Paradigm of Instructional Theory (Vol. II) (pp.69-89). Mahwah, NJ: Lawerence Erlbaum Associates.

Garisson, D.R. (1992) Critical Thinking and Self-Directed Learning in *Adult Education: An Analisis of Responsibility and Control Issues Adult Education*, Quaterly 42 (3), 136-148

Gaynor, P. (1981). The Effect of Feedback Delay on Retention of Computer-Based Mathematical Material. *Journal of Computer Based Instruction*, 8 (1981), 28-34.

Gerlach, V.C. & Ely, D.P. (1980). *Teaching and Media: A Systematic Approach* (2nd Edition). Englewood Cliffs, NJ: Prentice-Hall.

Gery, G. (1987). *Making CBT Happen*. Weingarten Publications, Boston, U.S.A..

Gick ML, Holyoak KJ. (1980). Analogical problem solving. *Cognitive Psych*. 12, 306-355.

Giesbrecht, N. (2007). Connectivism: Teaching and learning. http://design.test.olt.ubc.ca/Connectivism:_Teaching_and_Learning

Giesbrecht, N. (2007). Connectivism: Teaching and learning. http://design.test.olt.ubc.ca/Connectivism:_Teaching_and_Learning

Giustini D. (2010). Evidence-based teaching for health librarians: some questions and considerations. *JCHLA / JABSC*. 31(1):7–10.

Giustini D. (2010). Evidence-based teaching for health librarians: some questions and considerations. *JCHLA / JABSC*. 31(1):7-10.

Gobbo C, Chi MTH. (1986). How knowledge is structured and used by expert and novice children. *Cognitive Development*. 1:221-237.

Goldin-Meadow S, Nusbaum H, Garber P, Chruch RB. Transition in learning: Evidence for simultaneously activated strategies. *J Exp Psych: Human Percep Perform*. 19(1):92-107.

Good TL, Brophy JE. (1990). *Educational psychology: a realistic approach. White Plains*, NY: Longman.

Greeno, J. G. (1998). The situativity of knowing, learning, and research. *American Psychologist, 53*(1), 5-26.

Gustafson, K. (1991). Survey of Instructional Development Models. Syracuse: ERIC Clearinghouse on Information Resources (ED 211 097).

Habermas J. (1984). *The theory of communicative action*. Vol. 1: Reason and the rationalization of society. Boston: Beacon.

Hadley, M., & Sheingold, K. (1993). Commonalties and distinctive patterns in teachers'integration of computers. *American Journal of Education, 101,* 261- 315.

Hammond KJ. (1990). Case-based planning: a framework for planning from experience. *Cognitive Science*. 14:385-443.

Hannafin, M, Dalton, D. & Hooper, S. (1989). Computers in Education: Ten Myths and Ten Needs. *Educational Technology*, 27 (10) 8-14.

Hannafin, M. & Peck, K. (1988). Chapter 18 in *The Design, Development and Evaluation of Instructional Software*. Macmillan Publishing, New Year.

Hannafin, M., & Reiber, L. P. (1989). Psychological foundations of instructional design for emerging computer-based instructional technologies: Part I. *Educational Technology Research and Development, 37*(2), 91-101.

Hannafin, M.J. & Peck, K.L. (1985). *The Design, Development and Evaluation of Instructional Software.* Macmillan Publishers, New York.

Hannafin, R.D., & Freeman D. J. (1995). An exploratory study of teachers' views of knowledge acquisition. *Educational Technology, 35*, 49-56.

Hansen, D.N. (1970). The Role of Computers in Education During the 70's. Technical Memo # 15. Florida: Computer Assisted Instruction Center, Florida State University.

Harp, C., S. Taylor, et al (1998). "Computer Training and Individual Differences: When Method Matters." *Human Resource Development Quarterly*, 9(3): 271-283.

Hartemink, F.J.A. (ed.) (1988). Handbook for the Design of Educational Software. Version 3.0. PMI series 12, C.O.I., Enschede, Netherlands (in Dutch).

Hasselbring, T. & Carruthers, B. (1982). The Computerized Test of Reading Comprehension (unpublished manuscript). Nashville: Peabody College of Vanderbilt University.

Hasselbring, T. & Owens, S. (1983). Microcomputer Based Analysis of Spelling Errors. *Computers, Reading and Language Arts*.1, 26-31.

Healy, J. (1998). *Failure to Connect: How computers affect our children's mind and what we can do about it*. New York: Simon & Schuster.

Heer, A. & Sampin, A. (1997). Sulzer ruti: Computer-based training. *Textile World*, 47(4), 56-58

Henderson, A. (1991). 'A Development Perspective on Interface Design and Theory'. In: J.M Carroll (ed.), *Designing Interaction*, Cambridge University Press, pp. 254-269-8.

Herrington, J., & Standen, P. (2000). Moving from an Instructivist to a Constructivist multimedia learning environment. *Journal of Educational Multimedia and Hypermedia, 9*(3), 195- 205.

Higgins O, Sixsmith J, Barry MM. (2011). A literature review on health information-seeking behaviour on the web: a health consumer and health professional perspective. Stockholm: ECDC.

Hoffman S. (1997). Elaboration theory and hypermedia: is there a link? *Educational Technology*. 37(1):57-64.

Holmes, G. and M.E. Kidd. (1982). Second Language Learning and Computers. *Canadian Modern Language Review* 38 (3), 503-516.

Honev, M., & Moeller, B. (1990). *Teachers' beliefs and technology integration: Different values, different understanding*. New York: Center for Technology in Education. http://www.instructionaldesigncentral.com/htm/IDC_instructionaldesignmodels.htm#sthash.DeAxJXLJ.dpuf

Huang, A. (1997). "Online Training: A New Form of Computer-Based Training." *Journal of Education for Business* 73(1): 35-38

Ionel, V. (2002) Pedagogia situaþiilor educative, Editura Polirom, Ia°i

Irving, A. (1991). The educational value and use of on-line information services in schools. *Computers in Education, 17*, 213-225.

Issa N, Mayer RE, Schuller M, Wang E, Shapiro MB, Darosa DA. (2013). Teaching for understanding in medical classrooms using multimedia design principles. *Med Educ.* Apr; 47(4):388-96.

Janicak, C. (1999). "Computer-based training: Developing programs with the knowledge-based safety training system". *Professional Safety*, 44, 34-36.

Järvelä, S., Häkkinen, P., Arvaja, M. & Leinonen, P. (2003) Instructional support in CSCL. In P. Kirchner, J-W. Strijbos and R. Martens (Eds.) *What we know about CSCL in higher education* (pp.115-139). New York: Kluwer Academic Publishers.

Jolicoeur, K. & Berger, D.E. (1988). Implementing Educational Software and Evaluating Its Academic Effectiveness: Part I & II. *Educational Technology*, Vol. 28 (9-10).

Jonassen D, Ambruso D, Olesen J. (1992). Designing hypertext on transfusion medicine using cognitive flexibility theory. *J Educational Multimedia and Hypermedia.* 1(3):309-322.

Jonassen D. (1998). Designing constructivist learning environments. In: *Instructional theories and models*. Mahwah, NJ: Lawrence Erlbaum.

Jonassen DH, Mayes JT. (1993). A manifesto for a constructivist approach to technology in higher education.

Jonassen DH, Prevish T, Christy D, Stavrulaki E. (1999). Learning to solve problems on the web: aggregate planning in a business management course. *Dist Ed* 20(1):49-63.

Jonassen DH. (1999). Designing constructivist learning environments. In: *Instructional design theories and models: A new paradigm*. Mahwah, NJ: Lawrence Erlbaum.

Jonassen DH. (1999). *Learning with technology: a constructivist perspective*. Upper Saddle River, NJ: Prentice-Hall.

Jonassen DH. Cognitive flexibility hypertexts on the Web: Engaging learners in meaning making. In: *Web-based instruction.* New Jersey: Educational Technology Publications.

Jonassen, D. H. (1991). Objectivism versus constructivism: Do we need a new philosophical paradigm? *Educational Technology Research & Development, 39*(3), 5-14.

Jonassen, D. H. (2000). *Computers as mindtools for schools: Engaging critical thinking.* Columbus, OH: Prentice-Hall.

Jonassen, D. H., & Reeves, T. (1996). Learning with computers: Computers as cognitive tools. In D. H. Jonassen (Ed.), *Handbook of Research for Educational Communications and Technology* (pp. 693-719). New York: MacMillan.

Kaye AR. (1992). Learning together apart. In AR Kaye (Ed), *Collaborative Learning Through Computer Conferencing.* Springer-Verlag, London pp. 1- 24.

Kearsley G. (2001). Explorations in learning & instruction: the theory into practice database. Stanford Education Faculty.

Kearsley G. Structural learning theory. http://tip.psychology.org/scandura.html

Keller FS. (1968). Goodbye teacher. *J Applied Behavior Analysis.* 1:79–89.

Kemp, J. (1985). *The Instructional Design Process.* New York, NY: Harper Row.

Kennedy, C. (1998). *Reinventing Teaching in the Classroom of the Future: The political science laboratory experience.* New York: Penn State University. http://www.personal.psu.edu/faculty/c/l/clk8/reinvebtteach.html.

Kinzer, C.K, Sherwood, R.D. & Bransford, J.D. (1986). *Computer Strategies for Education* (Foundations and content area application). Merrill Publishing Company.

Kinzie MB. (2005). Instructional design strategies for health behavior change. *Patient Educ Couns.* Jan;56 (1):3-15.

Knuth RA, Cunningham DJ. (1992). Tools for constructivism. In: *Designing environments for constructive learning.* Springer-Verlag, Berlinpp. 163-188.

Kolb D. (1984). *Experiential learning: experience as the source of learning and development.* Englewood Cliffs, NJ: Prentice Hall.

Kolodner JL, Guzdial M. (2000). Theory and practice of case-based learning aids. In: *Theoretical foundations of learning environments.* Mahwah, NJ: Lawrence Erlbaum Associates.

Kolodner JL, Kolodner RM. (1987). Using experience in clinical problem solving: Introduction and framework. *IEEE Transactions on Systems, Man and Cybernetics.* 17(3):420-431.

Kolodner JL. (1992). An introduction to case-based reasoning. *Artificial Intelligence Review.* 6(3):3-34.

Koshmann T, Collins A, Klein G, Holyoak K, Kolodner J. (1997). The role of cases in learning. *Annual Conference of the Cognitive Science Society.*

Kovalik, S.J. & McGeehan, J.R. (1999). Integrated Thematic Instruction: From Brain Research to Application. In C.M.Reigeluth (Ed.), *Instructional Design Theories and Models: A New Paradigm of Instructional Theory* (Vol.II) (pp.371-396). Mahwah, NJ: Lawrence Erlbaum Associates.

Kuhn ME. (1990). Teaching material. Ways to enhance visual aids in staff development programs. *AORN J.* Feb;51(2):539–40, 542–3, 546–7.

Kulhavy, R.W & Anderson, R.C. (1972). The Delay-retention Effect with Multiple-choice Tests. *Journal of Educational Psychology*, 63, 505-12.

Kulik JA. (1979). A meta-analysis of outcome studies of Keller's Personalized System of Instruction. *Am Psych.* 34(4):307–18.

Kulik, C., Kulik, J., and Bangert-Drowns, R. (1985). The Importance of Outcomes: A Reply to Clark. *Journal of Educational Computing Research*, 7, 381-387.

Kulik, J.A., Kulik, C.C. & Cohen, P.A. (1980). Effectiveness of Computer Based College Teaching: A Meta Analysis of Findings. *Review of Educational Research*, 50, 525-544.

Lajoie, S., & Derry, S. (1993). *Computers as Cognitive Tools.* LEA: Hillsdale, NJ.

Laurillard, D. (1987). The different forms of learning in psychology and education. In J.

T. E. Richardson, M. W. Eysenck &D. W. Piper (Eds.), *Student Learning* (pp. 198-207). Milton Keynes, England: Open University Press.

Lave J, Wenger E. (1991). *Situated learning: legitimate peripheral participation.* Cambridge: Cambridge University Press.

Lave J. (1989). Cognition in practice. Mind, mathematics and culture in everyday life.

Lave, J., & Wenger, E. (1991). *Situated Learning: Legitimate Peripheral Participation.* New York, New York, USA: Cambridge, University Press.

Laws, P.W. (1991). Calculus-Based Physics Without Lectures, Physics Today, 44.

Lawson, R. (1999). *Computer-based training: Is it the next wave? Professional Safety, 44(1), 30-34.*

Lee, J. (1994). Effectiveness of Computer-Based Instructional Simulation: A Meta Analysis. *International Journal of Instructional Media*, 26 (1), 71-85.

Lehtinen, E. (2003) Computer-supported collaborative learning: An approach to powerful learning environments. In E. de Corte, L. Vershaffel, N. Entwistle, & J. van Merrieboer (Eds.), Powerful learning environments: Unravelling basic components and dimensions (pp. 35-54). Amsterdam: Pergamon.

Linger H, Warne L. (2001). Making the invisible visible: modelling social learning in knowledge management context. *Australasian J Information Systems*. 56–66.

Lipponen, L. & Lallimo, J. (2004) Assessing applications for collaboration: from collaboratively usable applications to collaborative technology. *British Journal of Educational Technology*, (35)4, 433-442.

Lowyck, J., & Elen, J. (1993). Transitions in the theoretical foundation of instructional design. In T. M. Duffy, J. Lowyck &D. H. Jonassen (Eds.), *Designing Environments for Constructive Learning* (Vol. 105, pp. 213-229). Berlin, Germany: Springer-Verlag.

Mager, R. F. (1984). *Preparing Instructional Objectives*. (2nd Edition). Belmont, CA: Pitman.

Maggio LA, Tannery NH, Chen HC, Cate OT, O'Brien B. (2013). Evidence-based medicine training in undergraduate medical education: a review and critique of the literature published 2006-2011. *Acad Med.* Jul;88(7):1022-1028.

Maher ML, Balachandran MB, Zhang DM. *Case-based reasoning in design*. Mahwah, NJ: Lawrence Erlbaum Associates.

Markle, S.M. (1969). *Good Frames and Bad: A Grammar of Frame Writing*. New York: John Wiley.

Martin TL, Pear JJ, Martin GL. (2002). Analysis of proctor marking accuracy in a computer-aided personalized system of instruction course. *J Appl Behav Anal*. 35:309–312.

Martin, J.M., Szabo, M. (1990). The Dialogue and Computer-Assisted Instruction in Chemistry. *Journal of Computer-Based Instruction*. 17, 41-45.

Mason, R., Rennie, F. (2007). Using web 2.0 for learning in the community. *Journal of Internet and Higher Education, 10*(3), pp.196-203. http://www.sciencedirect.com.

Maubant, P. (2004) Pédagogues et pédagogies en formation d'adultes. PUF, Paris

McClintock, R. (1992). *Power and pedagogy: Transforming education through information technology*. New York: Teachers College Press.

McDermoot, L.C. (1993). Guest comment: How We Teach and How Students Learn-A Mismatch? *American Journal of Physics*, 61, 295-298.

McKenna, P. (2004). *Constructivist or instructivist: Pedagogical concepts practically applied to a computer learning environment.* Proceedings of the Innovation and Technology in Computer Science Education, Leeds, UK, 166-170.

Means, B., & Olson, K. (1997). *Technology and education reform*. Washington, DC: U.S. Department of Education.

Mergel, B. (1998). Instructional Design & Learning Theory. Educational Communications and Technology, University of Saskatchewan.

Merrill MD, Li Z, Jones MK. (1991). Second generation instructional design (ID2). *Educational Technology* 30(1):7-11.

Merrill MD, Li Z, Jones MK. Instructional transaction theory. *Educational Technology*. 31(6):7–12.

Merrill MD. (1983). Component display theory. In: Instructional-design theories and models: an overview of their current status. Hillsdale, NJ: Lawrence Erlbaum Associates.

Merrill MD. (2002). First principles of instruction. *Educational Technology Research and Development*. 50(3):43–59.

Merrill MD. (2008). Effective peer interaction in a problem-centered instructional strategy. *Distance Education*. 29(2):199–207.

Merrill MD. Instructional design based on knowledge objects. In: *Instructional design theories and models*. VII. Mahwah, NJ: Lawrence Erlbaum Associates.

Merrill, M.D. (1997). Instructional Strategies That Teach. *CBT Solutions*, Nov./Dec., 1-11.

Merrill, M.D. (2000). Knowledge Objects and mental Models. In D.A. Wiley (Ed.). *The Instructional Use of Learning Objects*. Washington D.C.: Association for Educational Communications and Technology. On-line version at http://reusability.org/read.

Mezirow J. (1995). *Transformation theory of adult learning*. New York: SUNY Press.

Mezirow J. (2000). *Learning as transformation: critical perspectives on a theory in progress*. San Francisco: Jossey Bass.

Mezirow J. Transformative learning: theory to practice. *New Directions for Adult & Cont Ed*. San Francisco, CA: Jossey-Bass.

Miller N, Dollard J. (1941). *Social learning and imitation*. New Haven, NJ: Yale University Press.

Miller, G.A. (1956). The magical number seven, plus or minus two: Some limits on our capacity for processing information. *Psychological Review*, 63, 81-97.

Min, R. (1995). *Simulation Technology and Parallelism in Learning Environments*. De Lier: Academic Book Center. ISBN 90-5478-036-3.

Molnar, Andrew R. (1990). Computers in Education: A Historical Perspective of the Unifinished Task. *T.H.E Journal*, 18 (4), pp. 80-83.

Montazemi AR, Gupta KM. A framework for retrieval in case-based reasoning systems, *Annals of Operations Research*, 72, 51-73.

Moore, C. (1992). *Appropriate Technology*. Manchester: The British Council.

Morrison, G. R., Ross, S. M. and Kemp, J. E. (2001). *Designing Effective Instruction*. (3rd Edition). New York: John Wiley and Sons.

Nakhleh, B.M. (1983). An Overview of Microcomputers in the Secondary Science Curriculum. Computers in Mathematics and Science, Fall, 3 (1), pp.13-21

Nicola, I. (1996) Tratat de pedagogie °colarã, Editura Didacticã °i Pedagogicã, Bucure°ti

Nothnagle M, Goldman R, Quirk M, Reis S. (2010). Promoting self-directed learning skills in residency: a case study in program development. *Acad Med*. Dec; 85(12):1874-9.

Olson, J. (1988). School Worlds/Microworlds: Computers and the Culture of the Classroom.New York: Pergamon Press.

Ormrod JE. (1999). Human learning. 3e. Upper Saddle River, NJ: Prentice-Hall.

Owston, R.D & Dudley-Marling, C. (1988). A Criterion Based Approach to Software Evaluation. *Journal of Research in Computing in Education*, Vol. 20 (3).

Papert, S. (1982). Mindstorms (Children, Computers and Powerful Ideas). The Harvester Press Limited.

Pãun, E., (1999) ªcoala – abordare sociopedagogicã, Editura Polirom, Ia°i

Pear JJ. (2011). Web based computer aided personalized system of instruction. *New Dir Teach Learn*. (128):85-94.

Pearlman, R. (1993). "Restructuring with Technology". In T. Cannings and L. Finkel (Eds.), *The Technology Age Classroom* (612-617), Wilsonville, Oregon: Franklin, Beedle and Associates, Incorp.

Perry, William G. (1999). *Forms of Ethical and Intellectual Development in the College Years*. San Francisco: Jossey-Bass Publishers.

Piaget J. (1985). *The equilibration of cognitive structures: the central problem of intellectual development*. Chicago, IL: University of Chicago Press.

Piaget J. *Genetic epistemology*. New York: Columbia University Press.

Piaget J. *The equilibration of cognitive structures*. Chicago, IL: University of Chicago Press.

Piaget, J. (1951). *Play, Dreams and Imitation in Childhood*. New York: W.W.Norton & Company.

Piaget, Jean (1968). *Six Psychological Studies*. Anita Tenzer (Trans.), New York: Vintage Books.

Prewitt, M. (1998). "Darden execs share ins, outs of computer training". *Nation's Restaurant News, 32, 57-58.*

Provost, J.A. (1990). Work, Play and Type: Achieving Balance in Your Life. Palo Alto, CA: Consulting Psychologist Press.

Rasheed KS, Cohen PA. (1990). An evaluation of computer-based instruction versus printed study guides in a dental material course. *J Dent Hyg*. 64(1):36–9.

Reedy GB. (2008). PowerPoint, interactive whiteboards, and the visual culture of technology in schools. *Technology, Pedagogy and Education*. 17(2):143–162.

Reeves, T. C., & Reeves, P. M. (1997). Effective Dimensions of Interactive Learning on the World Wide Web. In B. H. Khan (Ed.), *Web-Based Instruction* (pp. 59-66). Englewood Cliffs, New Jersey, USA: Educational Technology Publications.

Reeves, T.C. (1993). Evaluating Technology Based Learning. In Piskurich A.S.T.D. *Handbook of Information Technology*.

Reeves, T.C. (1993)b. Research Support for Interactive Multimedia: Existing Foundation and New Directions (pp. 79-96). In C. Latchem, J. Williamson & L. Henderson-Lancett (Eds.), *Interactive Multimedia: Practice and Promise*. London: Kogan Page.

Reeves, T.C. (1994). Systematic Evaluation Procedures for Interactive Multimedia for Education and Training. In Reisman, S. (Ed.). *Multimedia Computing: Preparing for the 21st Century*. Harrisburg, PA: Idea Group.

Reeves, T.C. (1997). Evaluation Tools Available Online: http://mimi.marc.gatech.edu/MM_Tools/evaluation.html.

Rega MD. (1993). A model approach for patient education. *Medsurg Nurs*. Dec;2(6):477-9, 495.

Reid, T.A. (1992). Information Technology Strategic Planning Proposals Office of IT, University of Western Australia.

Reigeluth CM. (1979). In search of a better way to organize instruction: the elaboration theory. *J Instruction Dev*. 2(3):8-15.

Reigeluth CM. (1999). Instructional-design theories and models: a new paradigm of instructional theory. *Instructional Design Theories & Models*. Lawrence Erlbaum Associates.

Reigeluth CM. (1999). The elaboration theory: guidance for scope and sequences. In: *Instructional-design theories and models: a new paradigm of instructional theory*. Mahwah, NJ: Lawrence Erlbaum Associates.

Reigeluth, C.M. (1999). *Instructional Design Theories and Models: A New Paradigm of Instructional Theory* (Vol. II). Mahwah, NJ: Lawrence Erlbaum Associates.

Reinbold S. (2013). Using the ADDIE model in designing library instruction. *Medical Ref Serv Q*. 32(3):244-256.

Richardson, J. T. E. (1987). Research in education and cognitive psychology. In J. T. E. Richardson, M. W. Eysenck &D. W. Piper (Eds.), *Student Learning* (pp. 3-12). Milton Keynes, England: Open University Press.

Richardson, W. (2006).Blogs, wikis, and podcasts, and other powerful web tools for classroom. California: Corwin Press.

Rickel, J.W. (1989). Intelligent Computer–Aided Instruction: A Survey Organized Around System Components. IEEE transaction on System, Man and Cybernetics, 19 (1).

Riddle, E. M. (1995). *Communication through multimedia in an elementary classroom* (Report No. 143). Charlottesville, VA: Curry School of Education, University of Virginia. (ERIC Document Reproduction Service No. ED 384 346)

Rieber, L.P. (1994). Computers, Graphics and Learning. Dubuque. IA: Wm. C. Brown Communications.

Rieber, L.P. (1996). Animation as Feedback in a Computer-Based Simulation: Representation Matters. *Educational Technology Research & Development*, 44 (1), 5-22.

Rigney, J.W. & Lutz, K.A. (1976). Effects of Graphic Analogies of Concepts in Chemistry on Learning and Attitude. *Journal of Educational Psychology*, 68, 305-11.

Ritchie, D. C., & Hoffman, B. (1997). Incorporating Instructional Design principles with the World Wide Web. In B. H. Khan (Ed.), *Web-Based Instruction* (pp. 135-138). Englewood Cliffs, New Jersey, USA: Educational Technology Publications.

Rizo, F.M. (1991). The Controversy About Qualification in Social Research: An Extension of Gage's " Historical Sketch". *Educational Researcher*, 20 (12), 9-12.

Roblyer, M. D. *et al.* (1997). *Integrating Educational Technology into Teaching*, Merrill/ Prentice-Hall.

Rogers, J.B. (1984). Computer Use in Pre-College Education. IEEE Computer, 17 (4).

Roschelle, J. & Teasley, S. (1995) The Construction of Shared Knowledge in Collaborative Problem Solving. In C. O'Malley (ed.) *Computer-Supported Collaborative Learning* (pp. 69-97), Heidelberg: Springer-Verlag.

Rothfeder, J. (1998). "Computer-Based Training." *Forbes* 1(1): 34-35.

Rothman, M. (1972). *Discovering Natural Laws: The Experimental Basis of Physics*, Doubleday, New York

Rothwell, W.J., & Kazanas, H.C. (1997). *Mastering the Instructional Design Process: A Systematic Approach.* San Francisco: Jossey-Bass.

Rubenstein, E. (1999). "The learning imperative: Operators tap CBT, the 'net,' to train and retain employees". *Nation's Restaurant News*, 33, 51-52.

Rumelhart DE. (1981). Norman DA. Analogical processes in learning. In J.R. Anderson. *Cognitive skills and their acquisition*. Hillsdale, NJ: Erlbaum.

Rumelhart, D.E. & Ortony, A. (1977). 'The Representation of Knowledge in Memory' in Schooling and the Acquisition of Knowledge, eds. R.C. Anderson, R.J. Spiro & W.E. Montague. Hillsdale, NJ: Lawrence Erlbaum Associates.

Ryba, K., & Brown, M. E. (2000). How proficient IT teachers integrate computers into the curriculum. *Journal of Computing in Teacher Education, 16*, 6-11.

Sabeih, C. (1998). The Use of the Computer as a Tool and/or Tutor to Enhance Language Learning. Unpublished doctoral dissertation, University of the Holy Spirit Kaslik, Lebanon.

Sadaf S, Ali SK, Zuberi RW. (2009). Educational models and strategies in health education. Introduction. *Educ Health (Abingdon)*. May;22(1):96.

Sălăvăstru, D. (2004) Psihologia educaþiei, Editura Polirom, Ia°i

Salovaara, H. & Järvelä, S. (2003) Students strategic actions in Computer Supported Collaborative Inquiry. *Learning Environments Research*. 6(3), 267-284.

Samenow CP, Worley LL, Neufeld R, Fishel T, Swiggart WH. (2013). Transformative learning in a professional development course aimed at addressing disruptive physician behavior: a composite case study. *Acad Med.* Jan;88(1):117-123.

Sandler, R. (1998). *CBT boosts skills, improves attitudes to learning. Computing Canada, 24(23), 30.*

Sattler, P. (1990). The Evolution of American Educational Technology. Englewood, CO: Libraries Unlimited, Inc.

Scandura JM, Scandura AB. (1980). *Structural learning and concrete operations*. New York: Praeger Publishers.
Scandura JM. (1984). Structural (cognitive task) analysis: a method for analyzing content. Part II: Precision, objectivity, and systematization. *J Structural Learning*. 8:1-27.
Scandura JM. (2001). Structural learning theory: current status and new perspectives. *Instructional Science*. 29(4-5):311-336.
Scandura JM. (2003). Domain specific structural analysis for intelligent tutoring systems: automatable representation of declarative, procedural and model- based knowledge with relationships to software engineering. *Technology, Instruction, Cognition & Learning*. 1(1):7-58.
Scandura JM. (2007). Knowledge representation in structural learning theory and relationships to adaptive learning and tutoring systems. *Tech Inst Cognition Learning*. 5:169-271.
Scandura T. (1992). Mentorship and career mobility: an empirical investigation. *J Organ Behav*. 13(2):169-174.
Scandura TA. (1998). Dysfunctional mentoring relationships and outcomes. *J Management*. 24(3):449-467
Schank, R.C. (1995). *Engines for Education*. Hillsdale, NJ: Lawrence Erlbaum Associates.
Scheffler, F., & Logan, J. (1999). Computer technology in schools: What teachers should know and be able to do. *Journal of Research on Computing in Education,* 31, 305- 325.
Schunk DH. (1991). Learning theories: an educational perspective. New York: Macmillan.
Schwarz, H. & Lewis, M. (1989). Basic Concept Microcomputer Courseware: A Critical Evaluation System for Educators. *Educational Technology*, 29 (5), pp. 16-18.
Scollon, R., Wong Scollon, R. (1995) Intercultural Communication. Oxford, Blackwell
Scriven, M. (1967).The methodology of evaluation.In R. W. Tyler, R. M. Gagne, & M. Scriven (Eds.), *Perspectives of curriculum evaluation*, 39-83. Chicago, IL: Rand McNally.
Shachak A, Ophir R, Rubin E. (2005) Applying instructional design theories to bioinformatics education in microarray analysis and primer design workshops. *Cell Biol Educ*. 4(3):199-206.
Shank JD. (2012). Academic library administrators' perceptions of four instructional skills. *Coll Res Libr*. January 73(1):78-93.
Shank RC, Abelson R. (1977). Scripts, plans, goals and understanding. Hillsdale, NJ: Erlbaum.
Shank RC, Berman TR, Macpherson KA. Learning by doing. In: *Instructional Design Theories and Models*. Mahwah, NJ: Lawrence Erlbaum Associates.
Shank RC. (1982). *Dynamic memory: A theory of learning in people and computers*. Cambridge: Cambridge University Press.
Shank RC. (1990). Tell ma a story: narrative and intelligence. Evanston, IL: Northwestern University Process.
Siemens, G. (2004). A learning theory for the digital age. http://www.elearnspace.org/Articles/connectivism.htm
Siemens, G. (2006). Conectivism: learning and knowledge today. http://www.educationau.edu.au/jahia/webdav/site/myjahiasite/shared/globalsummit/gs2006_siemens.pdf
Siemens, G., (2005). Connectivism: A Learning Theory for the Digital Age. *International Journal of Instructional Technology and Distance Learning, 2, 1*. http://www.itdl.org/Journal/Jan_05/article01.htm
Siemens, G., (2005). Learning as network creation. *Learning circuits*. http://www.learningcircuits.org/
Skinner BF. (1950). Are theories of learning necessary? *Psych Rev*. 57:193-216.
Skinner BF. (1958). Teaching machines. *Science*. 128(967-77):137-58.
Skinner BF. (1972). Utopia through the control of human behavior. Readings in the Philosophy of Education. Belmont, CA: Wadsworth.

Skinner, B. F. (1976). *About Behaviorism*. New York: Vintage Books.

Skinner, B.F. (1954). The Science of Learning and the Art of Teaching. Harvard *Educational Review*, 24, 86-97.

Skinner, Thorndike, Watson. [On-line]. Available: http://userwww.sfsu.edu/-rsauzier/Thoendike.html.

Smaldino SE, Lowther DL, Russell JD. (2012). *Instructional technology and media for learning*. Upper Saddle River, NJ: Prentice Hall.

Smith, P. L., & Ragan, T. J. (1999). *Instructional Design*. 2nd ed. New York, NY: John Wiley & Sons, Inc.

Spector, J. Michael. (2000). Toward a Philosophy of Instructional Design. Annual Meeting of the American Educational Research Association. New Orleans, LA: AERA 2000.

Spencer, B. (2004). On-Line adult learning. In griff Foley (ed.), *Dimensions of adult learning: Adilt education and training in a global era* (pp.182-200). Berkshire: Open University Press.

Spille, A.H.; Galloway, W.S. & Stewart, W.D. (1985). How to Evaluate Courseware Designed for Use in Education or Training Programmes for Adult Learners? *Educational Technology*, 25 (3), pp. 40-42.

Spiro RJ, Feltovich PJ, Jacobson MJ, Coulson RL. (1991). Cognitive flexibility, constructivism and hypertext: random access instruction for advanced knowledge acquisition in ill-structured domains. *Ed Tech*. 24-33.

Spiro RJ, Jehng JC. (1990). Cognitive flexibility and hypertext: theory and technology for non-linear and multi-dimensional traversal of subject matter. Hillsdale, NJ: Lawrence Erlbaum.

Spring H. (2010). Theories of learning: models of good practice for evidence-based information skills teaching. *Health Info Libr J*. Dec;27(4):327-31.

Staats CK, Staats AW. (1957). Meaning established by classical conditioning. *J Exp Psychol*. 54:74-80.

Stanfield, D. (1973). *The Computer and Education*. The Educational Technology Review Series # 9. Englewood Cliffs, New Jersey: Educational Technology Publications.

Sternberger C, Meyer L. (2001). Hypermedia-assisted instruction: authoring with learning guidelines. *Comput Nurs*. Mar-Apr;19(2):69-74.

Stevens, R.S. (1994). Technology, Music, Teaching and Learning. Art and Music Technology Course. Deakin University.

Stollings L. Robert (2007). Gagne's nine learning events: instructional design for dummies.

Sugarman, R. (1978). "What's New Teacher?" Ask the Computer. *IEEE Spectrum*, 15 (9).

Sugarman, R. (1978). A Second Chance for Computer-Aided Instruction. *IEEE Spectrum*, 15 (8).

Surber, J.R & Anderson, R.C. (1975). Delay-retention in Natural Classroom Settings. *Journal of Educational Psychology*, 67, 170-73.

Szabo, M. & Flesher, K. (2002). CMI Theory and Practice: The Historical Roots of LMS. Paper presented at the E-Learning conference annual meeting, Association for the Advancement of Computers in Education.

Taylor EW. (1998). The theory and practice of transformative learning: a critical review. Columbus, OH: Center on Education and Training for Employment.

Taylor, R. (1980). *The Computer in the School: Tutor, Tool, Tutee*. New York: Teachers College Press.

Teasley, S., & Rochelle, J. (1993) Constructing a joint problem space: The computer as a tool for sharing knowledge. In P. Lajoie, & S.J. Derry (Eds.), *Computers as cognitive tools* (pp. 229-257). Hillsdale, NJ: Erlbaum.

Thomas, J. (2000). *A review of research on project-based learning*. San Rafael, CA: The Autodesk Foundation.

Tolman EC. (1951). *Behavior and psychological man: essays in motivation and learning*. Berkeley, Univ. of California Press.

Towler AJ, Dipboye RL. (2001). Effects of trainer expressiveness, organization, and trainee goal orientation on training outcomes. *J Applied Psych.* 86(4):664-673.

Tretten, R., & Zachariou, P. (1995). *Learning about project-based learning: Self-assessment preliminary report of results.* San Rafael, CA: The Autodesk Foundation.

UBC Faculty of Medicine Teaching Resources 2010

University of Calgary. Faculty of Medicine. Teaching Skills. Developing your skills as a Teacher. 2010.

Von Glasersfeld E. (2001). An exposition of constructivism: why some like it radical. In: *Constructivist views on the teaching and learning of mathematics.* Reston, Virginia: National Council of Teachers of Mathematics.

Vygotsky, L. S. (1978). *Mind in society: The development of higher psychology process.* Cambridge, MA: Harvard University Press. (Original published in 1930).

Wagner, E. D. (1994). In support of a functional definition of interaction. *American Journal of Distance Education, 8*(2), 6-29.

Weiler A. (2005). Information-seeking behavior in generation Y students: motivation, critical thinking and learning theory. *J Acad Librarianship.* 31(1):46–53.

Wenger E. (1998). *Communities of practice: learning, meaning and identity.* Cambridge: Cambridge University Press.

What We Know About CSCL and Implementing it in Higher Education edited by Strijbos, J-W, Kirschner, P.A. & Martens, R.L. (2004). Kluwer Academic Publishers, ISBN 1-4020-7779-3

Williams, A., & Williams, P. J. (1997). Problem-based learning: An appropriate method for technology education. *Research in Science & Technological Education, 15*(1), 91-104

Williams, M. (2008). Conectivism. http://design.test.olt.ubc.ca/Connectivism

Willis, J. "A Recursive, Reflective Model Based on Constructivist-Interpretist Theory," *Educational Technology*, 33(10), 15-20. (A constructivist model)

Wilson B, Cole P. (1992). A critical review of elaboration theory. *Educational Technology Research and Development.* 40(3):63-79.

Wilson BG, Myers KM. (2000). Situated cognition in theoretical and practical context. *Theoretical foundations of learning environments.* 57-88.

Winn W, Snyder D. Cognitive perspectives in psychology. In DH Jonassen, *Handbook of Research for Educational Communications and Technology.* New York: Macmillan.

Winn, W. (1999). Learning in virtual environments: A theoretical framework and considerations for design. *Educational Media International, 36*(4), 271-279.

Wittgenstein L. (1953). Philosophical investigations. New York: MacMillan.

Wood D. (1976). The role of tutoring in problem solving. *J Child Psych Psychiatry.* 17:89–100.

Woods HB. (2012). Know your RO from your AE? Learning styles in practice. *Health Info Libr J.* Jun;29(2):172-6.

Yaakub, M. N. (1998). *Meta-analysis of the effectiveness of computer-assisted instruction in technical education and training.* Unpublished doctoral dissertation, Virginia Polytechnic Institute and State University, Blacksburg, Virginia.

Young FY. (1993). Instructional design for situated learning. *Ed Tech Res Dev.* 41(1):43-57.

Zemelman S, Daniels H, Hyde A. (1993). Best practice: new standards for teaching and learning in America's schools. Portsmouth: Heinemann.